T0207458

Communications
in Computer and Information Science   1426

More information about this series at http://www.springer.com/series/7899

Arkady Yuschenko (Ed.)

Modern Problems of Robotics

Second International Conference, MPoR 2020
Moscow, Russia, March 25–26, 2020
Revised Selected Papers

 Springer

Editor
Arkady Yuschenko
Bauman Moscow State Technical University
Moscow, Russia

ISSN 1865-0929   ISSN 1865-0937 (electronic)
Communications in Computer and Information Science
ISBN 978-3-030-88457-4   ISBN 978-3-030-88458-1 (eBook)
https://doi.org/10.1007/978-3-030-88458-1

This Springer imprint is published by the registered company Springer Nature Switzerland AG
The registered company address is: Gewerbestrasse 11, 6330 Cham, Switzerland

Preface

The book contains the proceedings of the International Conference "Modern Problems of Robotics 2020", dedicated to RAS academician Evgeny Popov, which took place during March 25–26, 2020, in Moscow, Russia. E. P. Popov was one of the founders of scientific robotics in Russia. He worked as a professor at Bauman Moscow Technical University (BMSTU) till 1997. Since his departure the university has conducted an annual conference dedicated to him and devoted to the most interesting of today's investigations in robotics. Among our authors are known scientists and young investigators from Russia, Germany, Hungary, Armenia, and Kazakhstan.

Among the new trends in robotics is collaborative robotics - the branch devoted to the problem of co-working humans and robots. To work in an interactive mode with a human, a robot must be partially autonomous and "intelligent". The psychological problems of such interaction must also be considered. Some of the problems connected with human-robot interaction are considered in the first part of the book.

The second part is devoted to the problems of robot design and simulation, which is a necessary part of design. Among the problems under discussion are the locomotion algorithms for mobile robots including the underwater ones. For the area of robot design, the main focus is now on dynamics of movement and dynamic stability. Another important and modern problem is teaching a robot to move correctly. Reinforcement learning is one of the means to solve the problem.

The third part of the book considers the control of robots and robotic complexes. Here we find similar problems for industrial robots as for climbing, underwater, and flying robots. In fact, all types of control systems become more and more "intelligent" using different sensors and the distributed sensor systems necessary to work autonomously in partially undetermined environments.

We hope that our investigations will be useful for colleagues all over the world. We are sure that the increasing complexity of robotic systems needs the wide cooperation of all interested engineers and scientists.

March 2020   Arkady Yuschenko

Organization

General Chair

Anatoly A. Alexandrov — Bauman Moscow State Technical University, Russia

Program Committee Chair

Arkady S. Yushchenko — Bauman Moscow State Technical University, Russia

Steering Committee

Vladimir V. Serebrenniy — Bauman Moscow State Technical University, Russia

Ivan L. Ermolov — Russian Academy of Sciences, Russia

Roman V. Meshcheryakov — V.A. Trapeznikov Institute of Control Sciences, Russia

Program Committee

Paul G. Plöger — Hochschule Bonn-Rhein-Sieg, Germany

Oleg N. Gasparyan — National Polytechnic University of Armenia, Armenia

Yuriy V. Poduraev — Moscow State Technological University "STANKIN", Russia

Peter Zentay — Budapest University of Technology and Economics, Hungary

Contents

Collaborative Robotic Systems

Aspects of Industrial Applications of Collaborative Robots

Peter Zentay[✉], Lajos Kutrovacz, Mark Ottlakan, and Tibor Szalay

Budapest University of Technology and Economics, Budapest, Hungary
zentay.peter.zoltan@gpk.bme.hu

Abstract. In the automotive industry robots are widely used in the entire range of the production. In most cases, the isolation of the robots from human involvement can be easily achieved, by physically separating the production line or its elements from the workers (for example by a fence). In other cases, e.g.: in testing, measuring, quality control, mixed manual assembly, etc., humans have to work together with robots. In these cases collaborative robots (CoR, or CoBot) are starting to infiltrate into the production. With the strong promotion of Industry 4.0 and the introduction of cheaper robot designs the spread of CoR increased in a rapid rate. The management of factories also pushes the use of CoR in ever greater numbers. However the question still remains that the use of CoRs is necessary in all newly installed cells? Are the benefits greater than the disadvantages of these machines compared to classical industrial robots? In this paper a case study of a real industrial application in the field of automotive part supply is presented. The analysis is made on a control board-testing cell that utilises two UR10 type CoRs. The analysis tries to assess the question whether the advantage of collaborativeness of the whole cell, despite their current problems (higher price, the increase in cycle time due to the slower robotic motion, the varying rigidity and inferior accuracy), justifies the application of CoRs.

Keywords: Collaborative robots · Industrial robotics · Robotic production cell · Robotic operation analysis · Robot operation safety requirement

1 Introduction

Industry 4.0 and smart factory has certainly dominated the concept of industry in the last decade and collaborative robots play an important role in realising this concept. The application of collaborative robots has changed the whole concept of production lines and flexible manufacturing/assembly cells by being an organic part of the production instead of playing a central role. Usually they are surrounded by other machines, devices and a protective fence. This concept has changed from robots working separately from workers to being an equal partner in the production process and performing task among other humans. Many improvement and concept have been utilised and implemented in the development of CoRs to make them safer, user friendly, easier to work with; mainly to fit into the factory environment that would allow working in a shared palce together with humans. It also implied that new standards and recommendations had to be introduced

© Springer Nature Switzerland AG 2021
A. Yuschenko (Ed.): MPoR 2020, CCIS 1426, pp. 3–17, 2021.
https://doi.org/10.1007/978-3-030-88458-1_1

and new annexes and supplements of older standards had to be added to specify the application and design features of these robots. The operation of collaborative robots (Co-Robots, CoRs or CoBots) allows simultaneous and safe humans-robots participation in a common workspace and it may concern not only manipulators but also mobile robots that are able to accomplish autonomous navigation [1]. One of the most complicated of their task is the problem of human-robot interaction in a full collaborative system [1]. They should provide safe interactions with a human, when performing task in a joint working environment [2]. In this paper, we are analysing the possibility of automating a combined production and test cell of printed circuit boards (PCBs) used in electric machines in cars. It is not our aim to analyse the entire work process of automation but to evaluating a given production cell for robotic and collaborative robotic use. Most of the analysis was already made by the company together with a recommendation for the main concept of the cell. Our task was mainly to perform the detailed design of the process (such as designing: grippers, grasping methods and performing path and trajectory planning of robot motion), simulate (also to create the programming) and optimise the cell, outpoint its shortcomings and possible bottleneck, determine the cycle time and production volume. The analyses was performed according to recommendation of standards and on the bases of literature. Two different arrangements were developed for the simulation: one that contained two collaborative robots and another with a single conventional industrial robot. The two cells were compared to each other in respect of safety, efficiency, flexibility and price.

2   Method General Analyses of Collaborative Robot Application Based on Literature

2.1   Industrial Robots vs CoRs

Conventional industrial robots are designed to work separated without direct human interaction. In contrast, the main goal of a collaborative robot is to be an assistant to a human and to complement his work in his direct surroundings. The use of collaborative robots, due to their structural design and safety features, is significantly less likely to cause serious injuries during operation than conventional industrial robots [1]. One of the great advantage of collaborative robots is that the conventional security fence is no longer needed, therefor in the application the installation of the whole cell is reduced, saving workspaces and operation costs. The continuity of the workflow is improved compared to conventional arrangements. Operators can move freely, no need to halt the process when entering the cell resulting in decrease in downtime [2]. Production lines can be adapted configured and re-configured more easily due to having less equipment and safety features to move around and re-install.

However, on the downside, there are many drawbacks. One of the major problem is the use of any tool or process on the robot that may pose a hazard to humans due to sharp, pointed edges or hard surfaces. These include almost all the conventional hard jaw grippers, rotating tools, etc., including all the dangerous parts that are handled by the robot. This inflicts a limitation of the application of collaborative robots in the industry. Further limitation on the field of application is the smaller payload capacity of these robots. Although there are now collaborative robots that can handle considerable weight (e.g. up-to 35 kg in case of FANUC CR 35iA). Due to their low speed (in collaborative mode) their performance are a fraction compared to traditional industrial robots, resulting in a large increase in cycle times. This significantly extends their return of investment time. The investment of a collaborative robot is quite considerable at the moment. The cost of a collaborative robot compared to a classical industrial robot having the same performance characteristics is 1.5–2.5 times. Although in the near future as the technology will become more widely available, it will eventually be reduced.

2.2 Terminology

When analysing robotic working environment the type of human robot interaction has to be determined. There are usually three different types that are distinguished: coexistence, cooperation, collaboration:

In coexistence: there is no direct contact between the robot and the human in normal process, the workspaces are separated, although physical is possible but highly unlikely and unforeseeable.

In cooperation: there is direct contact between human and robot, they share part of the workspace. The work processes are only separated in time but not in space. Physical contact is possible, but unforeseeable in most cases and less likely.

In collaboration: the robot and the human worker is in physical contact in the same shared workspace. The human and the robotic work processes take place at the same time and there can be a full time direct contact between the worker and the machine.

Human-robot collaboration allow workers and robots into a shared workspace, conventional protective schemes established for industrial robotics no longer needed [6]. Standards such as, ISO 10218-1 [8], for robot safety and, ISO 10218-2 [9] robot system safety is still the governing standard, however collaborative applications (and robots), have properties that are not covered in these standards. To solve this problem a technical supplement was issued in 2016, that contains necessary information and provides guidelines for designing safer collaborative applications (such as Power and Force Limitation, PFL) in ISO/TS 15066 [6, 10]. This applies to industrial robot systems as mentioned in ISO 10218 1 & 2. It does not cover non-industrial robots, although these principles of safety described in the standard can be used in different fields of robotics. Even if this guideline is used for the design of collaborative applications (e.g.: PFL type collaboration) the proper risk assessment must be carried out according to ISO 12100 [6, 11]. ISO introduced four different methods of operation for human robot collaboration modes including:, safety-rated monitored stop (SrMS), hand guiding (HG), speed and separation monitoring (SSM), and power and force limiting (PFL) [4, 10].

- safety-rated monitored stop – (SrMS) is actually a powered standstill, when the controller monitors the brakes of the robot drives and allows no motion of the robot if the operator is inside the robot's workspace.
- speed and separation monitoring - the robot motion speed de- or increases dynamically depending on the distance between operator and robot. If the distance is closer than a set safety then a SrMS is initiated. By leaving the area, the robot can resume its operation.

– and guiding is when an operator is in full contact with a robot and guides the robot motion manually through a set of force/torque sensors. This method is not important in our concept, it will not be discussed further in this paper.
– power and force limiting, limits the actual force and moment that a robot can exert on the worker hopefully small enough not to cause significant injury. It allows the sharing of workspace and collision between the worker and the robot [10, 13].

PFL and Fence-less operation will be considered in the analyses, that is why some consideration will be taken in explaining them. One of the great advantage of collaborative robots is that the conventional security fence is no longer needed, therefor in this application the installation of the whole cell is reduced, saving workspaces and operation costs. The continuity of the workflow is improved compared to conventional arrangements. Operators can move freely, no need to halt the process when entering the cell resulting in decrease in downtime. Production lines can be adapted configured and re-configured more easily due to having less equipment and safety features to move around and re-install [3]. Sometimes the term fence-less is used in the same context as collaborative, however being fence-less is usually a base requirement of a system to be collaborative. Yet in the other way round the definition will not be correct: if an application is deemed fence-less does not directly mean that it is also collaborative [8]. Meanwhile a conventional fence-less system would only require the robot to stop when someone enters its workspace. The misunderstanding is caused by having the Safety-rated Monitored Stop (SrMS, see later) currently included among the collaborative methods in both ISO 10218-1/2 and ISO/TS 15066 standards [3, 4, 10]. However, this method will probably be de-listed from collaborative modes. The SrMS is actually a form of perimeter safeguard and it forbids the mutual movement of the robot system or humans in its workspace [3]. Although this method allows the entrance to a robots restricted area anytime, but only in a stopped condition. It is clearly not the recently expected collaborative usage. For example when a heavy part is held by the robot while the worker performs delicate assembly task the robot and the human has to move together in the same workspace. In a simple fence-less operation the worker would have to step out of the workspace when the robot transfers the work piece. Separation monitoring methods provide high flexibility and have widely adoptable field of use due to their application independency. These methods allows the robot and the human to work within the same workspace if a protective separation distance between them is met. One method of verifying this protective distance is the use of velocity dependent safety zones in bounding volumes, as explained in [14].

A real-time collision avoidance strategy is also an appropriate solution, for example applying artificial potential fields. Another applicable method is when the distance between the manipulator and the worker is evaluated to slow the motion of the manipulator or to stop the robot completely. Camera operated barriers can also be combined with depth sensing devices that possess body tracking capabilities [14]. Collaborative also does not mean that the contacts between human and robot are completely eliminated and injuries will not occur. Further development were introduced and protective devices were properly configured for achieving a proper physical interaction [3].

2.3 Possible Risks and Solutions in Collaborative Processes

The risk assessment process consists of an iterative process risk analysis, risk evaluation and risk reduction when in the end, the risks are considerably reduced and the residual risks are determined [6, 8]. The first step is the identification of all hazards that may occur during the operations and other activities [4]. During the operation of a robotic cell, the most typical hazards are mechanical ones, but others (such as electrical, thermal, vibration, noise) may also be important [12]. In this paper only mechanical hazards will be considered. The next step is to determine all relevant cases involving the risk of physical contact between the worker and the robot. According to the literature, the possible contacts are associated with either "quasi-static" (continuous) or "transient" (short-extent) type of contact [6]. Annex A of [10] collects limiting values for biomechanical loads. For quasi-static contact are the values are provided for maximum forces and maximum pressure that are considered safe for the worker. In the transient case, values of peak force and pressure may be twice as high as in the static case. If during the application these forces (or pressures) exceeds the prescribed limits, then the severity of the contact must be reduced with other measures. These can include active and/or passive safety design characteristics [6, 13]. Features may include increasing the size of the contact surfaces, eliminating sharp edges, smoothing down surfaces, using deformable parts, padding or energy absorption on hard surfaces to reduce impact. Active methods beside FPL could include reducing the speed of moving parts, using delimiters or using sensor signals to predict and detect possible contacts. These may also be pre-collision systems – control based limitations and sensor based surveillance of the workspace or post-collision systems – robot integrated sensors [7]. None the less even if all of these methods are applied but the risk assessment for a given application is performed improperly, as was described in an experimental setup in [13], the robotic application can still be hazardous to the operator. Therefore, even if ISO/TS 15066 is applied completely it will still not guarantee the existence of a safe robot, only a safe application if it is designed properly. In addition, this safety means that the risk of injury (even serious a one) can still occur [13]. This is of great importance in collaborative small parts assembly in a mixed environment with human workers and with robots operating according to PFL. Risk assessment is a difficult task in the situation when collaborative robots are constantly working together with many humans, since there is simply not enough experience gained in this area [6].

3 Analysing a Robotic Production Cell with Collaborative Robots - a Case Study

In this part, the working process of the production cell is analysed staring from the manual process to the proposed automated one. The purpose of the cell is to perform final assembly and testing of PCBs (see: Fig. 1a). It is divided in two stages in the present (manual) cell. In the first stage the final assembly of the PCB is performed. The assembly can be performed on three different products that can be assembled in two different ways, depending on the need of the production. This is done by attaching two or three (depending on the models) mechanical parts (flux condensers (FC)) to prepared sites (two opposites or three adjacent) on the PCB by two M5 screws each. These parts to be attached are identical and can be supplied from a common dispenser. In the second part of the cell, two different kind of electronic tests are performed in two separate machines. The cycle time of the testing machines are fixed and only varies slightly depending on the required processes and the product (see earlier: t = 60–65 s).

3.1 The Manual Process

Usually the PCBs arrive on a common transport plate of 6 pieces. The FC parts are stored on a mass palette. Screws are fed from a bowl feeder to a semi-automatic screwdriver unit. All the manipulation and transportation of the part and the assembly process is performed manually in the cell. The worker places the PCBs and the required number of F.Cs in a jig on the screwdriver unit and performs the screwing process semi automatically one-by-one. Then the assembled PCB is fixed on a transfer fixture (Fig. 1b) and placed on a manual transfer pathway (see: Fig. 2 T.Pw.).

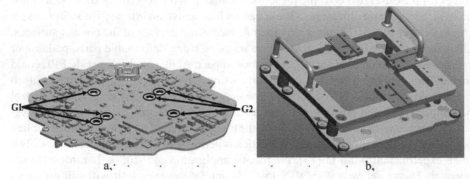

Fig. 1. a, The PCB to be tested (indicating the possible grasping surfaces with G1 & G2) and b, the transfer fixture used in the manual testing cell.

The worker moves the PCB with this fixture only on the allowed pathway. Firstly, the part placed in the first testing machine (T1 Fig. 2), where sensor calibration is performed. After it has cleared for perfect, the first test the part can only be moved to the second testing machine (T2 Fig. 2) where the entire board function test is performed. The testing machines are duplicated for productivity because of their slow cycle time (60–65 s depending on the machine and product). After the part performed the two tests is then removed from the fixture and placed on the outgoing transport plate. In-cell storage between testing processes can be performed on the transfer pathway. Usually the assembly is faster than the testing processes. Because of confidently reason of the automobile supply company only a 3D sketch of the production cell is illustrated in the paper (Fig. 2).

3.2 The Proposed Automatic Process

The analyses of a general automated assembly cell is discussed in detail in [5] by analysing the factors that are identified as attributes of information content for a human

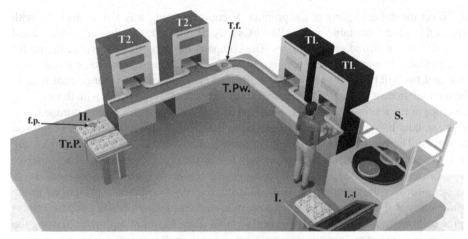

Fig. 2. Manual assembly and test cell of the analysed process[1].

robot collaboration (HRC) assembly process, these are: physical characteristics of the components, mounting, feeding, safety, fastening and miscellaneous.

Most of the mentioned task had already been evaluated earlier by the company; our task was to verify some of these topics for the given concept. Feeding and mounting does not change from the manual assembly process and fastening (placing screws) is done separately from the robot. Analysis of the characteristics of the components has to be made for robot grasping and safety analyses should decide the method to be applied. The requirement was to modify or change as little as possible to the original cell when performing the automating of the presented process with minimising human presence. The testing machines operate automatically and the screwdriver unit can be replaced with an off-the shelf automated one, leaving the robotisation solely to the handling of the parts. This consist of placing the PCBs from the transport tray to the screwdriver jig with the appropriate number of FCs, transporting and placing the assembled part in the testing machines in the given sequence and finally positioning them in one of the outgoing transport trays. The transport of the trays to the outside of the cell may also be performed by one of the robot using a compound gripper. In the automation process, the grasping of the part by the robot is also a question to be answered. The PCBs contain acceleration and gyro sensors that are very sensitive and could be damaged by accesses loads or improper handling. Manipulation of the part had to be designed in this consideration. When analysing the product, it became apparent that all PCBs possess positioning holes, that can be used for simple mechanical grasping (see: Fig. 1a, the grasping holes are marked with G1, G2). The accuracy of the wholes (diameter and position) is sufficient for the task and they are positioned in places that are safe for gripping. Force limitation of the grasping and acceleration limitation of the robot motion can be simply achieved

---

[1] Legend for all the figures in the paper are: I.: incoming storage, II.: outgoing storage, I-1, flux condenser storage: testing machine, S: screwdriver unit (semi-automatic or automatic), I.R.: industrial robot, C.R.: collaborative robot, T.Pw.: manual transfer pathway, f.p.: finished PCB, T.f.: transfer fixture, Tr.P.: transfer plate used for transferring PCBs outside the cell.

to protect the delicate parts of the product. Vacuum gripping was also considered with almost the same acceptable results. The FCs may be grasped with the same mechanical method using modified grasping jaws. The company has provided a possible layout for the cell that contained the same testing machines (T1, T2), a full automatic screwdriver unit, and two UR10 collaborative robots. Instead of a square type arrangement seen in the manual process a circular arrangement was chose complying better with the working envelope of the robots. Part storage consisted of an incoming and outgoing storage stack, where standardised transfer plates are stored on top of each other, containing six PCBs on each plate. There is also an in cell temporary storage between the assembly and the testing units to decrees waiting time. All parts has to follow the process sequence of screwdriver unit, T1 (testing machine 1) and T2. The layout arrangement and the robot motion was not set, however the company insisted on using the exact equipment prescribed in the initial concept. The task was not the automation of the processes (testing and assembly) in the cell but improving the entire process with a higher level of automation, using the same equipment but making the material flow inside the cell automatic. The arrangement of the testing machines was changed to an alternating pattern to equalise the path length of the robot motion. After some repositioning and adjustment of the layout the cell was designed in Process Simulate programming environment (See: Fig. 3). By analysing this concept, many questions arose about the choice of collaboration method, robot and the role robots play in the cell. This has effects on the outcome of the cell in almost all the important aspect: safety, initial cost, cycle time, reliability, return of cost, etc.

3.3 Requested Devices and Human Robot Interaction

The application request of the factory was to use two UR collaborative robots for the automation, mainly for flexibility and for safety reasons. The UR10 has a payload of 10 kg and a working radius of 1300 mm which makes it sufficient for its task. UR robots have full axis torque monitoring and a sophisticated control system that makes it capable of the highest degree of collaboration mode with the capability of PFL. A short list is presented to explain some of the reasons why the factory has chosen to apply CoRs:

- It is easier to install than conventional robots leaving out the protective fence,
- The cell takes up less space, (less or no space is needed for the static protection).
- It is easier to relocate the entire robotic arrangement. In a dynamic production environment, relocation of machines can be frequent.
- It also allows people to move more freely between the machines and around the factory with less care.
- It makes parts supply to and from the work-cells simpler, safer and allows a free access to the part stack.

3.4 Possible Risks in the Cell

Dynamic and quasi-static contacts may be possible if entering the cell when the robots are moving. In the presented case, workers entering the cell can have injuries to the arm, upper body and head (rarely upper thigh and genitals).

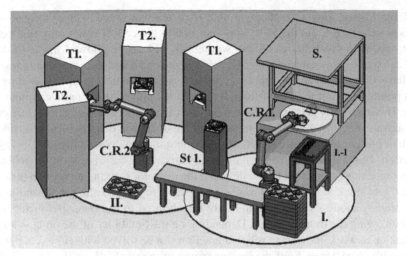

Fig. 3. Robotic production and testing cell simulation with two UR10 CoRs, developed accordance with factory requirement. Simulation made in Process Simulate.

Robots can collide with the workers if they enter into their workspace or can squash them if the worker stand between the robot and the machines. Evidently by having the workers allowed entering only to the appropriate places for their usual tasks (parts stack, finished parts palette, etc.), this risk can be considerably reduced. In addition, a quasi-static contact resulting in a squashing injury can occur even if not entering the cell. One obvious example if the hand of a worker would get between the robot gripper and a hard surface (table, transfer plate, etc.). Presently the robotic cell is designed for simple semi-manual supply of parts; therefore, it is inevitable for the workers to enter some parts of the cell, or reaching into the robot's workspace. A suitable palette changer or a conveyor could prevent this, however for supply, available space, adaptation and scheduling problems the company decided not to use these methods. A simple analysis was performed about the personnel required to enter the robotic area based on the recommendation described in [6]. A list of possible entrance to the cell is summarized in Table 1 by collecting the type of entries. For cleaning and dismantling, the severity is not indicated, because it is supposed to be performed correctly in a power-off mode. The normal admission frequency to the cell is not based on the current status of the cell (e.g. the stacks are full) but governed by external production conditions. In order not to disrupt the outside material flow in the factory workers have to replace the trays in both stacks in the cell according to the scheduling of the entire production line. This implies that only short or no delays are allowed.

3.5   Evaluation of the Cell

Analyses based on the literature and from the description of the process, it is clear that no direct human robot interaction is needed during the normal operation of the cell. Robots can perform all the handling tasks of the PCBs and all the components and the machines perform the assembly and the testing task fully automatically. It is also clear from Table 1 that during normal operation there is really no need to enter the cell while the robots are at work. So the HRC is not needed in the cell. It is not only that people are not needed in this robotic cell, but workers should not be allowed inside the main part of cell at all. They can get squashed between the robot and the other machines. The PCBs have sharp edges and the applied conventional mechanical gripper uses jaws that have a pointed geometry. Even if force limitation is applied, these parts can injure the worker. Having a body part quashed between one of these parts and a hard surface could cause serious injury. Workers have no place in the operation that takes place inside the cell. Their presence would just interfere in the robot motion, by slowing or stopping the production. Human entrance to the dangerous parts of the cell (between the robot and the other machines) should only be allowed if the operator is fixing a problem (example if a part gets stuck in one of the machine, or was dropped by the robot) and always in a stationary mode. Workers should only be admitted to the outer perimeter of the cell for changing the transfer plates. Depending on the flexibility of the process and the organization of work, the human robot interaction can be solved with either cooperation or even with coexistence. So if the worker arrives at the stacks (I. or II. in Fig. 3, 4) he can take the stacks if the robot is not in the vicinity or the cell would stop the robot if it is approaching. The conventional solution would be to have a simple mechanical gate that is constantly closed and only allows entry when the robot is stationary. Since the workers only approach the cell when changing the transfer trays and this happens for a short time, so slowing down the robot with Speed and Separation Monitoring or even using a monitored stop would be an acceptable solution. Admission to the cell can be made in a smarter way by defining accessibility authorisation to ID cards for all factory workers. A simple proximity or RFID identification can distinguish the workers and signal the cell what action to take. It can be efficient by not stopping the process when an operator is approaching and also be safe by stopping immediately if unauthorised or unintentional entry is detected. It is argued that creating and refreshing the permissions is a complex and tedious process, but in contrast, this method does not require the use of special robots and the authorisation database of the workers are usually established anyway. CoRs have the benefit that they can be easily reconfigured to fit the quickly changing environment in the production. In the present situation, there is no need for re-arrangement, due to the sequential manner of the procedures. Sometimes the relocation of the whole cell maybe required, but it would not interfere with its original layout. Arranging the components of the cell in an appropriate way, can limit unintentional access to the cell considerably. The static machines can be organised in such a way that approaching the dangerous part of the cell from behind is impossible (see: Fig. 3 or 4). Using this arrangement and combining with SrMS or SSM (possibly with real-time collision avoidance monitoring) the extensive fencing can be reduced or completely left out from the cell. This saves floor space and installation cost. Further arguments always emerge supporting the use of collaborative robots (mainly applying PFL) opposite to other collaborative methods. One is that a cell should not limit the freedom of movement of workers in the factory. The staff in the factory should be trained, disciplined, should always have a route to follow and the installation of the cell should not get in the way. In these circumstances only unintentional entries can occur.

Table 1. Analysis of human robot interaction within the robotic work cell (based on [6]).

Type of entry	Description	Possible severity	Frequency of entering cell	Personnel
Sc1: Setup	Programming/debugging	High	Rare	Highly trained
Sc2: Normal production 1 –automatic	Robotic cell functioning automatically	Low/none	None	None
Sc3: Normal production 2 – manual	Changing transporting parts	Moderate	Frequent	Simply trained operator
Sc4: Maintenance	In training mode or powered off	Moderate/high	Infrequent (monthly)	Highly trained personnel
Sc5: Cleaning	Performed at power-off	–	Infrequent (1–2/day)	Untrained personnel
Sc6: Dismantling	Performed at power-off	–	Once/rare	Untrained personnel
Sc7: Unintended entry	Accidental entry to the cell	Very high	Rare	Untrained personnel

The other argument is the problem of complex authority programming of the entry to the cell. The argument is founded on the bases that it is much easier to install a CoR and it will have a wider solution to this problem. But CoRs are not 100% safe, they can cause certain amount of pain or injury. It cannot use any appliance for grippers, since some would compromise its safety. A CoR is usually much slower and less efficient (resulting in a longer cycle time of a given task) than conventional industrial robots (even slower in safe mode). They are considerably more expensive. There is much less choice in the variety of robots that may be suitable for a given task. Currently a robot manufacturer have 20–30 different robot (with different working envelope and payload in the same category), while only having 2–3 CoR in their selection.

4 Results

Based on the presented analyses it can be concluded that this cell should operate on a certain collaborative bases but does not necessarily required to employ collaborative robots. Considering this result an alternative cell using a conventional industrial robot was designed at our department. The design and the simulation of the cell was made in the FANUC Roboguide environment (see: Fig. 4). It employs a modified arc welding robot (from FANUC M-10 series) with a longer arm reach of 2030 mms, faster maximum speed and about the same payload (12 kg). The semi-circular arrangement was kept with the alternating testing machine order. Incoming and outgoing storage was arranged on one side of the cell, with accomplishing restriction on any entry from any other sides. Cell operation is be based on either cooperation or coexistence applying SSM and/or SrMS methods for safety. This arrangement is better suited for the task because due to its parameters (size and speed) one robot is sufficient to serve all five machines in the cell.

5 Discussion

Since a collaborative robot is such an industrial robot that is able to interact safely with humans in a shared hybrid workspace [2], it would be strait forward that it may be widely used without any objection. Many factories consider the simple case of replacing a worker with collaborative robot will solve the problem of retrofitting a manual assembly cell with an automatic one without further intervening into the current (otherwise manual) production system [4]. This is however not as simple as that and may end-up in an otherwise non-optimal, slow and expensive system. The assessment of automation (or conversion from manual to automated) is usually made in a less comprehensive fashion assuming the application of collaborative robots is an ultimate solution, and need not be analysed further deeply. In the industry there is still a misconception that collaborative robot = safe robot. The origins of this misinterpreted safety terminology lie in the commercial success of the collaborative semantics, especially when referring to the imperfect term "collaborative robot" [3]. According to [3] robots alone are not collaborative, only applications can be rendered as collaborative when they also adopt sufficient safety features. The "collaborative robot" term is quite inaccurate in the sense that it may suggest to the user that a machine is actually safe in all situations. This is usually not the case and would have to be decided by further risk analysis [3]. By observing the analyses, it can be concluded that solution better suited to the task can be found than the previously proposed one. Over engineering and unnecessary use of complex methods does not result in an evidently better solution. This can be proven from the point of view of safety, efficiency and installing cost (one robot instead of two). The company's choice of UR robots would be evident and further analysing would have not be need required, if at present collaborative robots would be completely safe and would always offer an optimal solution. However, it is apparent from the previous chapters that it is not the case. Just by replacing an industrial robot with a collaborative one, the safety issues are not solved immediately, and productivity can decrease considerably. Still, the original cell is also an agreeable solution. Since UR robots are one of the cheapest CoRs that are available in the market and robot speed is not the paramount parameter (cycle time of the testing and screwdriver machine govern the overall time of the cell) this way their installation costs and application can be justified. However, they are not rugged industrial robots, that is why their reliability and lifespan still remains a question. It became apparent from the analyses that using robots capable of PFL in the cell does not eliminate all the possible injuries, because of the geometry applied grippers and the handled part. Cuts and wounds may still be acquired from the collision with these surfaces. One method would be to eliminate these sharp edges by rounding off or chamfering the edges or applying padding.

While this may be done easily on the gripper, but not on the PCBs. To achieve the increase of the safety of the cell an additional perimeter safeguarding method could be

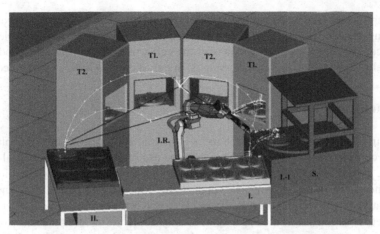

Fig. 4. An alternative realisation of the assembly and testing cell with the use of a conventional industrial robot. Simulation made in FANUC Roboguide.

introduced to eliminate this the hazard. Although, it would render the collaborative PFL method redundant. Proper training of workers is essential even if using CoRs, otherwise the false sense of safety would gain ground. Workers entering the cell have to be trained at least to a certain level; they should know that there is a possibility to be hit by a robot and a potential chance of suffering injury or pain. An untrained person would think that the robot would not collide with him and when it happens, it could cause fright or even panic. Even a minor incident could cause a huge problem if the person is not prepared. Emotional control and behaviour analysis of collaborative robotic cells would offer a suitable solution for this problem in the future. Some concept of human robot collaboration supplemented by emotion analyses were summarised in [1], such as recognising emotional or behaviour patterns. If someone is approaching the cell or entering its workspace the controller should know whether this is intentional or not, form analysing behaviour patterns from image or other sensors signals. In simple cases when someone is advancing towards the cell with facing away from it or backwards, approaching too fast from a distance, making too much unnecessary movements, would indicate the controller, that the person is nearing the cell either unintentionally, or without proper training. In this case, safety actions have to be taken immediately e.g. by halting all motion. If someone is approaching the cell in a calm fashion on a given route will give the impression that the person is trained and signal the controller, that the robotic cell can work normally and no other actions have to be taken. Comparing the two different design concept cells, it can be concluded that they both have advantages and disadvantages but they are marginal in this application. The collaborative one is a little more flexible and gives the smarter impression, while the conventional one is more efficient but needs careful consideration for making it safe while keeping a small installation area. Presently the cell is operating in a hybrid human-robotic production environment. The factory is planning to further automate the production line to another level when the material supply to and from the cell will also be automatic. The factory is planning to introduce an AGV system for the shop floor in the future that will reduce the number of person moving around the factory even further. In this case, the frequency of people approaching or entering the cell will be reduced to just maintenance, troubleshooting and cleaning. In this scenario, both designed versions of the cell would fit well into the production system, although the collaborative version is, in our opinion, a little over engineered.

6 Conclusion

By the introduction of collaborative robots for industrial use, the possibility of application widened considerably. In many places, where the use of conventional industrial robots would be previously considered impossible, a collaborative robot could function effi-ciently and safely. However, companies in the light of Industry 4.0 install more and more collaborative robots without deep analyses, because it is thought to be a simple solution to all safety regarded automation problems. Mainly due to the misuse of terminology and misguiding marketing, companies assume that just by replacing a worker with a CoR and with some tricky programming would instantly solve the automation of a given task. However as it was discussed it is not as simple as that. Although much improvement has been made towards this goal, it is by far not solved completely. Collaborative robots still have many drawbacks that has to be carefully considered when designing indus-trial applications. With the introduction of CoRs to the industrial palette the choice of finding a proper solution for a more extensive range of problems have broadened signif-icantly. The planning and pre-planning of the design phase of applications became more complex by having a much larger variety of machines and methods to choose from. So instead of simplifying the methods just by using collaborative robots, a more thorough consideration is needed for finding an optimal solution. Combining all the collaborative methods and using them all together would result in a very safe robotic environment. It must not be forgotten, that no matter what kind of safety methods are used it will not result in a 100% safe situation. Care should be always be take when designing these environment and workers have to be trained properly even in the safest situations. It is expected that price of CoRs will decrease in the future and with the improvement of the technology the speed and payload limitation will be overcome. The demands from the customer will encourage robot manufacturers to provide as wide a range of CoRs as of industrial robots. When these requirements will be met then the previous analyses will not be necessary anymore. Meanwhile finding an optimal solution among conflicting conditions of safety, efficiency and economy will be a great challenge. Despite all the technical aspect a human-robot environment is only successful if the workers trust these machines and enjoy working with them. Creating a really worker friendly environment will be the most important challenge in the future of collaborative robotics.

Acknowledgement. This study was supported by research project "Digital solutions for efficiency improvement of the workers in production logistics", (registration number: 2017-1.3.1-VKE-2017-00036). The help of Professor Mátyás Horváth, Maté Barabás, György Póka and Donát Huszák is greatly acknowledge.

References

1. Yuschenko, A.S.: Control and ergonomic problems of collaborative robotics. In: Kravets, A.G. (ed.) Robotics: Industry 4.0 Issues & New Intelligent Control Paradigms. SSDC, vol. 272, pp. 43–53. Springer, Cham (2020). https://doi.org/10.1007/978-3-030-37841-7_4
2. Galin, R.R., Meshcheryakov, R.V.: Human-robot interaction efficiency and human-robot collaboration. In: Kravets, A.G. (ed.) Robotics: Industry 4.0 Issues & New Intelligent Control Paradigms. SSDC, vol. 272, pp. 55–63. Springer, Cham (2020). https://doi.org/10.1007/978-3-030-37841-7_5
3. Vicentini, F.: Terminology in safety of collaborative robotics. Robot. Comput. Integr. Manuf. **63**, 101921 (2020). https://doi.org/10.1016/j.rcim.2019.101921
4. Gualtieria, L., Raucha, E., Vidonia, R., Mattab, D.T.: An evaluation methodology for the conversion of manual assembly systems into human-robot collaborative workcells. Procedia Manuf. **38**, 358–366 (2019)
5. Ahmad, A., Bilberg, M.A.: Collaborative robots in assembly: a practical approach for tasks distribution. Procedia CIRP **81**, 665–670 (2019)
6. Matthias, B., Reisinger, T.: Example application of ISO/TS 15066 to a collaborative assembly scenario. In: Proceedings of ISR 2016: 47st International Symposium on Robotics, pp. 1–5. Munich, Germany (2016)
7. Krüger, J., Lien, T.K., Verl, A.: Cooperation of human and machines in assembly lines. CIRP Ann. Manuf. Technol. **58**(2), 628–646 (2009)
8. ISO 10218-1:2011: Robots and Robotic Devices – Safety Requirements for Industrial Robots – Part 1: Robots. ISO, Geneva (2011)
9. ISO 10218-2:2011: Robots and Robotic Devices – Safety Requirements for Industrial Robots – Part 2: Robot Systems and Integration. ISO, Geneva (2011)
10. ISO/TS 15066:2016: Robots and Robotic Devices – Collaborative Robots. Geneva (2016)
11. ISO 12100:2010: Safety of Machinery – General Principles for Design – Risk Assessment and Risk Reduction. ISO, Geneva (2010)
12. ISO 13849-1:2015: Safety of Machinery – Safety-Related Parts of Control Systems – Part 1: General Principles for Design. ISO, Geneva (2015)
13. Rosenstrauch, M.J., Krüger, J.: Safe human-robot-collaboration-introduction and experiment using ISO/TS 15066. In: 2017 3rd International Conference on Control, Automation and Robotics (ICCAR), pp. 740–744. Nagoya (2017)
14. Shakhovska, N. (ed.): Advances in intelligent systems and computing. AISC, vol. 512. Springer, Cham (2017). https://doi.org/10.1007/978-3-319-45991-2

Control System Calibration Algorithm for Exoskeleton Under the Individual Specificities of the Operator

V. G. Gradetsky, I. L. Ermolov$^{(\boxtimes)}$, M. M. Knyazkov, E. A. Semenov,
and A. N. Sukhanov

Laboratory of Robotics and Mechatronics, Ishlinsky Institute for Problems in Mechanics RAS,
119526 Prospect Vernadskogo 101-1, Moscow, Russia
ermolov@ipmnet.ru

Abstract. Control approaches for the most modern exoskeleton devices are based on the use of the potentiometric proportional sensors. This allows setting the velocity of the movement of the exoskeleton links, but has significant peculiarities, which are concluded in a large time delay for processing the control signal and increased sensitivity of such sensors, which leads to increased injury risk during control. The use of muscle biopotentials for control of an exoskeleton device also makes it possible to take into account the physiological characteristics of the operator for using the exoskeleton in various areas of human activity. The development of control algorithms of the exoskeleton, along with the use of the activity of human muscle groups' data, is essential for expanding the functionality of a human-machine system such as the "operator-exoskeleton". The paper considers the interaction of a human and an exoskeleton drive based on mathematical models of a DC motor with a current feedback loop and a muscle duplex. A calibration algorithm is proposed to determine the parameters of the muscle duplex model in order to form a database that corresponds to an individual operator and reflects its individual characteristics. The technique for setting the parameters of the control system in the exoskeleton calibration mode is given. Paper presents the results of experiments with the developed algorithm on full-scale stand, simulating the arm exoskeleton with the electric drive, located in the elbow joint and controlling algorithms based on the electromyogram of the biceps brachii and triceps brachii of the operator. The structure and features of the stand developed in the laboratory of robotics and mechatronics of IPMech RAS are shown. A comparative characteristic of the control quality of the electric drive, which is part of the exoskeleton, with the proposed algorithm in relation to one operator when changing by another one was worked out. At the same time, the following control quality indicators were evaluated – over-regulation, time to set the specified position, and accuracy of positioning the control point of the exoskeleton link. The present work was supported by the Ministry of Science and Higher Education within the framework of the Russian State Assignment under contract No. AAAA-A20-120011690138-6.

Keywords: Exoskeleton · Electromyogram · Control · Experiment · Muscles · Motor control · Calibration

A. Yuschenko (Ed.): MPoR 2020, CCIS 1426, pp. 18–28, 2021.
https://doi.org/10.1007/978-3-030-88458-1_2

1 Introduction

The research and development of such a human-machine system as an exoskeleton is related with a number of tasks due to the interaction of the operator and the elements of the exoskeleton system [1, 2]. An important role is played by feedback, which allows evaluating the performed action, both on the operator and on the exoskeleton control system. The latter is necessary for the control system to adjust its parameters taking into account the appearance of a new operator, or to adjust these parameters in conditions of hard human work in the exoskeleton and the appearance of signs of fatigue. For example, in [3], the authors describe modern methods of qualitative evaluation of fatigue of individual muscle groups based on the analysis of surface EMG data under static and dynamic loads. The authors showed that continuous monitoring of local muscle fatigue when performing certain physical work is possible by measuring the myoelectric activity of individual muscles via surface electromyography techniques. The practical use of such methods in relation to an exoskeleton, which control system is based on the use of information about muscle biopotentials, is the possibility of creating an algorithm for configuring the exoskeleton control system for a specific user and for a specific type of task.

In addition to fatigue, which is expressed in a decrease in the frequency and increase in the amplitude of the electromyogram signal [4, 5], it is important to take into account the individual characteristics of each skeletal muscle involved in controlling the exoskeleton. These features include geometric parameters [6], force parameters [13], conduction conditions at the signal lead points [14, 15], the operator's age [7], the level of its vigor [12], and so on. However, many of these parameters cannot be obtained without surgery or long-term medical research [16–18], so when developing an exoskeleton control system, the question arises of creating databases for different groups of operators with similar characteristics. Based on the obtained characteristics, you can develop a set of values for each group, which will be a reference when calibrating the control system.

2 The Development of an Experimental Stand

In our previous works [8–10], the results of mathematical modeling of the interaction between the exoskeleton and an operator were presented, which showed the importance of taking into account the operating mode of the system (speed mode, object hold mode with compensation of external forces). The exoskeleton working situations were modeled in the conditions of interaction between the movement of the links and the operator's limbs, which allowed forming special requirements for control, accuracy of operations to ensure the safety of the movement. This work presents the creation of an exoskeleton system and presents results of experimental studies conducted at the laboratory of robotics and mechatronics of the Institute for problems in mechanics RAS.

Figure 1 shows a generalized scheme of the experimental stand developed for the given tasks. There is a controller unit that receives information about the current position of the exoskeleton elements in space, the state of activity of the operator's muscle groups. The exoskeleton link, driven by a DC motor, is equipped with force sensors that measure the reaction forces between the structural element of the exoskeleton and the operator's hand. The system is evaluated by the operator using visual and tactile channels.

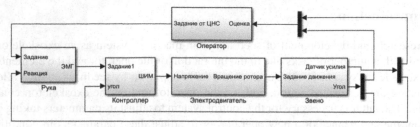

Fig. 1. Generalized scheme of the experimental stand

Two DC motors were selected for the experimental stand. One of the DC motors was selected without a motor-braking gearbox for the operator to sense the reaction forces in the conditions of holding the load in the isometric mode of operation. Another DC motor was equipped with a worm gear to simulate motion blocking when implementing an algorithm for detecting the maximum effort parameter of the biceps and triceps of various operators.

To quantify the reaction forces, we used an assembly of two strain gauges integrated into the exoskeleton handle and suitable for use under maximum load of 500 N, and an ADC unit HX711 with a resolution of 24 bits and a measurement frequency of 80 Hz. The location of the strain gauges is shown in Fig. 2.

Myoware Muscle Sensor AT-04-001 EMG sensors were used to obtain data on the activity of the biceps brachii and triceps brachii. Their applicability for the task of obtaining an electromyogram of the muscles was discussed in [11]. In this work, we used the possibility of receiving raw signal by these sensors to improve the performance and use their own software filter with dynamic adjustment of filtration parameters.

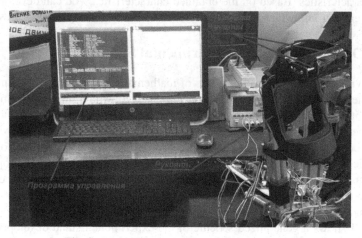

Fig. 2. Main elements of the experimental stand

To ensure safety, as well as to test the algorithm of restricting movement, limit switches and an angle sensor were integrated into the system (Fig. 3).

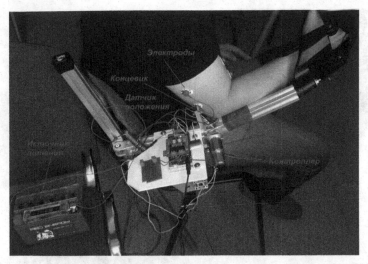

Fig. 3. Position of the operator during the experiment with limit switches and an angle sensor

A controller based on the Atmega2560 RISC processor with a clock frequency of 16 MHz and a 10-bit ADC was selected as the controller that processes data on the operator's muscle biopotentials, as well as forms the movement of the electric motor via PWM.

To change the various parameters transmitted to the controller and the generated control signals, a control panel with a set of variable resistors was implemented, which allows correcting the transmitted values according to the proposed algorithms (Fig. 4).

Special software was developed for processing experimental data and controlling the exoskeleton.

3   Conducting Experimental Research

Several groups of experimental studies were conducted on the developed stand. As part of a joint study of exoskeleton control with students of 10th "Λ" form, school N°. 1543 in Moscow, a group of 3 test subjects was created. The first group of experimental studies was conducted to determine the behavior of the total electromyogram of the biceps brachii and triceps brachii when the operator's arm moves with loads of different weights. The total electromyogram in this case means the readings of the potential difference on the biceps brachii EMG_{bic} and on the triceps brachii EMG_{tric} were obtained.

$$EMG_{sum} = EMG_{bic} + EMG_{tric} \tag{1}$$

In the control program, the data of the potential difference on the triceps brachii EMG_{tric} was taken with a negative sign in order to determine the direction of movement of the exoskeleton drive system from the resulting sign of the total electromyogram data EMG_{sum}.

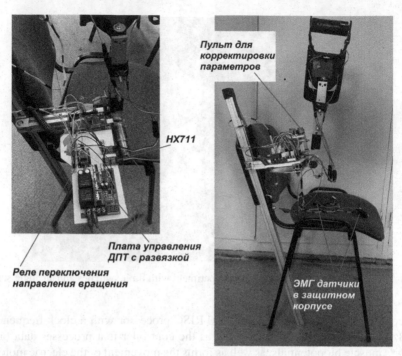

Fig. 4. General view of the experimental stand at the final stage of development

Figure 5 shows the results of an experiment on bending and unbending the arm at the elbow with a weight of 3 kg for each of the subjects. In this experiment, the behavior of an electromyogram without filtering was evaluated.

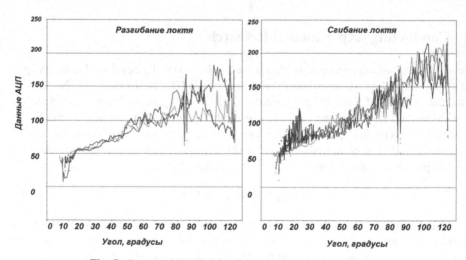

Fig. 5. Raw total EMG data of the biceps and triceps brachii

From the obtained data, we can see a tendency to increase the amplitude of the electromyogram with an increase in the bend angle. This is due to the fact that the arm compensates for the gravity of the load with the most active biceps of the shoulder. Thus it is seen that when extension arm triceps does not make a significant contribution to the work that can be explained by the arm position in space and the vector of force application during the experiment. As shown by further experiments, to obtain a negative value of the parameter EMG_{sum}, which means that when activating the reverse rotating of the exoskeleton's motor, it is necessary to take into account the position of the arm in space, as well as the individual characteristics of the muscles used. From this we can conclude that value of the parameter EMG_{sum} must be corrected.

$$EMG_{sum} = a * EMG_{bic} + b * EMG_{tric} \qquad (2)$$

Here, variables a and b are functions that depend on the maximum effort that a given muscle can develop. In the control system, these parameters are used as settings for the sensitivity of sensors to changes in the electromyogram amplitude. Table 1 shows the results of numerical adjustment of parameters a and b for each test subject in the group when setting the movement at a uniform speed.

Table 1. The results of the settings

	Parameter a	Parameter b
Subject 1	0,861	1,074
Subject 2	0,911	1,268
Subject 3	0,927	0,983
Average in the group	**0,899**	**1,108**

However, with such multipliers, the value of EMG_{sum} in the control program may go beyond the acceptable values transmitted by the ADC [−1024...1024], so the control program had to forcibly limit this range of values to prevent beats due to a sharp change in the variable EMG_{sum} at the border of the range.

Sharp changes in the amplitude of the graphs obtained in this experiment indicate the presence of noise that needs to be filtered. Therefore, the next group of experiments was devoted to configuring the noise filter [19] for the parameter EMG_{sum} entering the control system. For this experiment, the moving average algorithm was selected. This algorithm allows filtering out low frequencies. Implementing this filter in the control system requires setting two parameters – the time constant and the filtration coefficient. The value of the filtered parameter EMG_{sum} will depend on the parameter value on the current and subsequent sensor polling cycle:

$$EMG_{sum.k} = EMG_{sum.k} * (1 - N) + EMG_{sum.k+1} * N \qquad (3)$$

Here the parameter $N = [0...1]$ is the filtration coefficient. Increasing the value of this parameter leads to the return of the influence of noise on the received signal; however, as it was shown by experimental studies, a high value of this parameter reduces the sensitivity of the control system. If the filtration coefficient is high, it is difficult for the operator to make a sudden movement or change the direction of movement.

The time constant specifies the time interval during which averaging will occur. An increase in the time constant leads to smoother changes in the parameter EMG_{sum}, but introduces a noticeable delay in control. In the course of experiments, it was found that increasing the time constant parameter is suitable for slow movements characteristic of the exoskeleton load holding mode or for improving positioning accuracy. Sudden movements that are typical, for example, for fast technological operations, require reducing this coefficient.

As part of the experiment, the subjects were given the task to bend and unbend the arm at the elbow in an exoskeleton while holding loads of different weights and at the same time observe a constant speed. The speed constancy was controlled in the developed program. During the experiment, the settings for the filter time constant T and the filter coefficient n were changed. When the flexion-extension speed was constant for five approaches, the current parameters were recorded in the database. In this case, the angular range of 10°, set aside for acceleration and deceleration near the extreme positions defined by limit switches, was not taken into account. Table 2 shows the final values of the parameters after the experiment.

Table 2. The results of the settings

	Fast movements (1 s to overcome 100°)		Slow movement (4 s to overcome 100°)	
	Parameter T	Parameter N	Parameter T	Parameter N
Subject 1				
1 kg	2 ms	0,05	4 ms	0,1
3 kg	2 ms	0,05	5 ms	0,1
5 kg	3 ms	0,04	5 ms	0,08
Subject 2				
1 kg	2 ms	0,05	4 ms	0,1
3 kg	2 ms	0,05	5 ms	0,1
5 kg	2 ms	0,05	5 ms	0,09
Subject 3				
1 kg	2 ms	0,06	5 ms	0,1
3 kg	3 ms	0,05	5 ms	0,09
5 kg	3 ms	0,05	5 ms	0,08
Average in the group	**2 ms**	**0,05**	**5 ms**	**0,09**

From this table, one can see that increasing the weight of the load leads to the need of increasing the value of the filter time constant to obtain a constant speed of movement of the exoskeleton link. This can be explained by the fact that the increased load on the biceps led to the involvement of more motor units per unit of time, which led to an amplification of the EMG signal and an increase in the amplitude of noise, which had to be filtered by increasing the value of the time constant of the filter. When performing the movement in slow mode, the load on the biceps lasted longer, so the effect of fatigue is visible here, expressed in a decrease in frequency and an increase in the amplitude of the useful signal.

The next group of studies was aimed at identifying the value of the dead zone for the assigned biopotential. Experiments have shown that even in the state of rest and noise filtering, the value of EMG_{sum} will be different from zero, and since this value is used to form the motor speed, constant small deviations of the rotor from the current position are possible in the state of rest. Therefore, the speed calculation algorithm has been adjusted to take into account the dead zone parameter, which is configured individually for each operator. A verification condition was added to the control system algorithm (Fig. 6):

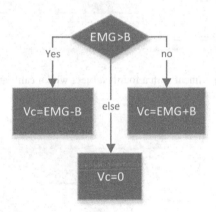

Fig. 6. Condition for calculating the speed of movement

This algorithm compares the value of the parameter EMG_{sum} and the selected value of the dead zone. The adjusted speed at the bend will be calculated from the difference between the calculated values of the EMG_{sum} parameter and the dead zone. These values are added together when moving for extension, since in this case the numerical value of the parameter EMG_{sum} will be less than zero. Thus, when reaching the border of the dead zone, the current speed will be formed from zero, thereby preventing sharp jerks of the motor rotor, which can be relevant when making small movements.

All other cases mean falling into the dead zone, which leads to the need to implement a PID controller that calculates the voltage on the motor windings, taking into account the maintenance of the current angular position. This case was described in detail in the previous paper (8). Experiments have shown that the numerical value of the dead zone should be adjusted in the direction of increase over time. This effect is due to an increase in the amplitude of the EMG signal when fatigue occurs.

The final experiments were devoted to checking the values of the control system parameters calibrated according to the found standards for the fourth untrained test subject. A load of 5 kg was placed on the handle of the test stand, and the task of moving at a constant speed was set (Fig. 7, 8).

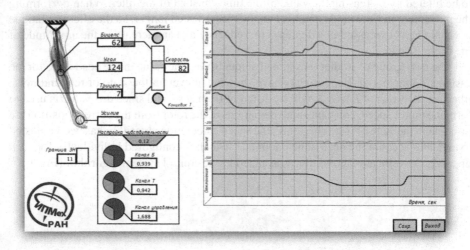

Fig. 7. The result of an experiment with a fourth subject with a calibrated control system when implementing slow movements.

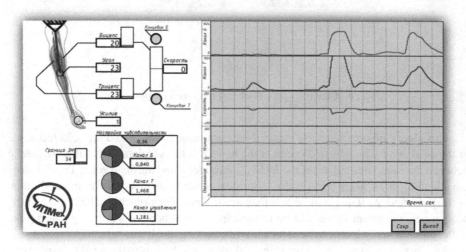

Fig. 8. The result of an experiment with a fourth subject with a calibrated control system when implementing fast movements.

The results of the tests have shown that the proposed algorithms for calibration and parameter setting of the exoskeleton control system work properly.

4 Conclusion

In the course of experimental studies, the influence of various parameters of the control system on the quality of movement control of the exoskeleton device was shown. The experimental stand and special software were developed to allow flexible configuration of the control system parameters. As part of the work, various data were obtained for several operators, on the basis of which reference values of control system parameters were obtained for calibration. The results of testing the developed algorithm on full-scale stand, simulating the arm exoskeleton with the DC drive, located in the elbow joint and controlling algorithms based on the pattern envelope electromyogram of the biceps brachii and triceps brachii of the operator were presented. The structure and features of the stand developed in the laboratory of robotics and mechatronics of IPMech RAS are shown. A comparative characteristic of the quality of control of the DC drive that is part of an exoskeleton, on which the proposed algorithm for configuring the control system in relation to one operator when changing to another was worked out. The following control quality indicators were evaluated – over-regulation (when evaluating the speed), time to set the specified position (when setting the filter coefficients and determining the numeric value of the dead zone parameter), and the accuracy of positioning the control point on the exoskeleton link.

References

1. Rukina, N.N., Kuznetsov, A.N., Borzikov, V.V., Komkova, O.V., Belova, A.N.: Surface elec-tromyography: its role and potential in the development of exoskeleton (review). Sovremennye tehnologii v medicine 8(2), 109–118 (2016). https://doi.org/10.17691/stm2016.8.2.15
2. Renato, V., Matamala, J.: Clinical neurophysiology standards of EMG instrumentation: twenty years of changes. Clin. Neurophysiol. 131 (2019). https://doi.org/10.1016/j.clinph.2019.08.023
3. Cifrek, M., Medved, V., Tonkovic, S., Ostojić, S.: Surface EMG based muscle fatigue eval-uation in biomechanics. Clin. Biomech. (Bristol, Avon) 24, 327–340 (2009). https://doi.org/10.1016/j.clinbiomech.2009.01.010
4. Dimitrova, N.A., Dimitrov, G.V.: Interpretation of EMG changes with fatigue: facts, pitfalls, and fallacies. J. Electromyogr. Kines. 13(1), 13–36 (2003)
5. De Luca, C.J.: Spectral compression of the EMG signal as an index of muscle fatigue. In: Sargeant, A.J., Kernell, D. (eds.) Neuromuscular Fatigue, pp. 44–51. Royal Netherlands Academy of Arts and Sciences, Amsterdam, The Netherlands (1992)
6. De Sapio, V.: An approach for goal-oriented neuromuscular control of digital humans in physics-based simulations. Int. J. Hum. Fact. Model. Simul. 4, 121–144 (2014). https://doi.org/10.1504/IJHFMS.2014.062387
7. Valderrabano, V., et al.: Muscular lower leg asymmetry in middle-aged people. Foot Ankle Int. 28(2), 242–249 (2007). https://doi.org/10.3113/FAI.2007.0242
8. Gradetsky, V.G., Ermolov, I.L., Knyazkov, M.M., Semenov, E.A., Sukhanov, A.N.: Switching operation modes algorithm for the exoskeleton device. In: Gorodetskiy, A.E., Tarasova, I.L. (eds.) Smart Electromechanical Systems. SSDC, vol. 261, pp. 131–142. Springer, Cham (2020). https://doi.org/10.1007/978-3-030-32710-1_10
9. Gradetsky, V., Ermolov, I., Knyazkov, M., Semenov, E., Sukhanov, A.: Features of human-exoskeleton interaction. In: Studies in Systems, Decision and Control, volume 261 of Robotics: Industry 4.0 Issues & New Intelligent Control Paradigms, pp. 77–88. Springer Nature Switzerland, Switzerland (2020)

10. Gradetsky, V., Ermolov, I., Knyazkov, M., Semenov, E., Sukhanov, A.: Osobennosti proektirovaniya aktivnoj ekzoskeletnoj sistemy s bioupravle-niem. In: Trudy XIII Vserossijskogo soveshchaniya po problemam upravleniya (VSPU-2019) 17–20 iyunya 2019 g. Moskva, IPU RAN, ISBN 978-5-91450-234-5, № gos. registracii: 0321902409, pp. 801–805. IPU RAN Moskva (2019)

11. Fuentes, S., Santos-Cuadros, S., Olmeda, E., Álvarez-Caldas, C., Díaz, V., San Román, J.: Is the use of a low-cost sEMG sensor valid to measure muscle fatigue? Sensors **19**, 3204 (2019). https://doi.org/10.3390/s19143204

12. Andersson, S.: Active Muscle Control in Human Body Model Simulations. Master's Thesis in Automotive Engineering, CHALMERS, Applied Mechanics, 62, p. 64 (2013)

13. Zajac, F.E., Gordon, M.E.: Determining muscle's force and action in multi-articular movement. Exerc. Sport Sci. Rev. **17**, 187–230 (1989) and Zajac, F.E. Muscle and tendon: properties, models, scaling, and application to biomechanics and motor control. CRC Crit. Rev. Biomed. Eng. **17**, 359–411 (1989)

14. Sancho-Bru, J.L., Pérez-González, A., Mora, M.C., León, B.E., Vergara, M., Iserte, J.L., et al.: Towards a realistic and self-contained biomechanical model of the hand (2011)

15. Wilkie, D.R.: The mechanical properties of muscle. Br. Med. Bull. **12** (1956)

16. Novoselov, V.S.: On mathematical models of molecular contraction of skeletal muscles. Vestnik SPbGU. Ser. **3** 88–96 (2016) (in Russian)

17. Grosu, V., Rodriguez-Guerrero, C., Brackx, B., Grosu, S., Vanderborght, B., Lefeber, D.: Instrumenting complex exoskeletons for improved human-robot interaction. Instrum. Meas. Mag. IEEE **18**, 5–10 (2015). https://doi.org/10.1109/MIM.2015.7271219

18. Matthew, W., et al.: Muscular activity and physical interaction forces during lower limb exoskeleton use. Healthc. Technol. Lett. **3**(4), 273–279 (2016)

19. Sado, F., Yap, H.J., Ghazilla, R.A.R., Ahmad, N.: Exoskeleton robot control for synchronous walking assistance in repetitive manual handling works based on dual unscented Kalman filter. PLoS ONE **13**(7), e0200193 (2018). https://doi.org/10.1371/journal.pone.0200193

Interactive Collaborative Robotics – New Results and New Problems

Arkady Yuschenko[✉]

Bauman Moscow State Technical University, 105005 Moscow, Russia
yusch@bmstu.ru

Abstract. A collaborative robotics in the last decade has gained significant popularity due to the fact that it allows to bring robots outside the boundaries of large engineering enterprises. It turned out that there are a significant number of small and medium-sized enterprises in which the robotics implementation was hindered by the two factors only – safety requirements for employees and the complexity of programming and operation. When these limitations were bridged, robotics started to be applied. However, the application of collaborative principles in more complex processes, such as patients' care in hospitals, prompt assistance to the surgeon during operations, rescue operations and etc. demanded to overcome a new barrier. Collaborative robots had to acquire elements of artificial intelligence in order to assist people in solving intellectual problems, by interacting with them actively. Perhaps, the date of birth of this trend in robotics should be considered the year 2016, when the first international conference on interactive collaborative robotics (Interactive Collaborative Robotics. ICR 2016, Budapest) took place. As the name of the conference implies, a new class of Co-robots involves the active interaction of humans and robots not only at the level of support when performing simple operations, but also some forms of dialogue, including verbal one. The article attempts to determine the current state of the issue and to examine in more detail some problems of fundamental importance, including those that require further research.

Keywords: Interactive collaborative robots · Human operator · Robotic system · Verbal dialogue · Emotional support · Information · Multimodal interface · Augmented reality · Deep neural networks

1 Introduction. Interactive Collaborative Robotics – Is a New Stage in the Human-Robot Relationships Development

One of the trends of the modern stage of scientific and technological development is the socialization of robotics – robots are included into various fields of human activity. In this regard, the term "*collaborative robots*", or *Co-Robots*, arose. In accordance with the international standard ISO 8373: 2012–03 "Robots and robotic devices" (2012), collaborative technological (robotic) operations include such operations that a person performs together with a robot in the same workspace. Robotic systems that allow such interaction with humans were called collaborative. Initially, this term was used in relation

© Springer Nature Switzerland AG 2021
A. Yuschenko (Ed.): MPoR 2020, CCIS 1426, pp. 29–43, 2021.
https://doi.org/10.1007/978-3-030-88458-1_3

to industrial manipulators, which were used to help a person when performing work on the conveyor. The basic principles of this relatively new direction are robot safety for the user and the possibility of using a robotic system (RS) without special training in the robotics and programming.

Today, collaborative robotics has begun to include the intellectual component to a considerable degree. A robot that has elements of artificial intelligence and a developed information-sensory system becomes a partner of a person in performing quite complicated tasks. In connection with this, a new term "Interactive collaborative robot" appeared. Let us take its acronym as ICo-Robot. For five years now, the annual international scientific and technical conference "Interactive Collaborative Robotics" has been held. The latest conference was held in 2019 in Istanbul [1]. The results represented, showed that the intellectualization of Co-robots has led to a significant expansion of the field of collaborative robotics application, covering all new areas of human activity. In fact, we are talking about a radical change in the interaction of man and the robotic system, which includes not only physical, labour activity, but also the intellectual component of human activity in the outside world.

The problem of the relationship between a robot and a person arose long period before the creation of robots themselves, capable of fully or partially replacing a person. Moreover, the main attention was initially paid to the social consequences of such a replacement [2]. A systematic study of technical problems associated with the interaction of man and the robotic system began in the middle of the last century. One of the first was studied in detail the master-slave manipulators allowing the operator to carry out the necessary operations remotely in the area, which he could not reach for some reason. The manipulator did not have any independence. The operator controlled the robot by moving a master manipulator with kinematics similar to the working one. It was shown that the operator's activity becomes much more effective when using not only visual, but also mechanoreceptor feedback in bilateral manipulators [3]. In other words, provided that the operator on a certain scale can perceive those forces that act on the manipulated object in the workspace. With the further development of such systems, the operator was able to carry out remote control, i.e. the operator observed the work on the monitor screen, and controlled the manipulator, which was in the working area. Further improvement of the remote-control systems made it possible to transfer some of the standard operations to the robot in automatic mode under the control of the operator. Ultimately, the evolution of remotely controlled manipulators has led to the emergence of a new type of system, which could be called collaborative robotic remote-control system. A well-known example of such a system is the Da Vinci robotic surgical system, which facilitates the work of a surgeon (Fig. 1). This system is not a robot in the generally accepted sense, but rather a smart robotic tool in the hands of a professional surgeon. This group also includes control systems for space and underwater manipulators with elements of artificial intelligence that are controlled by a person, but with active "support" from the RS.

Another area in the field of collaborative robotics, which focuses on the direct (physical) inclusion of a person in a robotic system, is exoskeletons. Such devices could be used to enhance the physical capabilities of a person, as well as for the rehabilitation of patients with impaired motor functions. The usage of these devices in medicine to restore such functions requires the usage of new information technologies, the complex

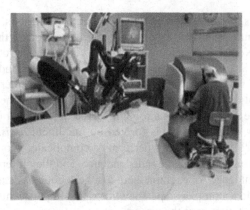

Fig. 1. Robotic system "Da Vinci"

Fig. 2. Exoskeleton HAL

processing of the bio-potentials of the muscles of human limbs. An example here is the HAL project (Fig. 2). In essence, this is a human-robot robotic system, which is controlled by a person not with his voice, and not with gestures, but with the direct movements of his limbs, or even the bio-potentials, corresponding to such movements. The term "collaborative" is also often applied to such systems, although it might be more correct to talk about a *robotic system with bio-technological control.*

A new class is formed by *interactive collaborative robots,* that perform autonomously various tasks according to the instructions of their operator, and maintain active interaction with a person during the operation. Such robots could be defined as the *"partner robots".* As an example, one could name rescue mobile robots that independently explore a certain territory, for example, after an accident or disaster. Such robots could not only be observers, but they are able to carry out some manipulation operations in environment at the direction of their operator. For example, to disassemble the rubble that arose after the disaster, to provide first aid to people, to remove victims from the disaster area. Actually, the term "control" is not quite acceptable here, for the relative independence of the technical partner. In this case, the robot has a system for recognizing and analysing environmental objects, perceives the operator's speech instructions, specifying them if necessary, independently plans and performs complex operations in the workspace under human supervision. Note that in this case the term "collaborative robot" does not seem entirely successful, since it means the interaction of the robot and the person in the labour process. Now, we include the robot in the execution together with the person in the implementation of different complicated operations. Perhaps the term "*cooperative robot*" would be more successful, i.e. a robot involved in joint operations.

A particular class of ICo-Robots is formed by intelligent *assistant robots*, whose task is precisely to help a person, who performs a complicated work. As it was in the previous case, these robots have some independence, and they interact with humans at the level of verbal dialogue. An example here can be robotic assistant of surgeons [4]. A robot assistant could accompany a person with visual impairments, could help orient a passenger at a train station or at the airport.

Interactive collaborative robotics in industry got a new development. In addition to the usage of collaborative robots to support the human labor activity directly during complicated operations, one more new direction could be noted. This is the organization of production as a *multi-agent collaborative RTS*, including both workers and robots at the individual stages of a single production process [5].

Multi-agent interactive robotics systems have a more complicated organization. In practice, in most cases, the usage of robotics gives an effect in case a group of robots is used, both of the same type a homogeneous and of different types robots for various purposes (heterogeneous RS) [6]. This means that a person or group of people controls a group of robots. This may be a group of transport unmanned vehicles, or UAVs. These robots could deliver cargo, conduct air or ground reconnaissance in the disaster area, and rescue operations. In this case the control task goes to a completely different level, both in relation to robots, and in relation to humans. Control methods are also changing radically, since a multi-agent interactive RS should automatically redistribute sub-tasks between group members at each stage of a task stated by human [7].

The development of collaborative robotics is directly related to the improvement of the interface, allowing operator to program the work of ICo-Robots on-line, even without special qualification. One possible solution of this problem is the programming using augmented reality. Recently, the term "intuitive programming" [21] has been used to designate such a process. Here, operator interacts not with the industrial robot itself, but with its virtual model, which ensures, on the one hand, safety, and on the other hand, makes it possible to consider the influence of numerous factors that are could be considered hardly during ordinary programming. A combination of augmented reality with verbal dialogue could be a very effective solution [9].

As in the previous stages of development of robotics, with the emergence of new directions it is assumed that this development only facilitates the tasks of man, to some extent, frees him from the need to perform routine operations. However, when using interactive collaborative RS, we could go beyond the objective capabilities of a person to effectively interact with his technical partner [10]. Human capabilities in interaction with collaborative robots have not been studied sufficiently yet.

2 The Concept of an Interactive Collaborative Robotic System

Previous researches allow us to define the general concept of an interactive robotic system. Let us assume that an interactive collaborative robot, in the general case, is a mobile platform on which actuators are installed to perform certain actions in the workspace, including manipulators, as well as the necessary information-sensor devices (Fig. 3, 4).

Functional diagram of an interactive collaborative system is shown in Fig. 5. In fact, the functional diagram of the ICo-Robot consists of two blocks – a control unit of an autonomous mobile robot with elements of artificial intelligence, and a block of an operator interface with enhanced intellectual capabilities. In the robot control system, which is equipped with the necessary external information sensors, including the technical vision system, laser scanning rangefinders, a preliminary analysis of sensory information is performed. On its basis a model of the current situation is formed in the operator interface unit, and the robot and surrounding objects are localized. Presentation of a visual image of the situation to the operator allows to clarify in the dialogue mode the description of objects, which are observed by the robot, or the general situation.

The ICo-Robot also has to plan operations in accordance with the tasks set by man. The operations planning is possible only if the robot creates an adequate image of the external environment in which the activity occurs, including the human-operator. Therefore, the recognition of the outside world objects and the situation in general becomes one of the tasks of ICo-Robot.

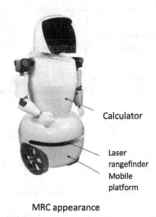

Calculator

Laser
rangefinder
Mobile
platform

MRC appearance

Fig. 3. Robot servicer (Neurobotics, Russia)

The ICo-Robot also has to plan operations in accordance with the tasks set by man. The operations planning is possible only if the robot creates an adequate image of the external environment in which the activity occurs, including the human-operator. Therefore, the recognition of the outside world objects and the situation in general becomes one of the tasks of ICo-Robot.

The main element of ICo-Robot, distinguishing it from the usual Co-robot, is a block of speech dialogue. This unit provides the interaction of the robot with a human partner

Fig. 4. Medical robot consultant (InTouch Health, USA)

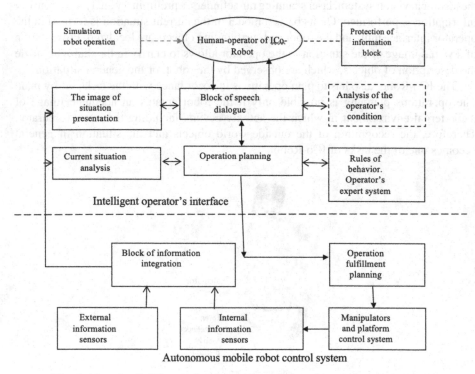

Fig. 5. Functional diagram of an interactive collaborative robot control system

through dialogue in a language close to natural, as a result of which a sequence of tasks is formed in the operation planning block. To represent the image of the current situation in an interactive control system, it is advisable to use the spatial-semantic representation of space, which includes a description of the objects of the working scene and the spatiotemporal relations between them [11]. The peculiarity of the interactive system is that this representation is created with the participation of a person – either in advance or directly in the process of work. Therefore, to describe it, it is advisable to use natural spatiotemporal fuzzy relations [12], which could be the basis of a more general approach to the organization of dialogue mode of control [13].

ICo-Robot is in permanent contact with a person and through the verbal dialogue could significantly facilitate the task of orientation in an unknown environment. In case of a loss of communication with the operator, another task arises – to find the operator. This problem could be solved using optical odometry – it is a method for estimating the linear and angular displacement of a robot by analysing a sequence of images taken with a pair of cameras, which are mounted on it [14]. Another problem in the controlling mobile assistant robots is to accompany moving objects, or to avoid collisions with them. For this, the task of predicting the future state of the working scene [15] must also be solved in the operations planning block. In order to perform a complicated operation in a limited space, it is advisable to simulate an operation on an accelerated time scale to determine its safe execution in relation to the objects in the workspace, including the operator. Simulation results could be presented to the operator in the form of virtual or augmented reality before the operation itself.

ICo-Robot must have the ability of self-diagnostics in order to inform promptly the operator about possible violations in the control system, communications, information processing, power restrictions, which are recorded by internal information sensors. Common requirements for interactive collaborative robots are information protection requirements, which exclude "control interception" by unauthorized persons. Here, in addition to the usual means of encoding control actions and commands, there may be applications such means as analysis of the speech features of the main operator, recognition of his face. These tools could be used to assess the state of the operator in the process of working with the control system of the Co-Robot, including his fatigue, emotional tension [16]. Finally, a developed control system of the Co-Robot, designed to perform certain operations in a specific environment, should contain an expert system for supporting operator decisions, which can accumulate both procedural knowledge ("situation-action") and knowledge about the features of the work of its operator.

3 Organization of the "Human-Robot" Dialogue

To organize a dialogue between a person and a robot, natural spatiotemporal relations introduced by D. A. Pospelov could be used [12]. Let us remind, that the introduced natural (extensional) relations include fuzzy relations of the position and orientation of objects, which are defined by membership functions. These functions correspond to the perception of above relations by human. The appropriate membership functions are the formalization of the corresponding psychophysiological scales that determine the capabilities of human receptors. To complete the description, the so-called intentional relations are added to such relations, such as $R1$ – touch; $R2$ – to be inside; $R3$ – be on the same plane, etc. Using the necessary means of observation (CVS, laser rangefinders, ultrasonic sensors of near location), as well as having membership functions preformed in the knowledge base, ICo-Robot could itself describe the situation in terms of natural spatial relations and report it to the operator in a verbal form. The same relations could be used by the operator in the formation of tasks for the robot in the process of dialogue.

The current situation, including M objects and the robot itself, or an external observer, is described by a system of binary frames (<object m>, <relation>, <object n>), m, n

= 1,2,...,M. If the fuzzy binary relationships between all the objects that the robot can observe during movement are established in advance, then we will get a fuzzy spatial-semantic network, or a fuzzy map. Using such a map, it is possible, in particular, to navigate the robot along the observed benchmarks, i.e. for objects whose position was known in advance.

The combination of designations (names) of given objects in the space of the working scene and fuzzy relations between them create a dictionary of the formal language to describe the situation. Using the terminology, which was introduced by D.A. Pospelov, one could name the language of formal-logical relations, which is used to describe situations, as a situational control language. In this language, a dialogue could be organized between the ICo-Robot and human operator during the control process.

The functional diagram of the dialogue control system is shown in Fig. 6.

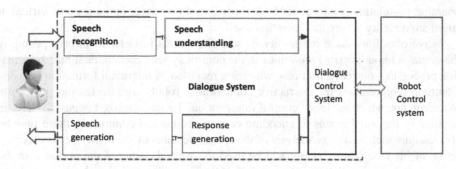

Fig. 6. Functional diagram of the dialogue control system of robot

For the means of speech recognition, today it seems the most effective way to use the deep neural networks Deep Neural Network (DNN), which have greater capabilities than conventional neural networks. However, neural networks are not in position to simulate voice signals directly. Therefore, in order to use the ability of neural networks to classify, a combined DNN-HMM model was proposed, including DNN and the Hidden Markov Model (HMM) [4]. The hidden Markov model is used to describe the dynamics of voice signals; the probabilities of the observed vectors are calculated by neural networks. This model has advantages in recognition accuracy over other methods for recognizing continuous speech. Neural network training is done using the Backward error propagation (BP) algorithm.

As the primary tool for speech recognition by robot, it is advisable to choose the n-gram model, which allows to calculate the probability of the next word from words that appeared earlier. In other words, the n-gram model is able to calculate the state of dialogue n from the previous $n-1$ states. The task of natural speech understanding is an interpretation of the meaning of the message in the text. In an object-oriented system, the task of interpreting meaning is greatly simplified due to the syntax – the rules for the formation of statements.

The dialogue process consists of the requests between the subject (person) making the request and the subject (robot) – responding to the request, which depend on the context of the discourse. The dialogue management system could create the following dialogue states according to its current state, or by the request of the subject. To solve the problems of monitoring the state of the dialogue and managing the dialogue, one could apply the technique of finite-state automation [17]. The system recognizes user requests using the DNN-HMM algorithm and generates a response to the request. In practice, in an object-oriented dialogue system for controlling a robot, the number of client input requests is limited (usually the number of requests is from 20 to 30). Therefore, it is advisable to develop in advance the main dialogue scenarios depending on the operations performed. For example, analysis of the current situation, the feasibility of the task, checking the status of the robot, etc. This simplifies the task of dialogue control. It should be noted that the operator's capabilities are significantly expanded if it is possible to connect the dialogue system to the Internet, which contains the necessary service for speech synthesis.

4 The Solution of the Task of Recognizing Objects by a Robot

An important feature of ICo-Robot is the ability to detect objects autonomously in the workspace, which is specified by the operator. Let us suppose, that as a result of the voice recognition system and the subsequent dialogue for the task clarification, if necessary, the subject, being specified by the operator, is defined. Then the task of this subsystem is to find this object and determine its position in space, in order to ensure it capture by the robot arm.

The traditional method of recognition (classification) of objects – is to use a database containing signs of objects, which are entered into it a priori. But in the current case this method is unacceptable, because it adds to the user the task of compiling such a database, which, moreover, is incomplete and could require the update during the work. Therefore, the approach that is more acceptable in the case of ICo-robotics is to use convolutional neural networks, which were mainly developed to solve problems of objects classification.

Both stationary cameras and miniature cameras, which are located directly on the last link of the manipulator, could be used as sensors of visual information. The problem of object recognition is understood well. It could be conditionally divided into several stages: the stage of searching for areas where the desired objects could be detected, the stage of distinguishing objects from the background of the environment and the stage of classification and determination of an object orientation in space.

In [18], to solve the problem of surgical instruments recognition on the operating table, a convolutional neural network, which consists of two parallel channels of information processing was used (Fig. 7). One of them (the upper one in the diagram of Fig. 7), scanning the workspace with a sliding window, finds the allocation area of the desired object, and the second (lower) channel solves the problem of distinguishing objects in each of the subdomains and classifying the objects using a convolutional neural network (CNN). This method turned out to be quite effective when the system observes several different objects simultaneously, among which the desired object is located.

The search for the necessary items was carried out by the manipulator using the camera, which was located on the last link. (Fig. 8, a). In order to determine the orientation of objects, the neural network divides recognition areas into three groups: the head of

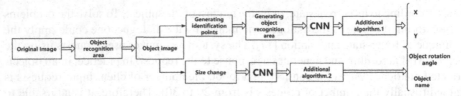

Fig. 7. Functional diagram of a parallel evolutionary network (CNN) for object recognition

the instrument, the tail of the instrument and the remainder. Based on the received data, algorithm 1 calculates the position and orientation of objects on the plane of the desktop (Fig. 8, b). The network consists of an input matrix, three convolution layers, two full-connected layers and it generates three signals.

a)   b)

Fig. 8. Results of recognition of objects and their spatial position

Each of the neural networks was trained separately by the back error propagation method. Let us note, that a sufficiently large number of iterations is required to achieve acceptable recognition accuracy. So, for recognition of the instrument as a whole with an accuracy of 90%, at least 2000 iterations are required. The step procedure is performed automatically and takes approximately 2 h. But after the learning process is completed, the system processes the 3968×2976 image in less than 1 s. The described experiments showed us the efficiency of objects recognition using a convolution network. However, the objects were almost flat, which made it possible to use the simplest electromagnetic device in order to capture. The task of capturing a 3-D object of complex shape used to be an independent task [19].

5   The Use of Augmented Reality and Intuitive Programming

Another way of human interaction with a collaborative robot is the use of augmented reality at the stage of programming its motions. Currently, the most common way to program Co-Robot is the direct capture of a working tool, held by the manipulator along the desired path, which is remembered automatically. It is safer for the operator to use augmented reality – the operator sets the desired movement, without manipulator activation itself. He observes in a real environment the motion of the 3D model of the manipulator gripper, or an object, or a working tool held in the gripper, or the manipulator in general. This is achieved through the usage of the transparent augmented reality glasses, being a miniature screen on which the movement of the manipulator model is displayed. At the same time, the operator sees the real space in which the motion is planned. This method could be called *programming a virtual Co-robot by demonstration.*

It should be noted that the augmented reality interface could also be used as a means of preliminary modelling of planned operations (see Fig. 5). Also, it could be used for the operations performing in a limited space, or for the operations, which could be associated with the risk of damage to the surrounding objects and to the manipulator itself. In this case operator could use his own experience and intuition to formulate the task for the robot. In this regard, this method is sometimes called – *the intuitive programming* [20].

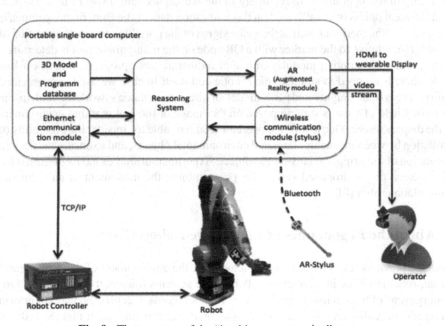

Fig. 9. The structure of the "intuitive programming" system

The structure of the intuitive programming system is shown in Fig. 9 [8]. The system consists of three parts: an operator interface, a portable single-board computer and a manipulator with its own control system. The operator is equipped with augmented reality glasses that allow one to see both the surrounding space and the additional information, which is generated by the augmented reality unit. The programming tool is a freely settable operator – AR (Augmented Reality) – pointer. The position and orientation of the AR-pointer in space is determined at each moment of time with the help of a miniature pinhole camera placed directly on augmented reality glasses. The continuous video signal of the camera is projected by the augmented reality (AR) software unit onto the portable screen, on the plane of the glasses, without distorting the operator's field of view. The portable screen is optically transparent for the operator, providing direct visibility of the work stage through the display. After processing the received information via a wireless communication channel in the augmented reality unit, it is entered into the manipulator motion planning unit. The latter is interconnected with a database including a 3D model of the manipulator itself, its capture, working tool, and manipulation objects. Reference points and trajectories obtained during the training of the robot and presented in the manipulator's own coordinate system are also entered into the database. The desired current position is transmitted to the manipulator via the wireless module from the side of the additional reality system, through the controller of the manipulator.

In the process of motion of the "virtual" gripper of Co-Robot (or of the object of manipulation) the operator could fix its positions, or keep in the robot's memory a completely given trajectory of the motion. The feature of the proposed solution is the ability of the operator to move freely in the workspace and inspect the workspace from different points of view. Based on the calibration data of the camera, the geometric parameters of the marks, as well as the video signal of the portable camera, the position of the observer relative to the marker with a QR code on the manipulator tool is determined in the portable computing module. Unlike of industrial robot programming in off-line mode, there is no need to simulate the robotic cell itself in case we use the augmented reality. The visual (augmented) 3D model of the manipulator's working tool in the operator's field of view is superimposed on the image of the real working environment on the display screen. Due to this, the operator would be able to consider the possibility of a collision between the manipulator and environmental objects, and to ensure the desired orientation of the gripper relatively the object. Experimental studies have confirmed the effectiveness of the proposed system for programming the movement of an industrial manipulation robot [8].

6   About the Ergonomics of Interactive Robotic Systems

From the previous review, one could conclude that the development of the "intelligent" human-robot interface in interactive collaborative systems follows the path of "anthropomorphism" of human intellectual activity. In other words, it copies the ways of human perception of reality and the ways of decision making. It would seem that the tasks of a person in interacting with a robot are simplified extremely and they become available to any user without prior preparation. A person could use his skills to work with another partner person just as well when interacting with a robot partner. This opinion, however, is erroneous. New requirements are also being imposed on the person, since he is (turning?) from controlling the movements of the robot to organizing the tactics of his "behaviour". And in the case of multi-agent robotic system, new requirements are also being imposed to the group control strategy. While this new type of human activity has been less studied, however, problems are already emerging that are related to psychology, perception, the possibilities of operation memory, imaginative thinking, and decision making.

First of all, to control the ICo-Robot, the developed imaginative thinking is required, which allows us to imagine not only the current situation in the workspace, but also the future that will arise when the robot executes the appropriate commands. Moreover, according to the information that the operator receives from a flat screen monitor with remote control, he must restore a three-dimensional image of the situation. An important role is played the stability of attention, as well as the possibility of the attention distribution since the working process could be realized in a complicated environment, in conditions when the robot is amongst another moving objects, including people. This requires certain skills related to the personality characteristics of a person – quick reaction, the ability to anticipate the consequences of own actions.

Additional requirements are applied to the operation memory. Control of ICo-Robots requires simultaneously observation of the situation visually, and at the same time adequately perceive the voice responses of the "partner". To realize this, one must possess the professional terminology, including both terms denoting objects of activity and those actions that must be performed. At the same time, the volume of the vocabulary of a professionally oriented language should be limited by the capabilities of the user's operation memory. Non-verbal signals, for example, gestures, which are recognized by the robot [21], could be used to clarify the operator's instructions together with speech commands. These gestures could be in the nature of individual commands, but they could also be a language similar to the language of the deaf [22]. It is important in the process of interaction with a robot (for?) persons with speech defects or those who do not possess the professionally-oriented language. However, the questions arise about the possibility of effective work, in case a person must simultaneously perceive imaginative, verbal, and textual information.

Recent work in this direction shows, that the efficiency of speech recognition by a robot can be significantly increased by using information about the facial expression of a person, especially in extreme situations [16]. It should be noted that such an analysis, performed by the robot, is also important for evaluation (by a robot!) the state of a person, which significantly affects the ability to perform those his tasks that could be transferred to the robot.

New problems arise when using systems with augmented or virtual reality. It should be borne in mind the features of the organization of the human visual apparatus, in which the accuracy of the perception of space depends on the location of the object in a particular observation zone. In addition, the limitations of the surveillance area of the camera itself, mounted on the operator's head, should be taken into account. In this area, both the control stylus and the working area in which the image of the working tool is moving should be constantly located. All the above requires certain skills to work with such a system. During the research done, it was revealed that the conditional effect of augmented reality requires the development of some skill in the three-dimensional representation of reality by an observer using a portable screen. Nevertheless, in all the studies performed for the operator, it was possible to acquire such a skill easily [8].

Particularly complex psychological problems arise when controlling multi-agent robotic systems, i.e. groups of robots. Despite the fact that methods have already been developed for the automatic distribution of tasks set by the operator for the entire group for each of the robots, anyway, a person must control the result of his task. However, the load on the operation memory of the operator, as well as the requirements for the stability of his attention, would increase significantly. Recent studies show that it goes beyond human capabilities already when managing more than 4–5 objects [23]. From this one could conclude that the robots forming the multi-agent Co-Robot systems must independently create associations, the number of which should not exceed the above value. It becomes obvious that, those tasks that a person must solve to control a group of robots, upgrade from the tactical to the strategic level, which also imposes certain requirements on the operator's operational thinking.

7   Conclusion

The emergence of collaborative robotics was a natural development of production systems that included robots in the direct work process of humans. In essence, collaborative robotics today – is a new stage in the development of the technogeneous human environment, which is characteristic of the 4-th industrial revolution, i.e. for a stage defined commonly as Industry 4.0.

Given the diversity of human activities, which now includes robots, let us assume that we are at the stage in the development of our society when robots become its integral part. Perhaps the main obstacle to this would be not technical, but psychological problems. First of all, the problems of human trust to such systems, especially when performing critical tasks. Starting from driving trains and ending with performing surgical operations associated with immediate risk to the patient. This problem could be solved only by achieving a greater anthropomorphism of interactive robots, but not in a visual appearance. The anthropomorphism should be in the ways of interacting with a person, ways of thinking, evaluation of the situation, making decisions. And on the other hand, a person should be ready to interact with an artificial partner, to understand it real opportunities and limitations. This may require training not only specialists in robotics, but also become one of the aspects of the education of any member of society in the near future. In all cases, the robot would remain the executor of the human will, other than slave, but a full-rights, friendly partner.

References

1. Ronzhin, A., Rigoll, G., Mesheryakov, R.: 4th International Conference, ICR 2019, Istanbul, Turkey, Aug 20–25, p. 340. Springer, LNAI 11659 (2019)
2. Wiener, N.: Cybernetics and Society, London (1954)
3. Kuleshov, V.S., Lakota, N.A.: Dynamics of Manipulators Control system, Moscow, p. 310 (1971)
4. Yin, S., Yuschenko, A.: Application of convolutional neural network to organize the work of collaborative robot as a surgeon assistant. In: Ronzhin, A., Rigoll, G., Meshcheryakov, R. (eds.) Interactive Collaborative Robotics: 4th International Conference, ICR 2019, Istanbul, Turkey, August 20–25, 2019, Proceedings, pp. 287–297. Springer International Publishing, Cham (2019). https://doi.org/10.1007/978-3-030-26118-4_28
5. Serebrenny, V., Lapin, D., Mokaeva, A.: The concept of flexible manufacturing system for a newly forming robotic enterprises. In: Lecture Notes in Engineering and Computer Science: Proceedings of the World Congress on Engineering 2019, pp. 267–271 (2019)

6. Nazarova, A.V., Zhai, M.X.: Organization of rescue robot team for post-disaster management. Robot. Tech. Cybern. **7**(1), 21–28 (2019). https://doi.org/10.31776/RTCJ.7103
7. Nazarova, A.V., Zhai, M.: Distributed solution of problems in multi-agent robotic systems. In: Smart Electromechanical Systems. Studies in Systems, Decision and Control, vol. 174, pp. 117–124. Springer, Cham (2018)
8. Schwandt, A., Yuschenko, A.: Robot manipulator programming interface based on augmened reality. Int. J. Recent Technol. Eng. **8**(284), 819–824 (2019). ISSN 2277-3878
9. Majewski, M., Kacalak, W.: Speech-based interfaces with augmented reality and interactive systems for controlling mobile cranes. In: Ronzhin, A., Rigoll, G., Meshcheryakov, R. (eds.) First International Conference, ICR 2016, pp. 89–98. Springer, LNAI 9812 (2016)
10. Yuschenko, A.: Ergonomic problems of collaborative robotics. Robot. Tech. Cybern. **7**(2), 85–93 (2019). https://doi.org/10.31776/RTCJ.7201
11. Konyshev, D.V., Yuschenko, A.S.: Collaborative mobile robotics as a new stage of service robotics. In: Transaction of the Conference Extreme Robotics. S-Pb. "Politechnika service", pp. 331–340 (2014)
12. Kandrashina, E.Y., Litvinceva, L.V., Pospelov, D.A.: Knowledge representation of time and space in intelligence systems, Moscow, Nauka, p. 307 (1989)
13. Yuschenko, A.S.: Dialogue mode of robot control on the base of fuzzy logic. In: Transaction of the Conference Extreme Robotics S-Pb. "Politechnika service", pp. 143–146 (2015)
14. Deveterikov, E.A., Mikhailov, B.B.: Visual odometer. Vestnik BMSTU Priborostroenie. Special issue no. 6 «Robotic Systems» M., pp. 68–82 (2012)
15. Yuschenko, A.S., Volodin, Y., Michailov, B.B.: Autonomous robot behavior in 3-D world. Mechatron. Autom. Control **11**, 11–15 (2014)
16. Konyshev, D.V., Vorotnikov, S.A., Yuschenko, A.S., Zhonin, A.A.: Mimic recognition and reproduction in bilateral human-robot speech communication, interactive collaborative robotics. In: Ronzhin, A., Rigoll, G., Mesheryakov, R. (eds.) First International Conference ICR, 2016 Budapest, Hungary, Aug 24–26, pp. 133–142. Springer, LNAI 9812 (2016)
17. Yin, S., Yushchenko, A.S.: Dialogue control system for a robot based on the theory of finite automata. Mechatron. Autom. Manage. **20**(11), 686–695 (2019). ISSN 1684-6427
18. Yin, S., Yuschenko, A.: Object Recognition of the Robotic System with Using a Parallel Convolutional Neural Network/Industry 4.0 Issues & New Intelligent Control Paradigms (2019)
19. Leskov, A.G., Seliverstova, E.V.: An algorithm for planning and selecting a method for gripping a deformable object with a multi-fingered gripping device of a handling robot. Mechatron. Autom. Manage. **11**, 739–743 (2017)
20. Akan, B., Ameri, A., Curuklu, B., Asplund, L.: Intuitive industrial robot programming through incremental multimodal language and augmented reality. In: IEEE International Conference on Robotics and Automation (2011)
21. Rogalla, O., Ehrenmann, M., Zöllner, R., Becher, R., Dillmann, R.: Using gesture and speech control for commanding a robot assistant. In: Proceedings of the 11th IEEE International Workshop on Robot and Human Interactive Communication (ROMAN), pp. 454–459. Berlin, September (2002)
22. Gruber, I., Ryumin, D., Hruz, M., Karpov, A.: Sign language numerical gestures recognition using convolutional neural network. In: Ronzhin, A., Rigoll, G., Meshcheryakov, R. (eds.) Third International Conference, ICR 2018, pp. 70–77. Springer, LNAI 11097 (2018)
23. Velichkovskiy, B.B.: Psychological problems of cognitive ergonomics. Mir Psyhologyi **4**, 102–114 (2018)

Development of Model for Labour Productivity Evaluation in Collaborative Technological Cells

Alisa Lapina$^{(\boxtimes)}$ (iD), Dmitriy Lapin (iD), and Vladimir Serebrenny (iD)

Bauman Moscow State Technical University, Moscow 105005, Russia

Abstract. The article considers the development of imitation model to evaluate the labour productivity in the concept of a transformable assembly system with the use of collaborative robotics. One of the key technologies in the development of the transformable assembly system under study is the use of collaborative robotic complexes. The property of collaboration is considered in the sense of interaction between deterministic agents – robots and non-deterministic agents – people within the framework of the described environment, where agents separate a single space and objects in the performance of joint tasks. Within the framework of the system under study the concept of partial operational automation of aircraft hull structures assembly is proposed. The essence of this solution lies in the joint work of a human and a collaborative robot within one technological process – drilling and riveting. Such tasks as primary analysis and concept detailing, development of simulation modeling design based on graphs and game model, formation of conclusions about the obtained results and their interpretation to determine the direction of further research are solved. The result was a baseline model for the implementation for the future virtual and in situ experiments.

Keywords: Collaborative robot · Assembly automation · Robotic manufacturing · Rivet · Fuselage assembly

1 Introduction and Task Definition

Modern tendencies of manufacturing development consist in widen use of automated and robotic complexes and tools [1, 2]. Thus continues to exist an essential barrier in application of robots in such stages of production life cycle which cannot process without participation of the human, as following: labour-consuming operations on assembling and the control, reorganisation and adjustment of manufacturing etc.

The key solution to this problem is the use of collaborative robotic complexes – systems that contain automatic devices that allow work to be performed together with a human. The use of collaborative robots (cobots) [3] in production is currently implemented in the following scenarios: the robot assists a human in the preparation of parts and tools [4–8], or a human performs the functions of an operator [9]. However, in both cases, the potential of the participants in the production process is not fully revealed.

On the basis of the given preconditions the concept which purpose is consideration of the human and the boat as equal participants of the industrial process, carrying out

A. Yuschenko (Ed.): MPoR 2020, CCIS 1426, pp. 44–52, 2021.
https://doi.org/10.1007/978-3-030-88458-1_4

operations simultaneously in uniform working space in uniform transformable assembly system on the basis of multiagent control is developed [10]. At the given stage for achievement of the set goal have been developed: the primary concept of robotization of assembly of hull structures of aircraft, a technique of an estimation of productivity by means of simulation modeling at various scenarios of interaction of the human and the boat is generated, conclusions about rationality of the given concept and ways of its development are made, directions of the further researches are defined.

2 Concept of Transformable Assembly System for Aircraft Body Structures

As an example, the concept of robotic production is discussed in the assembly of an aircraft fuselage. The core of this solution is the simultaneous work of man and cobot in a unified workflow – drilling and riveting.

The time spent on assembly operations is about 50–75% of the aircraft production cycle, and their labor input is 30–40% of it [12]. Riveting is the main method of joining the force components of the airframe structure (spars and ribs). Drilling and riveting operations take about 30–45% of the labor intensity of assembly work: drilling takes 30% of time, countersinking – 13%, rivet insertion – 4%, rivet riveting – 53%. The specifics of production, the complexity of the aircraft design, the variety of conditions of approach to the riveting area cause the usage of hand drills and riveting hammers. Their use does not allow to achieve high labor performance, does not guarantee the quality of joints and negatively affects the human wellness. In specific, it causes occupational diseases such as vibration sickness and hearing loss.

The performance of drilling and riveting work can be examined from a human and a cobot perspective. For the entity "Human" – H the monotony, in other words, the quantity of operations q, is the main factor of difficulty $Diff$. However, H has a high flexibility level, that makes the contribution of reachability d to $Diff$ relatively low and steady. For "Cobot" – K there is an opposite situation due to the limited working area, while the intensity of the work does not affect its performance.

These dependencies allow concluding about the possibility of the highly efficient combination of simultaneous human and robot performance. The collaborative robot performs the most of monotonous operations, the worker is involved when performing operations in a work area inaccessible to the robot. Such a combination makes it possible to reduce the total operational time and overall labor intensity with minimal interference with the existing process (Fig. 1) [13–15].

According to the Fig. 2, the following reference models are highlighted:

- sensor field model – the task of configuration from the theory of operations;
- inverse and forward kinematics – the task of quaternion algebra to obtain data on the current and possible positioning of the manipulator;
- operational control – the task of point generation using the game model – step-by-step matrix machine.

Game-based model is based on two submodels: the model of workpiece marking with the use of image processing and matrix game.

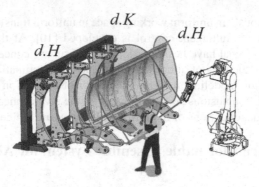

Fig. 1. Example of collaboration: d.H – Human workspace, d.K – Cobot workspace

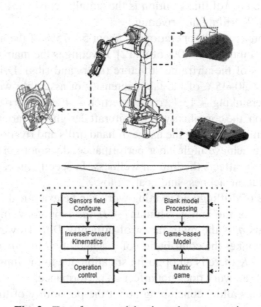

Fig. 2. Transfer to model-oriented representation

3 Approaches for Simulating Model for Labor Productivity Study in the Collaborative Cell

For definition of principles of the further simulation modeling we formalize representation of technological process from the point of view of its participants.

The following methodological and software implementation was developed as a baseline model.

Let's consider the functionality of the drilling and riveting process from the point of view of a Human and a Cobot. At the description of essence "the Human" – H the basic factor of labour performance complexity $Diff$ is its monotony or quantity of operations q. However, thus, H possesses high degree of mobility that makes a contribution of achievability d in $Diff$ rather small and constant. The reverse situation is observed in the essence of "Cobot" – K, associated with the limitation of the Cobot working area, while the monotony of the work done does not affect its performance. The basic hypothesis consists that their combination will allow to reduce total time on performance of operation: the most part of monotonous technological operations is carried out by the cobot, the human, thus, is involved at performance of operations in a working zone inaccessible to the cobot.

The following method based on game theory is used to compare time consumption under various scenarios of human-cobot interaction [14, 15]. On the basis of the image of the trim panel, a matrix was constructed, the elements of which characterize the values of the *Diff* function of complexity from the distance of the hole to the edge of the piece and the distance between the holes.

Further, in the cycle the vector-functions of mutual influencing entities "Human" – H and "Cobot" – K are implemented: when all matrix elements one-by-one are zeroed, the cycle is interrupted. They are characterized by a unique set of parameters, such as the working area, mobility, stock of rivets, fatigue, etc.

To estimate the cost of manufacturing all rivet connections in the part, a simplified model of the part is used, which was represented in this part of research as a 2D graph.

At the first stage it is necessary to build a coordinate grid of the aircraft paneling element. For this purpose, the colorized image of the paneling element shown in Fig. 3 is used.

Next, it is necessary to select the riveting points – the coordinates of the rivets. The scale-invariant feature transform (SURF) method is used for this purpose [16]. This method is used to extract distinctive invariant features from images that can be used to reliably match different views of an object or scene.

Fig. 3. Paneling image sample

The features are invariant to the scale and rotation of the image, which provides a reliable comparison over a significant range of affine distortions, 3D viewpoint changes, added noise, and changes in illumination [17]. The feature points search program was implemented in Python language with the help of OpenCV library. The results of finding points by coordinates of image are shown in Fig. 4.

Based on finding the points, the array of their coordinates is calculated and then converted into a graph. The vertices of the graph are the coordinates on the plane, the edges represent the value Euclidean distance [18] from the nearest points. Then the

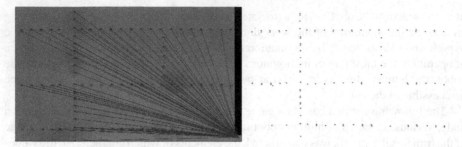

Fig. 4. Search result mask and overlay mask on image

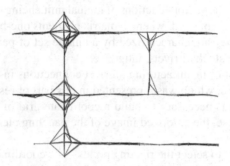

Fig. 5. Connected graph on feature points

graph is transformed to connected graph, presented on Fig. 5. Connection of graph is iteratively a gradual introduction of edges between vertices.

After receiving the connected graph, the salesman problem is solved as an example to form an optimal path for the manipulator for drilling and riveting. The solution is shown in Fig. 6.

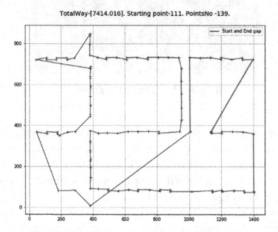

Fig. 6. Travelling salesman problem on graph

The solution determines the optimal starting points for the route as well as the total cost of the route. The results are shown in Fig. 7.

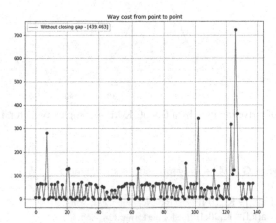

Fig. 7. Way cost from point to point on graph

4   Simulation Modeling Scenarios

The following drilling and riveting scenarios are considered: all operations are performed only by a human, only a robot, they work in series, when one second participant is idle during the work, and in parallel.

To estimate the complexity of the work performed by a human, a fatigue factor is introduced, which depends on the number of performed operations. To estimate the complexity of performing the work by a human, the complexity factor is introduced, which describes the attainability of a particular rivet for the robot due to the configuration of the tool and, as a consequence, the complexity of the geometry of the robot's working space. The heuristically given functions of the complexity coefficients for performing the work by man and by the moth are presented in Fig. 8 and Fig. 9, respectively (Fig. 10).

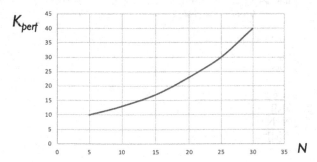

Fig. 8. Human physiological capacity curve: Kperf – fatigue coefficient, N – ordinal number of rivet joint

TOTAL = sum(A)//The sum of the modified matrix elements gives an estimation of labour input of performance of riveting connections on all detail.

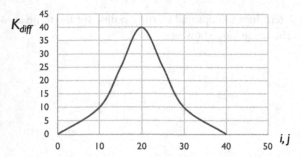

Fig. 9. Complexity of a riveting joint by a Cobot: Kdiff – complexity factor, i, j – distance deep from the part edge

```
while G // while navigation stack is not empty

        a[i,j]= Kperf(N) //cell is performed by Human
        a[k,l]= Kdiff(k,l) //cell is performed by Cobot
        s=(k-(i+1))*cols+cols-j+l-1 // cell spacing

        if S<Smin //if distance between Human and Cobot is less than
        required
        a[i,j]= Kperf(N)*M //M=1,5 – complexity "fine"
        a[k,l]= Kdiff(k,l)*M
        N=N+1
        G[i,j]=0
        G[k,l]=0

TOTAL=sum(A)
```

(a)

```
while G //while navigation stack is not empty

        if Kdiff< KdiffMax // Cobot starts and do work while difficutly is
        not max (there will be geometrically unreachable points)

        a[i,j]= Kdiff(i,j) // the cell records the complexity
        G[i,j]=0 // the cell coordinates are removed from the navigation
        stack

        else // Human finishes the rest of the cells
        a[i,j]= Kperf(N) // the fatigue estimation is recorded in the cell
        N=N+1
        G[i,j]=0 //the cell coordinates are removed from the navigation
        stack

TOTAL=sum(A)
```

(b)

Fig. 10. Pseudocode of simulation model execution at serial (a) and parallel operation (b).

5 Simulation Modeling Results

In case when a man and a robot work in series or in parallel, it is necessary to formalize the set of rules of the robot's behavior. All movements of a person in the vicinity of the selected point are considered equal. The choice of the starting point and the algorithm of traversing the neighboring points were accepted in the same way as when a man and a robot work separately. When working sequentially, the robot performs the maximum available to it due to the geometry of the workspace and the configuration of the connection tool, the man dazzles the remaining holes. The developed model will allow in the future various virtual experiments to check hypotheses about control and adaptation algorithms of the Cobot.

6 Conclusions

In the course of the work the concept of robotic assembly of aircraft hull structures was proposed. A simulation model was formed to assess the productivity of the collaborative work of the Cobot and the Human. In the future it is planned to consider game-based move by nature model to form rules of dynamic division of joint working zone from the point of view of cyber-physical system [19, 20].

References

1. Akberdina, V., Kalinina, A., Vlasov, A.: Transformation stages of the Russian industrial complex in the context of economy digitization. Probl. Perspect. Manage. **16**(4), 201 (2018)
2. Wang, L., Törngren, M., Onori, M.: Current status and advancement of cyber-physical systems in manufacturing. J. Manuf. Syst. **37**, 517–527 (2015)
3. Colgate J., Peshkin M.: US Patent No. 5952796: Cobots//Patent, Sep 1999.
4. Serebrenny, V., Lapin, D., Mokaeva, A.: The concept of an aircraft hull structures assembly process robotization. In: AIP Conference Proceedings, vol. 2171, No. 1, p. 170007. AIP Publishing LLC (2019)
5. Maurtua, I., Ibarguren, A., Kildal, J., Susperregi, L., Sierra Maurtua, B.: Human–robot collaboration in industrial applications: safety, interaction and trust. Int. J. Adv. Robot. Syst. **14**(4), 1–10 (2017)
6. Rosenstrauch, M.J., Krüger, J.: Safe human-robot-collaboration-introduction and experiment using ISO/TS 15066. In: 2017 3rd International Conference on Control, Automation and Robotics (ICCAR), pp. 740–744. IEEE (2017)
7. Cherubini, A., Passama, R., Crosnier, A., Lasnier, A., Fraisse, P.: Collaborative manufacturing with physical human–robot interaction. Robot. Comput. Integr. Manuf. **40**, 1–13 (2016)
8. Bütepage, J., Kragic, D.: Human-robot collaboration: from psychology to social robotics. arXiv preprint arXiv:1705.10146 (2017)
9. Vorotnikov, S., Ermishin, K., Nazarova, A., Yuschenko, A.: Multi-agent robotic systems in collaborative robotics. In: Ronzhin, A., Rigoll, G., Meshcheryakov, R. (eds.) Interactive Collaborative Robotics: Third International Conference, ICR 2018, Leipzig, Germany, September 18–22, 2018, Proceedings, pp. 270–279. Springer International Publishing, Cham (2018). https://doi.org/10.1007/978-3-319-99582-3_28
10. Drouot, A., Irving, L., Sanderson, D., Smith, A., Ratchev, S.: A transformable manufacturing concept for low-volume aerospace. IFAC-PahumanLine **50**(1), 5712–5717 (2017)

11. Serebrenny, V., Lapin, D., Mokaeva, A.: The perspective flexible manufacturing system for a newly forming robotic enterprises: approach to organization subsystem formation. In: Lecture Notes in Engineering and Computer Science: Proceedings of The World Congress on Engineering and Computer Science 2019, San Francisco, USA, 22–24 October, pp. 438–441 (2019)
12. Vashukov, Y.A.: Technology and Equipment of Assembly Processes [Electronic resource] Samara. https://docplayer.ru/31668726-Yu-a-vashukov-o-v-lomovskoy-a-a-sharov.html (2011). Accessed 15 Feb 2019 (in Russian)
13. Shannon, R.E., Long, S.S., Buckles, B.P.: Operation research methodologies in industrial engineering: a survey. AIIE Trans. **12**(4), 364–367 (1980). https://doi.org/10.1080/05695558008974528
14. Myerson, R.B.: Game Theory. Harvard University Press (2013)
15. Bütepage, J., Kragic, D.: Human-robot collaboration: from psychology to social robotics. arXiv preprint arXiv:1705.10146 (2017)
16. Panchal, P.M., Panchal, S.R., Shah, S.K.: A comparison of SIFT and SURF. Int. J. Innov. Res. Comput. Commun. Eng. **1**(2), 323–327 (2013)
17. Lowe, D.G.: Distinctive image features from scale-invariant keypoints. Int. J. Comput. Vis. **60**(2), 91–110 (2004)
18. Wang, L., Zhang, Y., Feng, J.: On the Euclidean distance of images. IEEE Trans. Pattern Anal. Mach. Intell. **27**(8), 1334–1339 (2005)
19. Sadrfaridpour, B., Saeidi, H., Burke, J., Madathil, K., Wang, Y.: Modeling and control of trust in human-robot collaborative manufacturing. In: Mittu, R., Sofge, D., Wagner, A., Lawless, W.F. (eds.) Robust Intelligence and Trust in Autonomous Systems, pp. 115–141. Springer, Boston, MA (2016). https://doi.org/10.1007/978-1-4899-7668-0_7
20. Volodin, S.Y., Mikhaylov, B.B., Yuschenko, A.S.: Autonomous robot control in partially undetermined world via fuzzy logic. In: Ceccarelli, M., Glazunov, V.A. (eds.) Advances on Theory and Practice of Robots and Manipulators, pp. 197–203. Springer International Publishing, Cham (2014). https://doi.org/10.1007/978-3-319-07058-2_23

Robotic Systems Design and Simulation

Increasing the Dynamic Characteristics of the Autonomous Mobile Robot by Adapting the Fuzzy Controllers of the Executive Level of the Specifics of Tactical Actions

Yuri A. Bykovtsev$^{(\boxtimes)}$, Genady G. Kalach, Valery M. Lokhin, Sergei V. Manko, and Alexander A. Morozov

Institute of Cybernetics, MIREA – Russian Technological University, Moscow, Russia
bykovtsev_yuri@vivaldi.net

Abstract. In recent years, the principle of hierarchical building of intelligent control systems for complex dynamic objects, including autonomous mobile robots of a range of base types, has been accepted. In accordance with this principle, the hierarchy includes, in addition to the information-gathering, three levels of control: executive (drive), tactical – provides a set of expedient actions and strategic – plans the behavior of a mobile object. The effectiveness of intelligent (and, in particular, fuzzy) executive level controllers is well justified. In this paper, we study the problem of increasing management efficiency by increasing the intellectual properties of the control system, i.e. due to the "movement" up the hierarchy and communication organization of the tactical and executive levels of the management system. In the presence of such a connection, smart executive level controllers can be rebuilt depending on the tactics of actions of a mobile robot. The combination of two levels provides a significant increase in the adaptive properties of a mobile robot, for example, improving patency or ensuring the accuracy of the required maneuvers by adjusting the wheel drive controllers when the mobile robot moves on various soils. The task of planning movements and controlling the movement of autonomous mobile robots allows for many options for the initial setting (depending on the operating environment, restrictions on control actions, properties of the mobile platform, etc.). Accordingly, there are very different approaches to its solution: potential fields, genetic algorithms, fuzzy logic, etc. The work shows that it is convenient to organize the communication between the executive and tactical levels on the basis of fuzzy logic. This approach allows to organize a quick reconfiguration of executive level regulators within 0.1 ms. The effectiveness of the proposed approach is illustrated on models, on a prototype of a servo-drive and on quadrocopter flights when making various maneuvers.

Keywords: Fuzzy logic · Control system · Navigation system · Expert system · Quadrocopter

1 Introduction

In recent years, with the development of autonomous and semi-autonomous robots, it has become increasingly obvious and promising to use intelligent technologies at all

© Springer Nature Switzerland AG 2021
A. Yuschenko (Ed.): MPoR 2020, CCIS 1426, pp. 55–71, 2021.
https://doi.org/10.1007/978-3-030-88458-1_5

levels of the control system hierarchy [1–16]. That is why, both in Russia and abroad, new methods and algorithms for planning behavior and organizing appropriate actions of mobile robots are being actively developed, i.e. the tasks of improving the tactical and strategic levels of control system are being addressed.

A certain reserve for increasing the effectiveness of the control system is laid in the organization of rational interaction of control system's levels among themselves. The following concept is developed in this article:

- For the studied mobile robot, a set of the most characteristic movements, called typical, is being formed
- A fuzzy controller is selected for each typical movement, providing the best dynamic performance of the robot
- During the movement of the mobile robot, the nature of its movement is identified, the closest typical movement is determined, and the corresponding controller is connected.

As an example of the mobile robot is considered quadrocopter.

2 Quadrocopter's Control System

The proposed structure of a multilevel quadrocopter's control system is presented in Fig. 1.

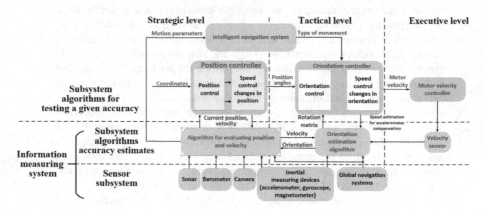

Fig. 1. The generalized structure of a quadrocopter's control system

As can be seen from Fig. 1, the tasks of the strategic level include controlling the position of the quadrocopter based on information received from the information-measuring system (IMS) and the current coordinates of the aircraft. The strategic level forms setpoints for the position angles necessary to perform the maneuver and transfers them to the tactical level of the control system.

At the tactical level, the quadrocopter is monitored in space along the three axes of the associated coordinate system (pitch, roll and yaw axes) and, based on the type of movement defined by the intelligent navigation system (INS), setpoints of velocity are made for the motors of the executive level motors. Information from the executive level, measured by velocity sensors, transfers to the IMS, namely, into the subsystem of algorithms for evaluating position and velocity, resulting in closing the control system.

Particular attention should be paid to the division of IMS into two subsystems: the sensory subsystem and the subsystem of algorithms for assessing accuracy. Since the quadrocopter is subject to increased requirements for maneuverability while maintaining high accuracy, the IMS also has higher requirements for the speed and accuracy of evaluating the parameters of the control system. The approach used, which involves the allocation of a subsystem for assessing accuracy, allows to work out these aspects in detail and, as a result, increase the accuracy and speed of the entire control system as a whole.

The second feature proposed in Fig. 1 of the structure consists in the fact that in order to organize commands for tuning of executive level controllers, it is necessary to "understand" the tactics of the quadrocopter, determined by the navigation system. Therefore, this navigation system is endowed with intellectual properties and is based on the combined use of expert systems technologies and fuzzy logic. The physical parameters as input expert minutes system perform readings from the inertial sensors, a global navigation satellite system and an optical system, and as output – quadrocopter motion type and motion parameters (navigation solutions) (Fig. 2).

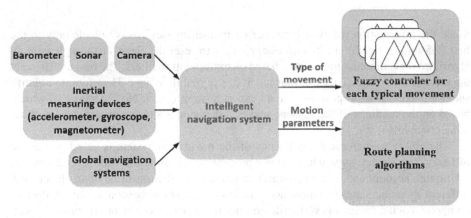

Fig. 2. Intelligent navigation system

Intelligent navigation system [17] solves, in essence, two important tasks:

- identification of the state (parameters) of movement
- identification of the type of movement (turns, acceleration, braking)

As can be seen from Fig. 3, the expert system is conventionally represented by three blocks. The first expert unit calculates the weighting coefficients for calculating the azimuthal angle, the second expert unit calculates the height of the object above sea level based on readings from the global navigation satellite system (GPS), and the third expert unit provides information on the dynamic state of the object by type: stop/moving.

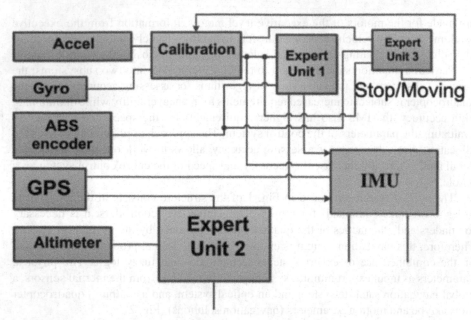

Fig. 3. General algorithm of the navigation system based on fuzzy logic technology

Since the information received from inertial measuring devices is reliable only in the first 2–5 min of operation, it is necessary either to reset the error, or to implement an algorithm for estimating the position based on extrapolation filters. The best time to reset the error is the complete lack of movement of the mobile object. Therefore, to identify such moments, it is proposed to use an expert system (block No. 3 in Fig. 3), which, based on the readings of the sensors, makes a decision about the dynamic state of the object (stop/moving).

The ability to increase the efficiency of the navigation system is based on the use of fuzzy logic technology, which allows processing information from several sensors, taking into account and revealing blurred boundaries of the transition of an object from different dynamic states (rotation, acceleration, etc.). Thus, as soon as the intellectual component of the navigation system determines the type of movement of a mobile object, the most suitable sensor can be used to improve the estimation of motion parameters. Based on the results of the identification, classical algorithms for the strapdown inertial navigation system (SINS) are included, taking into account the selected inertial sensors.

As a set of typical quadrocopter movements, a set of three components is proposed (Fig. 4):

- movement along the "square";
- movement along the trajectory of the "snake";
- circular motion.

The implementation of the concept of typical movements suggests the following (Fig. 5). At the tactical level of the quadrocopter control system, typical fuzzy controllers

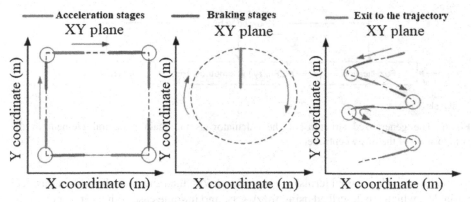

Fig. 4. Typical quadcopter trajectories

are pre-configured to go through typical trajectories. Based on the information received from the intelligent navigation system, the tactical level, "understanding" the current tactics of movement, activates a typical fuzzy controller that is most suitable for a specific movement.

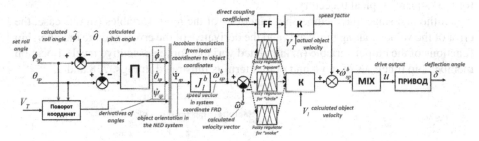

Fig. 5. Fuzzy quadcopter control system at the tactical level

The functioning process of each of the typical fuzzy controllers tuned to a specific type of movement involves the sequential implementation of the following main steps (Fig. 6):

1. fuzzification, which provides a comparison of the values of input variables with membership functions of the conditional part (antecedent) of individual rules;
2. fuzzy inference, ensuring the formation and aggregation of the desired conclusions based on the processing of the investigative part (consequential) of the rules available in the knowledge base, taking into account the results of fuzzification;
3. defuzzification, providing the conversion of the results of fuzzy inference to the final value of the output variable.

It should be noted that the knowledge base of fuzzy regulators is formed in the form of logical-linguistic models, which at the level of production rules determine the qualitative relationship of input and output variables. Moreover, the linguistic values of

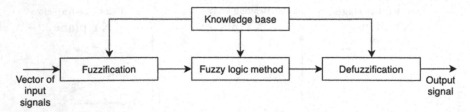

Fig. 6. The generalized structure of the calculator as the main structural element in the composition of the fuzzy controller

linguistic variables (called terms) are associated with the ranges of changes in physical variables, which are described using fuzzy sets, and in some cases other representations:

IF X_1 is A_{11} **AND**... **AND** X_m isA_{1m}, **THEN** Y isB_1;
IF X_1 is A_{p1} **AND**... **AND** X_m isA_{pm}, **THEN** Y isB_p;

There are several schemes for constructing the logical-linguistic models and the organization of their further processing. As part of this work, it was decided to use a Mamdani fuzzy model [3]. Let's show an example of synthesis process of fuzzy controller for the "square" typical trajectory.

At the first stage, the membership functions of the input variables (in this case, the error of the velocity along the X axis and the derivative of the error) and the membership functions of the output variable (manipulated variable for the executive level). Location membership functions of input and output term is illustrated in Figs. 7, 8 and 9.

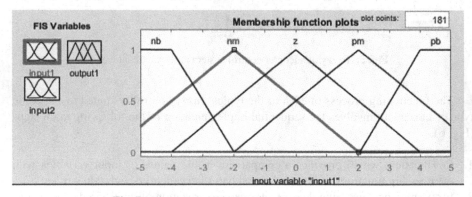

Fig. 7. The membership function for the speed error

The base of production rules, linking the input and output linguistic variables, has the following structure:

1.   If (input1 is nb) and (input2 is nb) then (output1 is nb)
2.   If (input1 is nb) and (input2 is nm) then (output1 is nb)
3.   If (input1 is nb) and (input2 is z) then (output1 is nm)

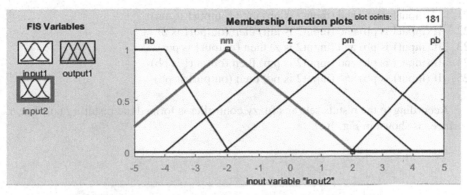

Fig. 8. The membership function for the derivative of the speed error

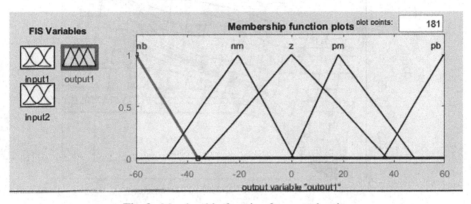

Fig. 9. Membership function for control action

4. If (input1 is nb) and (input2 is pm) then (output1 is z)
5. If (input1 is nb) and (input2 is pb) then (output1 is pm)
6. If (input1 is nm) and (input2 is nb) then (output1 is nm)
7. If (input1 is nm) and (input2 is nm) then (output1 is nm)
8. If (input1 is nm) and (input2 is z) then (output1 is nm)
9. If (input1 is nm) and (input2 is pm) then (output1 is z)
10. If (input1 is nm) and (input2 is pb) then (output1 is pm)
11. If (input1 is z) and (input2 is nb) then (output1 is nm)
12. If (input1 is z) and (input2 is nm) then (output1 is z)
13. If (input1 is z) and (input2 is z) then (output1 is z)
14. If (input1 is z) and (input2 is pm) then (output1 is z)
15. If (input1 is z) and (input2 is pb) then (output1 is pm)
16. If (input1 is pm) and (input2 is nb) then (output1 is nm)
17. If (input1 is pm) and (input2 is nm) then (output1 is z)
18. If (input1 is pm) and (input2 is z) then (output1 is pm)
19. If (input1 is pm) and (input2 is pm) then (output1 is pm)
20. If (input1 is pm) and (input2 is pb) then (output1 is pb)

21. If (input1 is pb) and (input2 is nb) then (output1 is nm)
22. If (input1 is pb) and (input2 is nm) then (output1 is z)
23. If (input1 is pb) and (input2 is z) then (output1 is pm)
24. If (input1 is pb) and (input2 is pm) then (output1 is pb)
25. If (input1 is pb) and (input2 is pb) then (output1 is pb)

According to the results settings fuzzy controller is formed the resulting non-linear surface, as shown in Fig. 10.

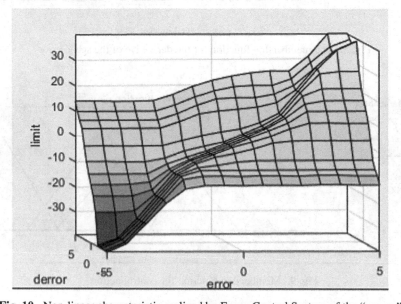

Fig. 10. Non-linear characteristic realized by Fuzzy Control System of the "square"

Thanks to the description at the level of the logical-linguistic model, it is possible to synthesize the nonlinear law of the fuzzy controller without analyzing the complex and multiply connected model of the quadrocopter control system for all other typical trajectories.

3   Experimental Studies of Quadrocopter's Control System

In the course of research on a real quadrocopter (Clever 4) and its model, a series of experiments was carried out, the purpose of which was:

- assessment of the quality of the passage of typical trajectories (square, circle, snake) by a quadrocopter using fuzzy controllers at speeds up to 0.2 m/s,
- assessment of the quality of the passage of a series of typical trajectories by a quadrocopter using fuzzy controllers at a speed of 0.5 m/s,
- development of the switching mode of typical fuzzy regulators.

Figures 11, 12 and 13 show the trajectories of the quadrocopter during the passage of the entire set of typical trajectories using one typical controller at low speeds.

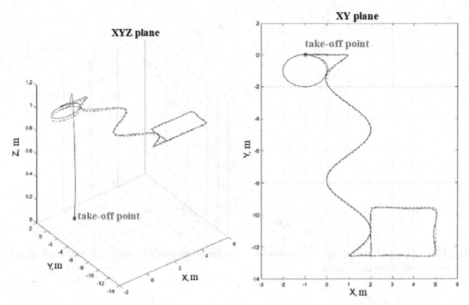

Fig. 11. Passage of a set of typical trajectories by a quadrocopter with a standard regulator configured for circular motion

This experiment shows that at low speeds a fuzzy controller of one type fulfills all typical trajectories at a satisfactory level. As the speed of the aircraft increases, the difference in the accuracy of working out the same paths by different standard controllers becomes apparent (Figs. 14, 15 and 16).

From an analysis of Figs. 14, 15 and 16, we can conclude that at high speeds, a fuzzy controller tuned to a certain type of movement provides a path accuracy of 10–15% better than other typical controllers when moving along the same path.

The experiment on practicing switching between regulators during movement is interesting primarily because the control system of a mobile object in the mode of switching the motion path can be considered as a non-stationary system. This, obviously, raises the question of the stability of the control system at the time of switching. Figures 17, 18, 19 and 20 show various switching options between the controllers, with the switching time being 0.1 ms. Experimental studies show that control system of a quadrocopter in the mode of switching typical controllers remain stable, which corresponds to the results set forth in [18, 19] on studies of nonstationary system.

Based on the results of the experiments, the following conclusions can be drawn:

1. The introduction of fuzzy controllers for predefined standard trajectories can improve the accuracy of the control system, while the advantages of this approach become more pronounced with increasing speed of the quadrocopter.

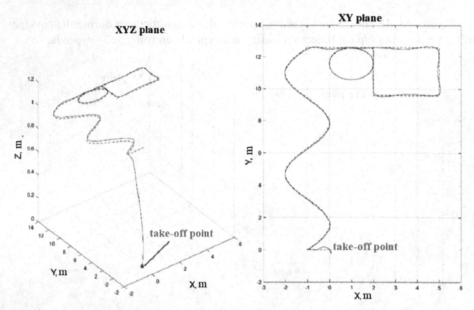

Fig. 12. Passage of a set of typical trajectories with a quadrocopter with a typical controller, mood for movement along the "snake"

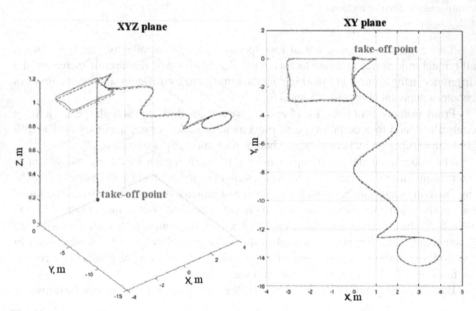

Fig. 13. Passage of a set of typical trajectories by a quadrocopter with a standard controller configured to move along the "square"

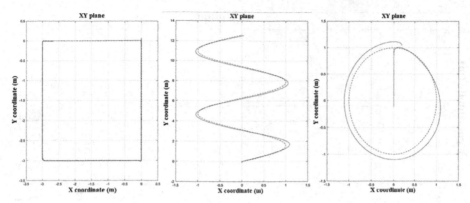

Fig. 14. Movement along typical trajectories with a fuzzy regulator tuned for "square"

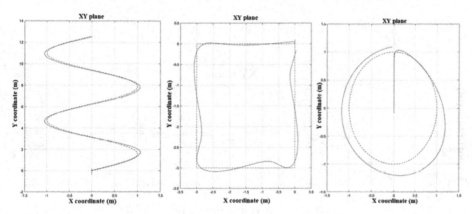

Fig. 15. Movement along typical trajectories with a fuzzy controller tuned for "snake"

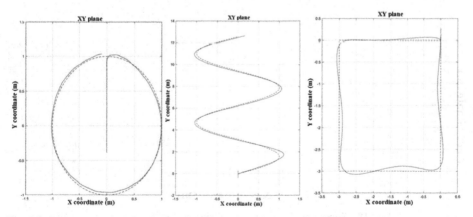

Fig. 16. Movement along typical trajectories with a fuzzy controller tuned for flying around the circle

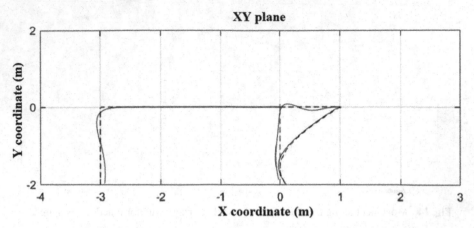

Fig. 17. Switching from the "square" path to the "snake" path

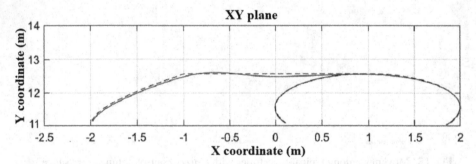

Fig. 18. Switching from the "snake" path to the "circle" path

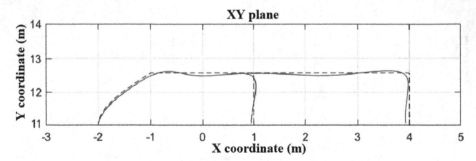

Fig. 19. Switching from the "snake" path to the "square" path

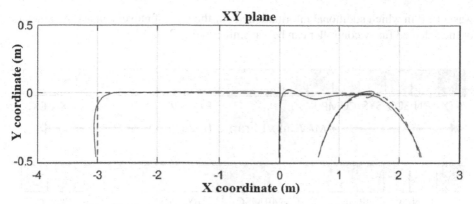

Fig. 20. Switching from the "square" path to the "circle" path

2. At the moment of switching the regulators, the control system does not lose stability.

The developed quadrocopter control system has close integration of all control levels, moreover, the appearance of an intelligent navigation block imposes requirements on the scheme of information exchange between levels. In this regard, the question arises about the availability of existing information exchange protocols that satisfy the requirements of scalability, easy implementation, and small requirements for management interfaces or developing new ones.

Existing on-board hardware and software systems allow the integration of third-party modules via open protocols and software interfaces and have open source code that allows modification of existing flexible solutions to fit your needs.

One of these protocols is the MavLink protocol [20], which is used as the main one for the exchange of control information between control units in onboard navigation systems of aircraft.

Since during the interaction of additional algorithms at the tactical or strategic levels the information transfer may not be synchronized due to specific signals that are not included in the protocol description, it is proposed to use the second version of the protocol (Fig. 21), which has bytes INC and CMP flags signaling compatibility transmitted information.

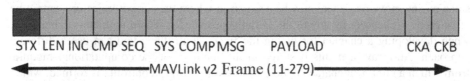

STX LEN INC CMP SEQ SYS COMP MSG   PAYLOAD   CKA CKB
◄──────────────────MAVLink v2 Frame (11-279)──────────────────►

Fig. 21. The frame size and description of the second version of the protocol Mavlink (INC – incompatibility flag, CMP – Compatibility flag)

Considering the specifics and information transmitted between the strategic and tactical levels through the intelligent navigation system, an AI flag (information byte) was added in which additional information about the type of movement and parameters of the selected fuzzy controller can be transmitted (Fig. 22).

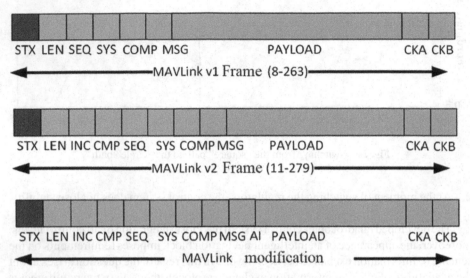

Fig. 22. Comparison of the first two revisions Mavlink with modernized version of the protocol

In the context of the approach being developed, the presence of two additional bytes in the packet header will tell the control unit about the addressee and source of information, and the size of the Payload buffer will not be wasted on encapsulating this information.

With this organization of the channel for transmitting information from the intelligent navigation system to the tactical level of the control system, the parameters of the entire set of typical fuzzy controllers must be stored in hardware memory in advance, and the software and algorithmic software should activate the corresponding set of controller parameters that best suits the current tactical task. Of the pronounced advantages of this approach, it is worth noting the fast switching speed between the regulators (it was approximately 100 µs), however, two drawbacks cannot be noted. Firstly, the presence of several controllers instead of one increases the requirement for the amount of memory required to store the entire set of controllers. Secondly, this approach has less flexibility, since during movement there may be a situation where the current trajectory cannot be effectively worked out by any of the initially provided standard regulators. Therefore, when developing a channel for tuning the fuzzy controllers, you can use a different approach. An array of points is stored in the memory of the computational module, from which a nonlinear characteristic of the required fuzzy controller is formed, which is a piecewise linear approximation of the initial nonlinear transformation. When a command for restructuring appears, the algorithmic software can both completely rewrite the structure of the nonlinear control law and change only the necessary part of the characteristic. The data transfer protocol used in this work is depicted in Fig. 23.

This protocol is based on the Modbus protocol. Unlike the Mavlink protocol, there is practically no overhead information (parity, compatibility flags, and so on) to reduce the

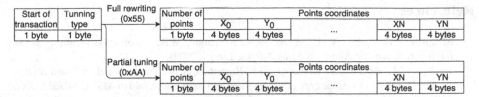

Start of transaction	Tunning type	Full rewriting (0x55)	Number of points	Points coordinates					
				X_0	Y_0		...	XN	YN
1 byte	1 byte		1 byte	4 bytes	4 bytes			4 bytes	4 bytes

		Partial tuning (0xAA)	Number of points	Points coordinates					
				X_0	Y_0		...	XN	YN
			1 byte	4 bytes	4 bytes			4 bytes	4 bytes

Fig. 23. Data transfer protocol for tuning a fuzzy controller

time required to reconfigure the controller. During experimental studies, it was found that the maximum time required for a complete rewrite of the nonlinear characteristics of a fuzzy controller does not exceed 150 ms. Although this approach is somewhat inferior to the previous one in terms of tuning speed, it has greater flexibility, since it is possible to set almost any nonlinear characteristic of the controller. It is also worth noting that the indicated time represents the maximum time that will be spent only in the event of a complete rewriting of the characteristic, which is not always necessary – in some cases, you can change the values of only individual points.

4 Conclusion

In the scope of this work, we study the possibility of improving the quality of the quadrocopter control system by introducing the concept of typical trajectory movements. The use of an intelligent navigation system, built on the basis of a combination of expert system technologies and fuzzy logic, allows to determine not only the current parameters, but also the type of object movement based on MEMS readings from the information-measuring system. After that, fuzzy regulators are switched, pre-configured to the corresponding standard ones. Experimental studies have shown that the introduction of fuzzy controllers for predetermined typical trajectories can improve the accuracy of the control system by 10–15%, while the advantages of this approach become more pronounced with increasing speed of the quadrocopter. At the same time, the control system at the time of switching the regulators remains stable. In conclusion, two methods of organizing a channel for transmitting information from an intelligent navigation system to the tactical level of a control system are presented, their main advantages and disadvantages are given.

In this paper, the concept of typical motions was considered in relation to an aircraft. However, it seems promising for other complex objects, while requiring a small modernization. For example, for autonomous ground-based mobile robots, the considered concept is transformed into the concept of typical underlying surfaces, for which the appropriate regulators are pre-selected. The structure and justification of the principles of the functioning of the system do not change (only the composition of the sensors changes). For underwater vehicles, a combination of different underwater currents can be considered as typical.

Funding. This work was supported by the Russian Science Foundation, according to research project 16-19-00052.

References

1. Makarov, I.M., Lohin, V.M., Manko, S.V., Romanov, M.P.: Automation synthesis study intelligent automatic control systems, Nauka, 228 p. (2009)
2. Lokhin, V.M., Manko, S.V., Romanov, M.P., Romanov, A.M.: The universal on-board control system for robots of various type of deployment and purpose. Herald of MSTU MIREA **3**(8), 230–248 (2015)
3. Lokhin, V.M., Kazachek, N.A., Ryabcov, V.A.: Complex research of dynamics of control systems with fuzzy P-controller. Int. J. Mater. Mech. Manuf. **4**(2), 140–144 (2016). https://doi.org/10.7763/IJMMM.2016.V4.242
4. Kalach, G., Kazachek, N., Volosnyh, G.: Fuzzy controllers in the control system of a brushless electric motor using HIL technology. MATEC Web Conf. **132**, 02001 (2017). https://doi.org/10.1051/matecconf/201713202001
5. Kalach, G., Kazachek, N.: Strategic level of mobile robot control system based on fuzzy logic. Int. J. Eng. Technol. **7**(4.38), 1615–1619 (2018)
6. Nadezhdin, I.S., Goryunov, A.G., Manenti, F.: Fuzzy adaptive control system of a non-stationary plant. IOP Conf. Ser. Mater. Sci. Eng. **142**(1), 1–8 (2016). https://doi.org/10.1088/1757-899X/142/1/012048
7. Siddique, N.: Fuzzy control. Stud. Comput. Intell. **517**, 95–135 (2014). https://doi.org/10.1007/978-3-319-02135-5
8. Lamamra, K., Batat, F., Mokhtari, F.: A new technique with improved control quality of nonlinear systems using an optimized fuzzy logic controller. Expert Syst. Appl. **145**, 113148 (2019). https://doi.org/10.1016/j.eswa.2019.113148
9. Errouha, M., Derouich, A., Motahhir, S., Zamzoum, O., El Ouanjli, N., El Ghzizal, A.: Optimization and control of water pumping PV systems using fuzzy logic controller. Energy Rep. **5**, 853–865 (2019). https://doi.org/10.1016/j.egyr.2019.07.001
10. Sabahi, K., Ghaemi, S., Badamchizadeh, M.A.: Designing an adaptive type-2 fuzzy logic system load frequency control for a nonlinear time-delay power system. Appl. Soft Comput. **43**, 97–106 (2016). https://doi.org/10.1016/j.asoc.2016.02.012
11. Ren, Y.-Q., Duan, X.-G., Li, H.-X., Chen, C.: Multi-variable fuzzy logic control for a class of distributed parameter systems. J. Process Control **23**, 351–358 (2013). https://doi.org/10.1016/j.jprocont.2012.12.004
12. Eltamaly, A., Farh, H.M.H.: Maximum power extraction from wind energy system based on fuzzy logic control. Electric Power Syst. Res. **97**, 144–150 (2013). https://doi.org/10.1016/j.epsr.2013.01.001
13. Vandegrift, M.W., Lewis, F.L., Jagannathan, S., Liu, K.: Adaptive fuzzy logic control of discrete-time dynamical systems. In: Proceedings of Tenth International Symposium on Intelligent Control, pp. 395–401. Monterey, CA, USA (1995)
14. Bergh, L., Yianatos, J., Olivares, J., Durán, J.: Predictive expert control system of a hybrid pilot rougher flotation circuit. IFAC-PapersOnLine **49**, 155–160 (2016). https://doi.org/10.1016/j.ifacol.2016.10.113
15. Soyguder, S., Karaköse, M., Alli, H.: Design and simulation of self-tuning PID-type fuzzy adaptive control for an expert HVAC system. Expert Syst. Appl. **36**, 4566–4573 (2009). https://doi.org/10.1016/j.eswa.2008.05.031
16. Jones, A.V., Vingerhoeds, R., Rodd, M.G.: Real-time expert systems for flight control. IFAC Proc. Vol. **29**, 203–208 (1996). https://doi.org/10.1016/S1474-6670(17)43721-9
17. Kalach, G.G., Romanov, A.M., Tripolskiy, P.E.: Loosely coupled navigation system based on expert system using fuzzy logic. In: 2016 XIX IEEE International Conference on Soft Computing and Measurements (SCM), St. Petersburg, pp. 167–169 (2016)

18. Berdnikov, V., Lokhin, V.: Synthesis of guaranteed stability regions of a nonstationary non-linear system with a fuzzy controller. Civ. Eng. J. **5**(1), 107 (2019). https://doi.org/10.28991/cej-2019-03091229

19. Berdnikov, V., Lokhin, V., Uvaysov, S.: Determination of guaranteed stability regions of systems with a pid controller and a parametrically perturbed control object. In: 2019 International Seminar on Electron Devices Design and Production (SED), Prague, Czech Republic, pp. 1–5 (2019)

20. Marty, J.A.: Vulnerability analysis of the mavlink protocol for command and control of unmanned aircraft. Air Force Institute Of Technology, Wright-Patterson AFB OH Graduate School Of Engineering and Management. AFIT-ENG-14-M-50 (2013)

Teaching Real Robots: The Right Way to Set up Learning-Based Systems for Your Robot

Ali Younes[1] and Arkady Yuschenko[2(✉)]

[1] Technische Universität Darmstadt, Darmstadt, Germany
ali@robot-learning.de
[2] Bauman Moscow State Technical University, Moscow, Russia

Abstract. The typical robotics system consists of perception, planning, and control modules. Each module is built upon information about its components, where modeling each part of the system plays an essential role in the design process. In practice, working with the non-linear models in robotics systems involves a lot of approximations which hinders reaching the optimal behavior for the goal task. Alongside the difficulties in redeploying the system to solve other similar tasks. Learning-based methods provide a promising approach for robotic systems. In the last decade, the interest in incorporating machine learning into robotics systems has been evolving rapidly. The benefit of using learning is the possibility to design systems that are independent of the dynamical model of the robot, with the flexibility to adopt new tasks and learn to excel in performance over time. The theory behind designing a learning-based system is still under development, ranges from end-to-end systems to hybrid systems that use inaccurate approximate models. In this paper, we are proposing the results of our research in learning-based systems, presenting our view for the right way to set up learning systems for robotics. The results are a whole learning-based framework for robotics applications, works efficiently (1 h of training – 10 min robot movement) with minimum human intervention (user has to provide video demonstrations only).

Keywords: Robotics · Reinforcement learning · Self-supervised learning · Contrastive learning

1 Introduction

The ingredients to design robotics systems start from understanding the needed components to be included in it. The standard structure of a robotic system consists of perception, planning, and control modules. The choice of each one of these modules depends on the application, the desired performance, and some design criteria.

A perception system is responsible for interpreting the data from the sensors to compatible state signals. The type of the output of the perception system depends on the set value's type in a simple system (e.g. voltage and current). In a more advanced system, the perception system (state estimation block) has to infer informative states from the sensor data e.g. localization of the robot [1], or the position and velocity of

© Springer Nature Switzerland AG 2021
A. Yuschenko (Ed.): MPoR 2020, CCIS 1426, pp. 72–84, 2021.
https://doi.org/10.1007/978-3-030-88458-1_6

objects. Designing a perception system is a challenging task [2], in robots lots of research done with states given by positioning systems. Recently, the interest shifted to extract informative states from more accessible sensors (systems), like images from cameras, depth information from laser sensors, and torque from motors [3].

We argue that using machine learning to learn representation is the future for perception modules in robotics systems. The positional and movement information of the object doesn't describe the correct step of the progress of the task, a higher latent representation could be more beneficial [4]. Using self-supervised learning to learn an embedding representation [5] for each set of sensor data in the latent space helps in forming a suitable perception system for each task.

The task of planning is the process of building a trajectory for the robot to follow. Giving the fact that the robot is moving from a state to state (in a state-space), possible trajectories are all combinations of actions that lead to getting the robot moved from an initial state to the desired goal state. The most common uses of planning [6] are planning over grids; where each node of the grid corresponds to the coordinates of a point in a map. Another common type is planning over graphs, where we represent possible states of the robot as nodes of the graph, and the edges are the possible transition. The goal of the planning over grids is to reach the target with minimum transitions, the same for unweighted graphs. For weighted graphs, we have to minimize the sum of the weights over the path, from the source state to the goal.

We are interested in planning in the Markov decision process (MDP) [7]. The environment can be represented as a Markov decision process, by defining the state and action states (possible states and actions), a transition model (the conditional probability of going from a state to another by executing an action), and a reward\cost function (how likely this transition will get us closer to the goal state). The goal of the planning in the Markov decision process is to maximize the reward, which likely leads to find the best trajectory from the current state to the goal. Planning is used in reinforcement learning [8] explicitly when we have the transition model of the environment (in model-based reinforcement learning [9, 21]). In model-free reinforcement learning [10], trajectory optimization is used instead of direct planning.

Model predictive control [11] proposes planning over a finite horizon instead of planning to the goal, while it couldn't guarantee the best trajectory from the source to the target states, but it provides a practical online planning algorithm to work with physical systems. Another important property of the model predictive control is natively considering the constraints (safety or desired conditions), as it formed based on the optimal control paradigm. The result of planning is a sequence of actions to follow, this sequence represents a trajectory that the robot has to follow.

The control part of the robot system is the process of interpreting a trajectory of action to actuators' commands. It depends on the type of states and actions in the planned trajectory, i.e. for rotation, velocity, or voltage state of the motors we can use simple low-level controllers for the motors (e.g. PID controllers [12]). If the states are the position of the robot, and the actions are movements of the center of the mass of the robot; then we have to use the model of the robot to find the corresponding motor commands. In the case of serial robots (e.g. manipulators) [13], the inverse kinematic and the dynamic model of the robot are used, which suffer from approximations and linearization when forming controllers, as they are nonlinear models.

Having a general view over the robotics systems, we are proposing a learning-based approach for controlling robots. We aim to have our method to (1) be independent of the robot's dynamical model (applicable to teach tasks to any robot) (2) achieve tasks effectively (works with small datasets), (3) learn fast (to make the robot able to adapt to unforeseen cases, with low computational cost), (4) work with real robot directly (little time of interaction on the real robot) and (5) need minimum human intervention to set-up a new task.

The structure of the paper starts by presenting the proposed learning-based system, starting by introducing its architecture, the Markov decision process representation, perception system, and the reinforcement learning system. We will discuss our experiments and results in each system, to conclude with high-level results and the possible future direction building on our work.

2   The Proposed Learning-Based Robotics System

2.1   The General Architecture

The proposed learning-based robotics system consists of the following.

1. The environment (green block in Fig. 1):

   It is the part that is responsible to interact with the physical system or the system in the simulation. For robotics systems, the environment contains the robot and the sensors, it receives an action from the control system, executes it on the control object (robot in our case), then collects the data from the sensors, and sends it to the perception system to form states.

2. The perception system (red block in Fig. 1):

   The perception system receives sensor data from the environment and uses it to form informative states. In our proposed system, we use the output of the perception system to compute the reward, by computing the distance to a goal image stored in the environment (white circle Fig. 1).

3. The reinforcement learning system (blue block in Fig. 1):

   The reinforcement learning system performs the planning and control part in our system, where instead of having the output of the reinforcement learning system in the end-effector's coordinate space, the output in our case is in the joints' space (direct commands to the motors). This idea helps in making our system independent of the robot dynamical model and can be used to any robotic arm with minimum effort. The goal of the reinforcement learning system is to maximize the expected long-term reward.

2.2   The Proposed System as a Markov Decision Process

A Markov Decision Process (MDP) is defined for the proposed system. This MDP describes the transitions between states. To make a connection between the architecture of our system, and the MDP in Fig. 2. We will define the following terminology:

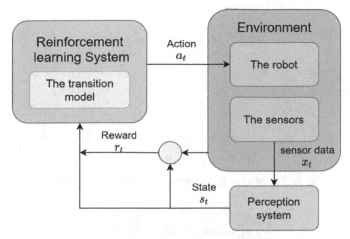

Fig. 1. The general architecture of the proposed learning-based robotics system (Color figure online)

1. The policy (of the Reinforcement learning systems in Fig. 1).

   The policy $\pi_\theta(s_t)$ is a function of the state, to be optimized in the reinforcement learning procedure to give the action corresponds with the highest predicted long-term return.

2. Execution and data acquisition (Environment block in Fig. 1).

   Given an action a_t from the policy, the action to be transformed into primitive commands, by executing these commands the state of the environment will change, sensors will be used to collect data x_t (data acquisition).

3. The embedding model (the model of the perception system in Fig. 1).

   By feeding the data x_t to the embedding model, we get the state of the system $s_t = y_e(x_t)$, the embedding model should be trained beforehand, and states will be used to compute rewards (or state_cost).

4. The transition model (to be learned in the reinforcement learning system).

   Given the current state of the system s_t and the chosen action a_t, the transition model predicts the probability of the next state $p(s_{t+1}|s_t, a_t)$, the transition model is learned over the training process (using the transition dataset $D = \{s_t, a_t, s_{t+1}\}$).

2.3 The Environment

The environment contains the robot and the sensors, it is defined following the rules of OpenAI gym [14] environments. The gym environment is defined as a class with the main methods; initialization, reset, and step methods (Fig. 3).

The initialization method sets up the components of the environment, by checking the connection to the simulator or the real robot, connection to the sensors, define the initial state of task-related objects, and move the robot to its initial position, it may also ask the user to provide some hyperparameters or to set the goal state. In our system, we

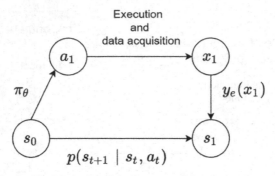

Fig. 2. The Markov decision process of the proposed system

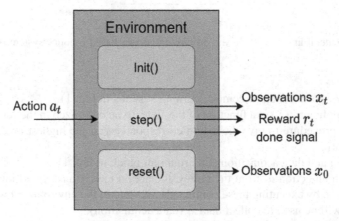

Fig. 3. The environment class

propose to load a pre-trained embedding model to be used to get states out of sensors' data.

As noted earlier, the environment receives an action a_t, the execution of this action is done in the step method. Where first the action is checked for its validity (e.g. doesn't exceed the limits of the motors), then given the current joints' angles, the action vector is scaled to an angle offset change, and the resulted angles are sent to the motors directly while moving the robot we have to check the lockdown cases (we have used a limit on the current used by each motor). The control of the robot done using RestAPI request, we prefer using low-level API control as it gives better flexibility than high-level APIs. When the robot finishes its movement, the data acquisition step is performed by collecting the output of the sensors, the raw data is called observations x_t, which will be forwarded to the perception system. Reward value is computed using the observation of using the states after using the perception system. In our system, we studied the use of low-cost RGB cameras and sensors equipped with the robot (encoders, current sensors). A done signal is returned whether the task was achieved or the robot fell into a lockdown case.

When receiving a done signal, the reset function returns the environment to its initial state, and it may ask the user to change the position of some objects, or do this randomly if possible (depends on the task properties).

Technically, we need a helper class to control the robot using RestAPI requests, also when working with cameras, we need a buffer-less video capture class (instead of an ordinary video capture class from OpenCV).

In our proposed learning-based system, the user doesn't have to care about the environment or change anything to train the robot on a new task, he just wants to collect some video demonstrations to train the perception system and provide one of them to the learning system, this one will be used to define the goal state, the reward will be the distance rot he goal state in the latent space.

2.4   The Perception System

The Model

Consider we have an input image $x \in \mathbb{R}^{W \times H \times 3}$. The output of the model is an embedding of the image in a latent space $y_e \in \mathbb{R}^E$. W, H are the width and the height of the image, E is the size of the embedding vector. The base CNN network (blue block in Fig. 4) is taken from the inception model [15] pre-trained on ImageNet [16], the parameters of this part are frozen and won't be re-trained. We add two additional convolutional layers, followed by a spatial softmax layer. A fully connected layer is added to get the embedding of the input image $y_e = f_\theta(x)$. The parameter to train embedding model θ is the training parameters of the model (weights and biases of the 2CNN layers and the feed-forward layer – green blocks in Fig. 4).

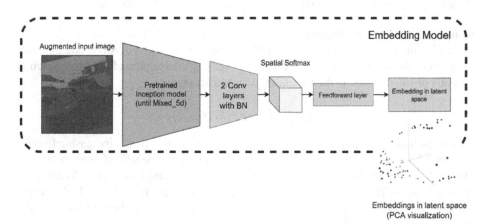

Fig. 4. The architecture of the embedding model (Color figure online)

The Dataset Formulation

The dataset is formed by extracting images from video files and form triplets for learning. In contrastive learning, the process starts by sampling an image from a video, this image is called anchor, a positive range is defined as all the images that far from the anchor by less than a positive margin, the negative margin is the rest of the images. One positive and one negative image is sampled from the positive and negative ranges respectively. The triplet consists of an anchor x_i^a, a positive image x_i^p, and a negative image x_i^n.

All images normalized and augmented before feeding them to the network. The normalization is needed because the pre-trained part trained on normalized images. The augmentation was done by using a color jitter (random coloring) and random rotation. The augmentation is useful for transfer learning, and to avoid overfitting to the training dataset.

Time Contrastive Training

Given a triplet of images; an anchor x_i^a, a positive image x_i^p, and a negative image x_i^n, the time-contrastive loss is [17] the loss tries to ensure that the anchor and the positive images are closer to each other in the latent space than the negative image. i.e. the aim is to learn an embedding such that:

$$\left\| y_e(x_i^a) - y_e(x_i^p) \right\|_2^2 + \alpha \leq \left\| y_e(x_i^a) - y_e(x_i^n) \right\|_2^2$$

The time contrastive loss is defined as:

$$L = \min\left(0, \alpha + \left\| y_e(x_i^a) - y_e(x_i^p) \right\|_2^2 - \left\| y_e(x_i^a) - y_e(x_i^n) \right\|_2^2\right)$$

Training of the embedding model starts by sampling a triplet of augmented images from the dataset, feeding them to the model, and use the output to compute the sequential time contrastive loss, the loss then is used to update the parameters of the model. The margins are updated every while.

Sample Results After Training

The embedding model was trained for 100 epochs (10000 triplets), Alongside the visualization of the latent space (embeddings) in Fig. 4, we have plotted a reward function depends on the distance to the target image in latent space:

$$r(x_i) = -\left\| y_e(x_i) - y_e(x_{target}) \right\|_2^2$$

For each video file, the reward function should be monotonically increasing to zero, smoother function means better performance. To judge the benefit of using time contrastive learning, we have plotted the latent space and reward before (Fig. 5) and after training (Fig. 6). The reward/cost function corresponds to each latent space. Before training, random distribution led to a bad reward function. After training, better monotonically increasing function, could be used in RL and control.

2.5   Reinforcement Learning System

We propose using a model-based reinforcement learning system (Fig. 7), with some key features to fulfill our requirements. Reinforcement learning will (1) interact with the environment (which is formed as a Markov Decision Process). (2) Learn the transition

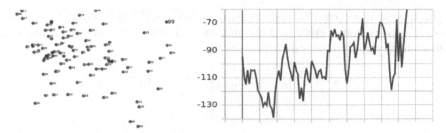

Fig. 5. Latent space and reward function before the training

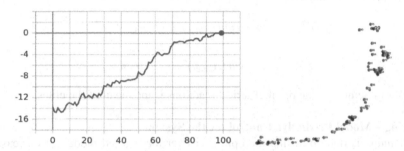

Fig. 6. Latent space and reward function after the training

model, which has to handle uncertainty, we used Ensemble neural network to learn the model. (3) Plan using the learned model, we are following the model predictive control in planning. (4) In the planning, we have to use an optimizer, that fits our system, we used Cross-Entropy Maximization optimizer.

The Transition Model – Ensemble Neural Network

The goal of learning the transition model of the environment is to predict the dynamics of the task. Learning the model is an essential part of the model-based reinforcement learning as it will be used in the planning.

The model should work efficiently in the cases of small and large datasets; i.e. learns good dynamics at the early stages of learning, and enhance the performance further with time. This is done by choosing a model that can handle uncertainty (to learn from small datasets), and deep enough to have the capacity to infer from large datasets.

We have chosen Ensemble neural networks [18], as it can handle the uncertainty by using the prediction from several deep neural networks, and have the needed capacity because of the deep structure in its components. Alongside the low computational cost when parallelized on the graphical processing units.

The Optimizer – Cross-Entropy Maximizer

The cross-entropy maximization (CEM) [19] is a gradient-free stochastic optimization algorithm, based on Monte-Carlo methods. Given a state cost function (negative reward from Sect. 2.3), and a learned transition model, CEM chooses the optimal series of actions (with length equal to the planning horizon) corresponds to the biggest predicted cost.

In our system, we use a Random-shooting method in CEM, this is done by sampling series of actions from a predefined distribution, evaluating them, and separating ones with the highest reward (we call them elites):

$$A_i = \left\{ a_0^i, a_1^i, a_2^i, \ldots a_{H-1}^i \right\}; \quad a_t^i \sim N\left(\mu_t^m, \Sigma_t^m\right)$$

$$A_{elites} = sort(A_i)[: J]$$

The mean and variance of the sampling distribution updated according to the mean and variance of the elite sets.

$$\mu_t^{m+1} = \alpha * mean(A_{elites}) + (1 - \alpha) * \mu_t^m$$

$$\Sigma_t^{m+1} = \alpha * var(A_{elites}) + (1 - \alpha) * \Sigma_t^m$$

After m iterations, the optimal series of actions is the mean of the elites.

Planning – Model Predictive Control for the System
The planning is done by using the optimizer over the learned model. In our case we have to use the ensemble neural network to find the predicted states after executing each action because the output of the ENN is a distribution, we used particles of the initial state, and propagate them using the ENN model:

$$s_{t+1}^p \sim f_\theta\left(s_t^p, a_t\right); \quad s_{t=0}^p = s_0$$

Then we use state cost function to find the cost of the series and continue the optimization.

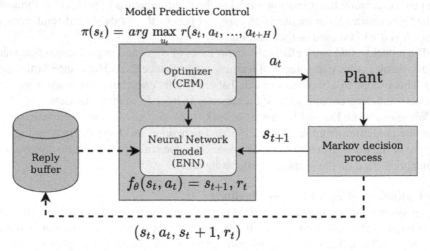

Fig. 7. Model-based reinforcement learning with ensemble neural networks

Sample Results for Experiments

To evaluate the Reinforcement learning system, we build an environment in simulation (VREP simulator [20]), contains a KUKA manipulator, a USB flash desk was attached to its end effector, and a USB socket placed on the ground in its workspace.

The state consists of the position of the object (flash desk and USB socket) and joints' angles. The control in the joint's space (actions are commands to motors). The transition model in Fig. 8.

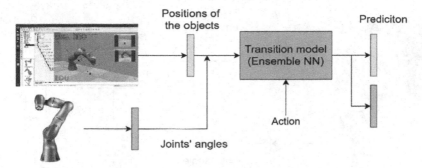

Fig. 8. Transition model for the experiment in simulation

In the simulation, we have tested the reinforcement learning system to reach a specified point in its workspace, similar to the step response in evaluating control systems.

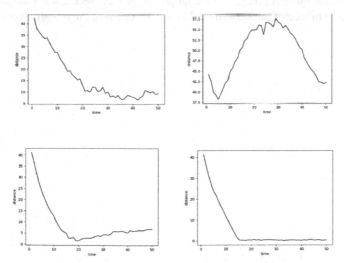

Fig. 9. The results for reaching a point in the workspace (step response analysis), from upper-left to lower right: iterations 1, 5, 8, 50

We have plotted the distance between the end effector over the training process (Fig. 9), we can notice that the system started to learn a correction from early iteration

(iteration 8), and by further training perfected its response (iteration 50), without any overshoot and holding the goal after reaching it. These results match our goal of learning efficiently from small datasets and improve the performance when larger datasets are available.

To test the whole system, we have to use the learned embedding model (trained according to Sect. 2.4), to extract image embeddings from RGB images, and replace the states in the last experiment (Fig. 10).

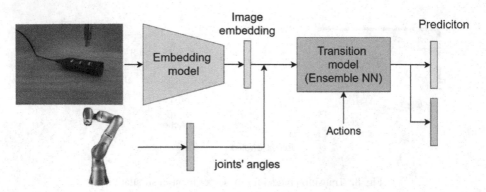

Fig. 10. The transition model of an experiment with the whole system

The reward (and state cost) depends on the distance in the latent space between the embedding of the current image and the target image (see Sect. 2.4 for details). We can judge the performance of the system on this task by drawing the reward over the training time (Fig. 11).

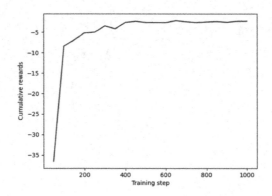

Fig. 11. The reward function over time, bigger is better.

We can notice the system can optimize its performance over the training time, and learns a good policy after 800 timesteps (30 min on the robot).

3   Conclusion

We have proposed a learning-based framework for learning robotics manipulation tasks. The framework uses self-supervised representation learning for perception, and reinforcement learning for planning and control. The framework doesn't depend on the dynamical model of the robot, data-efficient, learns tasks fatly, can be run the training process on the real robot directly, and works with minimum human intervention.

Perception systems have to be pre-trained before run the training process for the reinforcement part. The user has just to provide the system with some videos demonstrating the task, and then the learning process runs in a self-supervised way. The learning process takes around 30 min on a PC with single GPU (low computational cost, and short training time), the result is an embedding model to infer a representation in the latent space for an image on its input.

After that, we should define an environment as a Markov decision process, then we can run the reinforcement learning part. By using the trained perception system, the user can use our predefined environment, by just providing a goal image (the user doesn't have to change anything in the environment).

The reinforcement learning system will be trained lastly, in a fully automated way, its goal is to minimize the Euclidian distance between the current state and the goal image. The reinforcement learning system uses a model-based approach, with a probabilistic model, and the training time in our experiment between 30–45 min.

The whole framework provides a promising way to run robotics experiments, the user have just to collect some videos (possibly with a smartphone) demonstrating the task and run the learning process for the perception system, then provides a goal image and run the reinforcement learning part, without the need to any coding or engineering experience.

Open-source code is made available for reproducibility and validation: https://github.com/Alonso94/Self-supervised-RL.

Future direction for our research is to make the extend the framework for life-long learning, where the robot learns skills instead of learning just tasks, this needs an extension for our perception system, and an algorithm for planning over skills, not just states, but we believe this would be essential to have fully intelligent robotic systems.

References

1. Mihajlov, B.B., Nazarova, A.V., Yushchenko, A.S.: Avtonomnye mobil'-nye roboty-navigaciya i upravlenie. Izvestiya YUzhnogo federal'nogo universiteta. Tekhnicheskie nauki **2**(175) (2016)
2. Bagutdinov, R.A.: Princip razrabotki algoritmicheskogo obespecheniya si-stemy tekhnicheskogo zreniya robotov. Naukoemkie tekhnologii v kosmicheskih issledovaniyah Zemli **9**(5) (2017)
3. Lee, M.A., et al.: Making sense of vision and touch: self-supervised learning of multimodal representations for contact-rich tasks. :In 2019 International Conference on Robotics and Automation (ICRA), pp. 8943–8950. IEEE (2019, May)
4. Zhu, H., et al.: The ingredients of real-world robotic reinforcement learning. arXiv preprint arXiv:2004.12570 (2020)

5. Sermanet, P., et al.: Time-contrastive networks: self-supervised learning from video. In: 2018 IEEE International Conference on Robotics and Automation (ICRA), pp. 1134–1141. IEEE (2018, May)

6. Носков, В.П., Рубцов, И.В.: Ключевые вопросы создания интеллектуальных мобильных роботов. Инженерный журнал: наука и инновации **3**(15) (2013)

7. Bellman, R.: A Markovian decision process. Indiana Univ. Math. J. **6**(4), 679–684 (1957). https://doi.org/10.1512/iumj.1957.6.56038

8. Sutton, R.S., Barto, A.G.: Reinforcement Learning: An Introduction, vol. 1. MIT Press, Cambridge (1998)

9. Chatzilygeroudis, K., Vassiliades, V., Stulp, F., Calinon, S., Mouret, J.B.: A survey on policy search algorithms for learning robot controllers in a handful of trials. arXiv preprint arXiv: 1807.02303 (2018)

10. Schulman, J., Levine, S., Abbeel, P., Jordan, M., Moritz, P.: Trust region policy optimization. In: International Conference on Machine Learning, pp. 1889–1897 (2015, June)

11. Camacho, E.F., Alba, C.B.: Model Predictive Control. Springer Science & Business Media (2013)

12. Рогач, В.Я: Расчет настройки реальных ПИД-регуляторов. Теплоэнергетика **10**, 31–35 (1993)

13. Jazar, R.N.: Theory of Applied Robotics: Kinematics, Dynamics, and Control. Springer Science & Business Media (2010)

14. Brockman, G., et al.: Openai gym. arXiv Preprint arXiv:1606.01540 (2016)

15. Szegedy, C., Ioffe, S., Vanhoucke, V., Alemi, A.A.: Inception-v4, inception-resnet, and the impact of residual connections on learning. In: the Thirty-First AAAI Conference on Artificial Intelligence (2017, February)

16. Deng, J., Dong, W., Socher, R., Li, L.J., Li, K., Fei-Fei, L.: Imagenet: a large-scale hierarchical image database. In: 2009 IEEE Conference On Computer Vision and Pattern Recognition, pp. 248–255. IEEE (2009, June)

17. Sohn, K.: Improved deep metric learning with a multi-class n-pair loss objective. Adv. Neural Inform. Process. Syst. 1857–1865 (2016)

18. Pearce, T., Zaki, M., Brintrup, A., Neel, A.: Uncertainty in neural networks: Bayesian ensembling. arXiv Preprint arXiv:1810.05546 (2018)

19. De Boer, P.T., Kroese, D.P., Mannor, S., Rubinstein, R.Y.: A tutorial on the cross-entropy method. Ann. Oper. Res. **134**(1), 19–67 (2005)

20. Rohmer, E., Singh, S.P., Freese, M.: V-REP: a versatile and scalable robot simulation framework. In: 2013 IEEE/RSJ International Conference on Intelligent Robots and Systems, pp. 1321–1326. IEEE (2013, November)

21. Chua, K., Calandra, R., McAllister, R., Levine, S.: Deep reinforcement learning in a handful of trials using probabilistic dynamics models. Adv. Neural Inform. Process. Syst. 4754–4765 (2018)

Evaluation of Dynamic Models of a Mobile Robot's Movable Platform

Evgeniy Anatolyevich Kotov$^{(\boxtimes)}$ and Dmitriy Alexeevich Dolzhenok

Bauman Moscow State Technical University, Moscow 105005, Russia

Abstract. There is an analysis of research questions of a mobile wheeled robot platform movement. For these purposes, based on Gauss principle of least compulsion, a mathematical model of a platform of a certain class has been developed that takes into account the dynamics of all its mobile elements. A platform with two independently controlled coaxial wheels and two passive wheels, called "differential drive", is considered. The obtained model is analyzed for such indicators as versatility, accuracy, and cost-effectiveness. The research results were compared with similar results obtained when considering a simplified model based on Appel equations. Computer modeling allowed us to implement dynamic processes for changing model parameters, such as accelerations, speeds, generalized coordinates, and position coordinates. This approach is the basis for testing the performance of the future device and taking into account the main disadvantages of the system. The importance of this task is determined by the need of building dynamically correct and accurate control. The comparative analysis of the conducted research can serve as a basis for purposeful rational decision - making on the designs and effective control systems of mobile robots.

Keywords: Mobile robot · Mobile platform · Simulation · Dynamic model · Gauss's principle of least constraint

1 Introduction

Currently, the range of areas in which the achievements of mobile robotics are actively applied is significantly expanding in various areas of human activity. One of the most common and used classes of mobile robots is wheeled robots. However, they can not effectively move on previously unprepared surfaces. But for movement on prepared surfaces, the use of wheeled robots is most justified in comparison with the use of other classes of mobile robots (for example, tracked vehicles) due to their superior ease of operation, maximum possible travel speed, and energy efficiency.

The expansion of the application areas of wheeled robots determines the increase in requirements for the quality of their functioning, which can be characterized by such parameters as, for example, versatility, speed, accuracy of working out the specified trajectories, and efficiency. One of the most powerful tools for identifying the rationality of design solutions and the effectiveness of control algorithms is the modeling of the dynamic behavior of complex mechanical systems, in particular, mobile robots. Many

© Springer Nature Switzerland AG 2021
A. Yuschenko (Ed.): MPoR 2020, CCIS 1426, pp. 85–97, 2021.
https://doi.org/10.1007/978-3-030-88458-1_7

issues that arise at all stages of the existence of a mobile platform can be solved using this method. In this regard, it is important to develop rational mathematical models that most fully describe the system and give fairly close to reality results. For these purposes, we compared the results of modeling the movement of a mobile robot along different trajectories using two models obtained from Appel equations and based on Gauss principle of least compulsion.

2 Model Moving Platform of a Mobile Robot

The article considers mathematical models of a mobile platform of a certain class. The mobile platform (Fig. 1) consists of two drives (right 1 and left 2) located along the same axis and providing with the help of the driving wheels movement without slipping in the horizontal plane, the base 3 mass m_1, brackets 4, 6 mass m_2 and m_3, respectively, the support wheels 5, 7. Using a mathematical model of a mobile platform, accelerations, speeds and positions are determined depending on the vector of moments $Q = \begin{pmatrix} Q_1 \\ Q_2 \end{pmatrix}$, developed by the right and left drives [1–4], and the angles of rotation of the driving wheels are represented as a vector of generalized coordinates $q = \begin{pmatrix} q_1 \\ q_2 \end{pmatrix}$.

To determine unambiguously the position of the platform and its elements, it is required to enter the following coordinate systems: fixed $\{x_0; y_0; z_0\}$; associated with the base $\{x_1; y_1; z_1\}$, the beginning of which is located at the point O_1 on the axis of rotation of the driving wheels, equidistant from them; associated with the brackets $\{x_2; y_2; z_2\}$ and $\{x_3; y_3; z_3\}$, $\rho_{x2}, \rho_{y2}, \rho_{z2}, \rho_{x3}, \rho_{y3}, \rho_{z3}$– the coordinates of the brackets in the system $\{x1; y1; Z1\}$, $\rho_{x4}, \rho_{y4}, \rho_{z4}, \rho_{x5}, \rho_{y5}, \rho_{z5}$– coordinates of the mass centers of the driven wheels in systems $\{x_2; y_2; z_2\}$ and $\{x_3; y_3; z_3\}$, respectively.

φ_1 – the angle between the x_0 and x_1 axes;

$\varphi_2 = \varphi_1 + \varphi_{12}$ – the angle between the x_0 and x_2 axes;

$\varphi_3 = \varphi_1 + \varphi_{13}$ – the angle between the x_0 and x_3 axes;

r_{xi}, r_{yi} – coordinates of the center of mass of the i-th element of the system in the i-th coordinate system (i-th element of the system: 1 – base 3; 2 – bracket 4; 3 – bracket 6);

I_i – moment of inertia of the i-th element of the system regarding to the z_i axis;

R_1, R_2 – radii of the drive wheels;

R_4, R_5 – radii of the support wheels;

L – distance between the drive wheels;

d_1, d_2 – moments of inertia of the driving wheels 1, 2 regarding to the axes of rotation;

d_4, d_5 – moments of inertia of the driven wheels 4, 5 regarding to the axes of rotation.

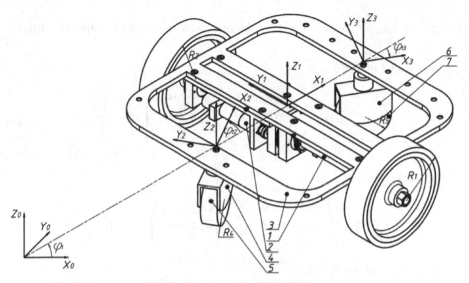

Fig. 1. Diagram of the mobile robot

2.1 Dynamic Model Based on Appel Equation

The model under consideration [5] takes into account only the dynamics of the base of the mobile platform and is expressed by the following calculation formulas:

$$\begin{cases} \dot{V}1 = -|rx1|\omega_1^2 + \dfrac{1}{Rm}(Q1 + Q2) \\ \dot{\omega}1 = \dfrac{|rx1|\, m\omega 1 V1}{I} + \dfrac{L}{2RI}(Q1 - Q2) \end{cases} \tag{1}$$

where V_1 – linear velocity of the base,
ω_1 – angular speed of rotation of the base.

2.2 Dynamic Model Based on the Gauss Principle of Least Compulsion [6, 7]

The distinguish characteristic of this approach is that it takes into account the dynamics of all moving elements of the platform structure: the base, two brackets, driving and supporting wheels. The acceleration vector of generalized coordinates is defined by the expression given below, which represents the solution of a linear equation obtained as a result of minimizing the constraint measure (acceleration energy) under restrictions determined by non-holonomic relations between the speeds and accelerations of the mobile elements of the object in question.

$$q \overset{..}{=} D^{-1}G \tag{2}$$

The symmetric matrix D(2 × 2) and the vector G(2 × 1) are defined by expressions (3) and (4), respectively.

$$D = A_1^T W_1 A_1 + A_2^T W_2 A_2 + A_3^T W_3 A_3 + \text{diag}\,\{d1, d2\} + d_1 A_4^T A_4 + d_5 A_5^T A_5 \tag{3}$$

$$G = Q + A_1^T W_1 \ddot{z}_1 + A_2^T W_2 \ddot{z}_2 + A_3^T W_3 z_3 - A_1^T W_1 B_1 - A_2^T W_2 B_2 - A_3^T W_3 B_3 - d_4 B_4 A_4^T - d_5 B_5 A_5^T \tag{4}$$

A_1 – matrix of size 3×2:

$$A_1 = \begin{pmatrix} \frac{1}{2} R_1 \cos\varphi_1 & \frac{1}{2} R_2 \cos\varphi_1 \\ \frac{1}{2} R_1 \sin\varphi_1 & \frac{1}{2} R_2 \sin\varphi_1 \\ \frac{R_1}{L} & -\frac{R_2}{L} \end{pmatrix} \tag{5}$$

B_1 – matrix of size 3×1:

$$B_1 = \frac{dA_1}{dt} q = \begin{pmatrix} -\frac{1}{2} R_1 \sin\varphi_1 & -\frac{1}{2} R_2 \sin\varphi_1 \\ \frac{1}{2} R_1 \cos\varphi_1 & \frac{1}{2} R_2 \cos\varphi_1 \\ 0 & 0 \end{pmatrix} \frac{1}{L} (R_1 q_1 - R_2 q_2) \dot{q} \tag{6}$$

A_2 – matrix of size 3×2:

$$A_2 = \left(\left(0; \ -\rho_{x4}^{-1} \right) \cdot L_2 \tilde{A}_2 \right) + \begin{pmatrix} 0 & 0 \\ \frac{R_1}{L} & \frac{R_1}{L} \end{pmatrix} \tag{7}$$

B_2 – matrix of size 3×1:

$$B_2 = \left(\left((0; \ -\rho_{x4}^{-1}) \cdot L_2 \tilde{B}_2 + \rho_{y4} \cdot \rho_{x4}^{-1} \cdot \omega_{12}^2 \right) \right) \tag{8}$$

$\tilde{A}_2$ – matrix of size 2×2:

$$\tilde{A}_2 = \begin{pmatrix} \dfrac{R_1}{2} - \dfrac{\rho_{y2} R_1}{L} & \dfrac{R_2}{2} - \dfrac{\rho_{y2} R_2}{L} \\ \dfrac{\rho_{x2} R_1}{L} & -\dfrac{\rho_{x2} R_2}{L} \end{pmatrix} \tag{9}$$

$\tilde{B}_2$– matrix of size 2×1:

$$\tilde{B}_2 = \begin{pmatrix} -\rho_{x2} \\ -\rho_{y2} \end{pmatrix} \frac{1}{L_2} (R_1 \dot{q}_1 - R_2 \dot{q}_2) \tag{10}$$

$A_3, B_3, \tilde{A}_3, \tilde{B}_3$ matrices for the other bracket have a structure similar to the Eqs. (7)–(10).

The equation linking the angular acceleration of rotation of the driven wheel $\ddot{q}3$ with velocities and accelerations of the generalized coordinates:

$$\ddot{q}_4 = A_4 \cdot \ddot{q} + B_4,$$

where

$$A_4 = \left(R_4^{-1}; \ \rho_{y4} \rho_{x4}^{-1} R_4^{-1} \right) L_2 \tilde{A}_2, \tag{11}$$

$$B_4 = \left(R_4^{-1}; \; \rho_{y4}\rho_{x4}^{-1}R_4^{-1}\right)L_2\tilde{B}_2 + R_4^{-1}\left(-\rho_{x4} - \rho_{y4}^2\rho_{x4}^{-1}\right)\omega_{12}^2 \tag{12}$$

Similar for the other support wheel:

$$A_5 = \left(R_5^{-1}; \; \rho_{y5}\rho_{x5}^{-1}R_5^{-1}\right)L_3\tilde{A}_3 \tag{13}$$

$$B_5 = \left(R_5^{-1}; \; \rho_{y5}\rho_{x5}^{-1}R_5^{-1}\right)L_3\tilde{B}_3 + R_5^{-1}\left(-\rho_{x5} - \rho_{y5}^2\rho_{x5}^{-1}\right)\omega_{13}^2 \tag{14}$$

W_i – symmetric matrix of the mass-inertial characteristics of size 3×3:

$$W_i = \begin{pmatrix} m_i & 0 & -m_i(r_{xi}\sin\varphi_i + r_{yi}\sin\varphi_i) \\ 0 & m_i & m_i(r_{xi}\sin\varphi_i - r_{yi}\sin\varphi_i) \\ -m_i(r_{xi}\sin\varphi_i + r_{yi}\sin\varphi_i) & m_i(r_{xi}\sin\varphi_i - r_{yi}\sin\varphi_i) & I_i \end{pmatrix}, i = 1, 2, 3 \tag{15}$$

Acceleration of free movement of the base and brackets:

$$\ddot{z}_i = \begin{pmatrix} \ddot{z}_{xi} \\ \ddot{z}_{yi} \\ \ddot{z}_{\omega i} \end{pmatrix}, \quad i = 1, 2, 3,$$

where $\ddot{z}_{xi}$, $\ddot{z}_{yi}$ – linear accelerations along the x_0, y_0 axes, respectively, $\ddot{z}_{\omega i}$ – angular acceleration.

In this task $\ddot{z}_i$ are determined only by inertia forces, i.e. the vectors of total acting forces measured in a fixed coordinate system and the total acting moments relative to the z_i axes are equal to 0.

Therefore, we have:

$$W_i\ddot{z}_i = \begin{pmatrix} L_i r_i m_i \\ 0 \end{pmatrix}, \omega_i^2 \; i = 1, 2, 3 \tag{16}$$

When viewed in a horizontal plane the transition from the coordinate systems $\{x_1; y_1; z_1\}$, $\{x_2; y_2; z_2\}$, $\{x_3; y_3; z_3\}$ to the system $\{x_0; y_0; z_0\}$ can be performed using orthogonal matrices of the following type:

$$L_i = \begin{pmatrix} \cos\varphi_i & -\sin\varphi_i \\ \sin\varphi_i & \cos\varphi_i \end{pmatrix}, \quad i = 1, 2, 3 \tag{17}$$

Thereby, the modelling algorithm can be constructed as follows:

1. Calculation of the orientation matrices L_1, L_2, L_3 (17);
2. Calculation of coupling equations matrices A_i, B_i, $i = 1, 2, 3, 4, 5$ (5)–(8), (11)–(14);
3. Calculation of mass-inertia characteristics matrices W_1, W_2, W_3 (15);
4. Calculation of the vectors $W_i \ddot{z}i$, $i = 1, 2, 3$ (16);
5. Calculation of the matrices D и G in the expressions (3), (4);
6. Determination of the desired acceleration vector $\ddot{q}$ by the expression (2);
7. Integration of accelerations in order to obtain the values of the vectors $\dot{q}$, q and determine the coordinates of the mobile platform on the plane.

The structurally functional diagram of the dynamic model of a mobile platform, based on Gauss principle, is summarized in Fig. 2.

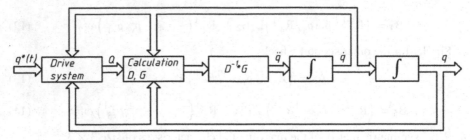

Fig. 2. The structurally functional diagram of the platform model

3 Results of Modeling the Movement of the Mobile Robot Platform

To evaluate the obtained models, we used the MatLab Simulink software package. Based on expressions (1) and (2), models were constructed and the results of their work were analyzed [9]. The experimental scheme is shown in Fig. 3. To determine the degree of influence of the mass of moving elements on the system parameters, it was decided to create an additional model with an increased weight of brackets. The Subsystem block is a simplified model based on the Appel equation. Subsystem1 and Subsystem2 blocks are models based on the Gauss principle of least compulsion that differ in the mass of the brackets by 4 times (in all three models, the total mass of the mobile robot's mobile platform is unchanged).

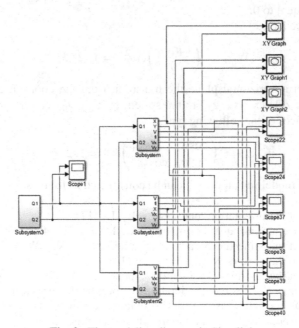

Fig. 3. The modeling diagram in Simulink

To get visual results of the models, let us start moving the mobile platform along an S-shaped trajectory. The model receives the signals shown in Fig. 4, which are processed by the drives, and the results are calculated in accordance with expressions (1), (2).

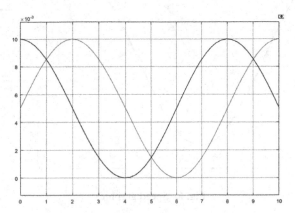

Fig. 4. Graphics of control signals

The results of modeling these methods are shown in Figs. 5, 6 and 7.

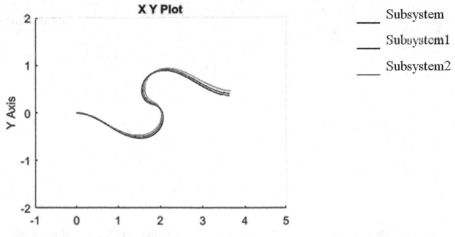

Fig. 5. Graphics of mobile robot trajectories

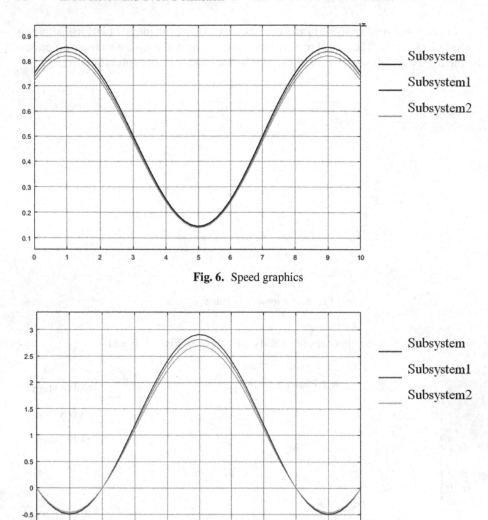

Fig. 6. Speed graphics

Fig. 7. Graphics of angle

Based on the graphs, we can conclude that taking into account the movable elements of the structure slows down the speed of changes in the model parameters: speed and angle of rotation. The increase in the mass of moving elements is directly proportional to the degree of deceleration of the model.

To assess the difference in the results produced by the models, a diagram was compiled, which is shown in Fig. 8. The Subsystem Block is a simplified model based on Appel equation, and the Subsystem1 block is a model based on Gauss principle of least compulsion. From the parameters of the Subsystem model, subtract the corresponding parameters of the Subsystem1 model. When evaluating percentages, the results of the simplified model were taken as the base values.

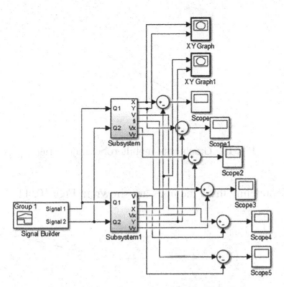

Fig. 8. The modeling diagram in Simulink

To identify differences in the results of the methods considered by coordinates and angle, it is necessary to work out a straight section and a turn section. To reflect them more clearly on the trajectory graph, add another straight section. The model receives the signals shown in Fig. 9, which are processed by the drives, and the results are calculated in accordance with expressions (1), (2).

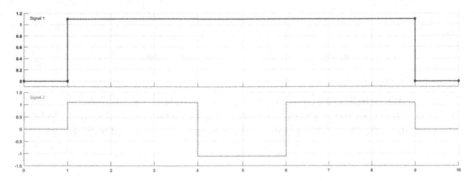

Fig. 9. Graphics of control signals

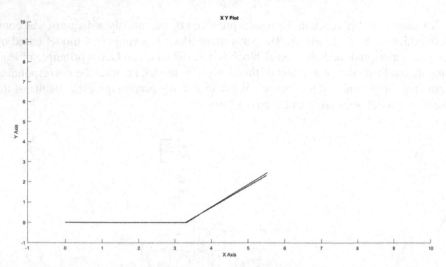

Fig. 10. Graphics of mobile robot trajectories

The results of modeling these methods are shown in Figs.10, 11, 12 and 13.

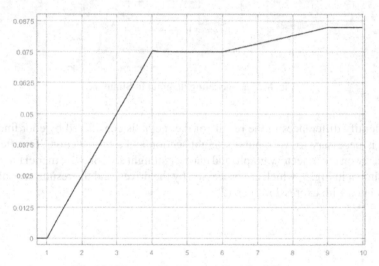

Fig. 11. The graphic of x coordinate's difference

The difference in the results of the considered methods by coordinates is 2,27%.
The difference in the angle of rotation is 3,89%. Thus, when the full rotation is performed, the difference in the results of the methods under consideration is 14°.

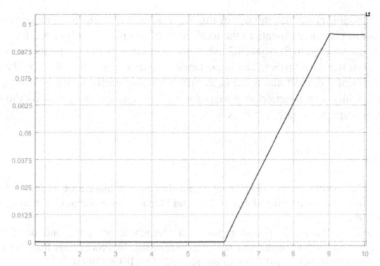

Fig. 12. The graphic of y coordinate's difference

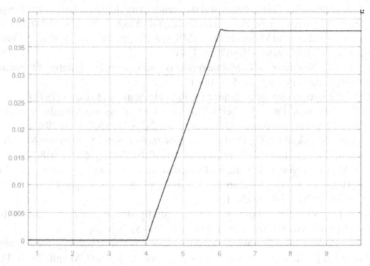

Fig. 13. The graphic of rotation angle's difference

4 Conclusion

In this article, we proposed a mathematical model of a mobile robot platform with two independent driving wheels, taking into account the dynamics of all its mobile elements. Using this model allows you to check more accurately the performance of the future device and take into account the main disadvantages of the system. However, it requires a lot of computing power. According to the geometric features of the mobile platform under consideration, the number of mathematical operations at each step of the model based on the Gauss principle of least compulsion is ~8.2 times greater than for the simplified model. However, the use of this method is important for a large percentage of the mass of mobile elements to the total mass of the mobile robot. As, for example, in the case considered in Subsystem2, when the mass of moving elements exceeded 8% of the mass of the entire robot. The importance of the task is determined by the need to build dynamically correct and accurate control. A comparative analysis of models was conducted, which can function as a basis for making rational decisions on the designs and control systems of mobile robots.

References

1. Kobrin, A.I., Martynenko, Y.G.: Nonholonomic dynamics of mobile robots and its simulation in real time. In: Works of the Mobile Robots and Mechatronic Systems Conference, pp. 107–123 (1998)
2. Campion, G., Bastin, G., D'Andrea-Novel, B.: Structural properties and classification of kinematic and dynamic models of wheeled mobile robots. In: Proceedings IEEE International Conference on Robotics and Automation, pp. 462–469. IEEE (1993)
3. Quaglia, G., Butera, L.G., Chiapello, E., Bruzzone, L.: UGV Epi. q-Mod. In Advances on Theory and Practice of Robots and Manipulators, pp. 331–339. Springer, Cham (2014)
4. Tang, Q., Schiehlen, W.: From lawnmower dynamics to modeling, simulation and experiments of a differentially driven robot. In: Ceccarelli, M., Glazunov, V.A. (eds.) Advances on Theory and Practice of Robots and Manipulators. MMS, vol. 22, pp. 365–374. Springer, Cham (2014). https://doi.org/10.1007/978-3-319-07058-2_41
5. Zenkevich, S.L., Nazarova, A.V.: Mobile robot control system. In: Bulletin of Bauman MSTU, Machine Building Series. pp. 31–51 (2006)
6. Pars, L.A.: Analytical dynamics. Science. 636 p. Heinemann, London (1971)
7. Kotov, E.A., Ivanov, E.O.: Mathematical model of a system containing mobile robot interconnected mobile platforms. AIP Conf. Proc. **2195**(1), 020026 (2019)
8. Karakaya, S., Kucukyildiz, G., Ocak, H.: A new mobile robot toolbox for Matlab. J. Intell. Rob. Syst. **87**(1), 125–140 (2017). https://doi.org/10.1007/s10846-017-0480-2
9. Bricogne, M., Le Duigou, J., Eynard, B.: Design processes of mechatronic systems. In: Hehenberger P., Bradley, D. (eds.) Mechatronic Futures, pp. 75–89. Springer, Cham (2016). https://doi.org/10.1007/978-3-319-32156-1_6
10. Pazderski, D.: Waypoint following for differentially driven wheeled robots with limited velocity perturbations. J. Intell. Robot. Syst. **85,** 553–575 (2016)
11. Nielsen, I., Dang, Q.-V., Bocewicz, G., Banaszak, Z.: A methodology for implementation of mobile robot in adaptive manufacturing environments. J. Intell. Manuf. **28**(5), 1171–1188 (2015). https://doi.org/10.1007/s10845-015-1072-2
12. Kheylo, S., Glazunov, V.: Kinematics, dynamics, control and accuracy of spherical parallel robot. In: Ceccarelli, M., Glazunov, V. (eds.) Advances on Theory and Practice of Robots and Manipulators. Mechanisms and Machine Science, vol. 22, pp. 133–140. Springer, Cham (2014). https://doi.org/10.1007/978-3-319-07058-2_15
13. Volodin, S.Y., Mikhaylov, B.B., Yuschenko, A.S.: Autonomous robot control in partially undetermined world via fuzzy logic. In: Advances on Theory and Practice of Robots and Manipulators, pp. 197–203. Springer, Cham (2014)
14. Muir, P.F., Neuman, C.P.: Kinematic modeling for feedback control of an omnidirectional wheeled mobile robot. In: Cox, I.J., Wilfong, G.T. (eds.) Autonomous Robot Vehicles, pp. 25–31. Springer, New York (1990). https://doi.org/10.1007/978-1-4613-8997-2_2

15. Yun, X., Yamamoto, Y.: Internal dynamics of a wheeled mobile robot. In: Proceedings of 1993 IEEE/RSJ International Conference on Intelligent Robots and Systems (IROS1993), pp. 1288–1294. IEEE (1993)
16. Zhao, Y., BeMent, S.L.: Kinematics, dynamics and control of wheeled mobile robots. In: Proceedings 1992 IEEE International Conference on Robotics and Automation, pp. 91–96. IEEE (1992)
17. Wang, D., Xu, G.: Full-state tracking and internal dynamics of nonholonomic wheeled mobile robots. IEEE/ASME Trans. Mech. 8(2), 203–214. IEEE (2003)
18. Tlale, N., de Villiers, M.: Kinematics and dynamics modelling of a mecanum wheeled mobile platform. In: 2008 15th International Conference on Mechatronics and Machine Vision in Practice, pp. 657–662. IEEE (2008)
19. Park, B.S., Yoo, S.J., Park, J.B., Choi, Y.H.: Adaptive neural sliding mode control of nonholonomic wheeled mobile robots with model uncertainty. IEEE Trans. Control Syst. Technol. 17(1), 207–214. IEEE (2008)
20. Yun, X., Yamamoto, Y.: Internal dynamics of a wheeled mobile robot. In Proceedings of 1993 IEEE/RSJ International Conference on Intelligent Robots and Systems (IROS'93), pp. 1288–1294. IEEE (1993)

Low-Cost In-Hand Slippage Detection and Avoidance for Robust Robotic Grasping with Compliant Fingers

Eduardo Cervantes, Sven Schneider, and Paul G. Ploeger[✉]

Hochschule Bonn-Rhein-Sieg, 53757 Sankt Augustin, Germany
eduardo.cervantes@smail.inf.h-brs.de, {sven.schneider,
paul.ploeger}@h-brs.de

Abstract. The act of grasping is fundamental for a robot to purposefully interact with its environment. However, all too often roboticists treat it as a singular event that can be solved with elaborate prior information such as kinematic models and planning thereupon. Instead, we advocate the view of grasping as a process that requires continuous adaptation to handle cases like (i) uncertainty in the objects' shape or mass that may result in imperfect grasps; or (ii) objects slipping in the robot's fingers. Recently, compliant fingers have been employed to address those challenges. However, it is still an open question how to properly integrate sensors to estimate the fingers' grasping state.

We propose the integration of low-cost – in terms of monetary expenses and integration effort – bend sensors and proximity sensors into a pair of flexible fingers. The resulting system enables the robot to detect and react to object slippage by relying on a simple sensor fusion scheme. We successfully demonstrate those capabilities over a set of objects that feature varying characteristics in terms of geometric shape, mass or rigidity. Two specially challenging objects are a fragile chocolate egg and a key chain that the robot still handles successfully.

Keywords: Robust grasping · Compliant fingers · Slippage detection

1 Introduction

Even after decades of research, industrial manipulators still rely on highly engineered environments – including the handled objects, the grasping mechanisms or the software solutions – to achieve their tasks. However, such approaches do not scale well to small lot sizes of highly variable objects as, for example, envisioned in the "factory of the future" that demand for flexible, yet robust grasping and manipulation solutions. We investigate similar, scaled-down scenarios in the context of robotics competitions in the RoboCup@Work league where we employ KUKA youBot robots (see Fig. 1) with a custom gripper. This gripper consists of a pair of compliant Festo fingers [1] (see Fig. 2) that are each mounted on a Dynamixel AX-12A servo motor. It is well known that compliant systems are a prerequisite for a robot to physically interact with its environment, as realized by *active compliance* on the level of the robot's control system (e.g. impedance

© Springer Nature Switzerland AG 2021
A. Yuschenko (Ed.): MPoR 2020, CCIS 1426, pp. 98–109, 2021.
https://doi.org/10.1007/978-3-030-88458-1_8

control [2]) or *passive compliance* in the robot's hardware – traditionally via Remote Centre Compliance devices [3, 4]. The former approach requires more elaborate, model-based control schemes and additionally more advanced sensors in the manipulator such as torque sensors in the robot's joints or force-torque sensors attached to the robot's end-effector. Thus, we focus on the cost-efficient solution of flexible and compliant fingers that passively adapt to the shape of the grasped objects.

Fig. 1. youBot robot low-cost sensor integration for robust grasping with flexible robotic fingers. *Image courtesy of Padmaja Kulkarni.*

Fig. 2. Flexible fingers low-cost sensor integration for robust grasping with flexible robotic fingers. *Image courtesy of Padmaja Kulkarni.*

All too often roboticists treat grasping as a singular *event* that is supposed to be solved with elaborate planning approaches using prior information like geometric models or information extracted from the robot's vision system. Detailed surveys on such approaches can be found in [5, 6]. Instead, we advocate the view of grasping as a process that requires (*i*) additional tactile or force feedback; and (*ii*) continuous adaptation or control, to handle cases like uncertainty about objects' shape or mass that may result in imperfect grasps or objects slipping in the robot's fingers. Similar approaches can also be observed in human beings that rely on a mixture of sensory inputs from exteroceptive sight and touch, fused with proprioceptive motion and force information to estimate the robustness of their grasps.

To address some of those issues, in [7] we have recently presented a low-cost, non-intrusive and easy-to-integrate state estimation method for flexible fingers using a proximity sensor (VCNL4010 [8]). While this approach has delivered promising performance for binary grasp verification and demonstrated the general feasibility of detecting object slippage, a further investigation has shown that the extracted information was not yet sufficient for designing a closed-loop system that can handle fragile objects. Hence, in this work, we incorporate additional sensory data – namely from a newly-integrated, flexible bend sensor [9] and the already present motor load sensors – into the grasping architecture. This approach enables the detection and avoidance of in-hand slippage for arbitrary objects.

We evaluate the system's performance on a set of objects with different characteristics in terms of geometric shape, mass or rigidity. The two most challenging objects, that our system is able to handle, are a fragile chocolate egg and a key chain that consists of rigid objects but is highly deformable due to its articulation.

2 Related Work

There exists a rich body of knowledge on the integration of sensors into *rigid* hands and fingers. However, as motivated above, we focus on soft and flexible hands and, hence, also limit this section to related work in this field.

Flexible and soft robotics is a rather young field of research that has gained momentum with the availability of affordable rapid prototyping technology in the recent years. As a result, designs of flexible hands and fingers vary widely, ranging from grippers that are based on the jamming of granular materials [10], over pneumatically-actuated soft fingers [11] to designs like the one in our use case. Since flexible grippers have not yet converged to particular designs there are even less established best practices for tactile sensing in those hands. Consequently, many approaches rely on the attachment of external sensors or the design and fabrication of custom soft hands with embedded sensors.

Still, prior research has demonstrated that soft hands with built-in sensors are capable of handling inherent uncertainty in grasping tasks that originates, for example, from imperfect object localization or prior knowledge associated with the objects' geometry, mass or rigidity. In particular, Dollar *et al.* [12] mold a film of piezoelectric polymer into the robot's compliant fingers which allows them to localize contacts and react to deviations. Similarly, Homberg *et al.* [13] integrate flexible bend and force sensors into completely molded soft fingers. The soft hand composed of such fingers is able to detect contacts and even identify objects. Ho *et al.* [14] demonstrate that soft fingers can passively adapt to delicate objects with limited risk of causing damage to the grasped objects. The authors integrate pressure sensors in a self-fabricated soft finger to detect contacts with objects. Tenzer *et al.* [15] present a tactile sensor to detect contact points on a soft finger. They employ a barometric pressure sensor embedded into a self-contained air bubble, from which the sensor can determine the pressure exerted by an external force. Zhao *et al.* [16] integrate photonic strain sensors into a custom-molded hand which enables bend and pressure sensing capabilities. While the previous approaches deliver promising results, they also require specialized fabrication techniques to integrate the sensors. Hence, from our perspective they are neither low-cost nor do they facilitate easy integration.

In [17] the authors employ an underactuated hand where each of the four fingers consists of two compliant phalanges. They attach hall-effect sensors to the phalanges to measure the joint angles. As such, those sensors are insufficient for directly localizing contacts, but an active perception strategy still allows the robot to infer those locations. While this design is an interesting crossover of rigid and flexible mechanisms it also means that it is not applicable to our fingers that are manufactured as one flexible element without explicit joints.

3 Approach

In a more elaborate evaluation of the previous setup, that only relied on the proximity sensors, we have observed the following specific drawbacks. Firstly, while the VCNL4010 employs a separate sensor and a specific signal modulation to attenuate the influence of ambient light, it fails to fully suppress this disruptive factor. We even observe this impact when operating the sensor's infrared LED at its maximum current of 200 mA. Since grasp verification relies on sufficiently high thresholds it is able to cope with those disruption, but slippage detection must continuously react to small changes in the measurement and hence suffers from the biased signal. Secondly, all VCNL4010's have one common and statically baked I^2C address so that additional actions must be taken to connect them to the same communication interface. Additionally, the VCNL4010's measurement principle in combination with the I^2C communication protocol limit the measurement frequency to a maximum of 250 Hz which maybe too low for highly dynamic situations, for example, discerning slippage induced vibrations.

3.1 Hardware Selection and Integration

In order to address the first issue, we have attached a bend sensor to each flexible finger. The bend sensor produces a measurement result that corresponds to the curvature of the finger while grasping an object as shown in Fig. 2. This decision aligns with our prior design criteria of a low-cost solution in terms of monetary expenses, integration effort and computational demands for processing the sensor data. Furthermore, mounting the sensors on the outside of the fingers reduces the risk of damage since they are not involved in the finger-object contact. Finally, we have observed that this design does not measurably interfere with the deformation of the fingers and hence the grasping *process*. The VCNL4010 proximity sensors remain in the same location as presented in our prior work, i.e. rigidly mounted on the base of the fingers. There, they operate in their optimal measurement range and stay in a static position, even at extreme deformations of the fingers. To summarize, Fig. 3 shows the selected locations of all sensors.

Additionally, that figure depicts the connectivity of the sensors to an Arduino Nano microcontroller. This microcontroller processes the sensory inputs and also commands the fingers' motions via the Dynamixel AX-12A servo motors. A SN74LS241N tri-state buffer acts as a circuitry conditioner to establish a half-duplex asynchronous serial communication between the daisy-chained servo motors and the microcontroller. To address the second issue, we have added a TCA9548A I^2C multiplexer that allows us to dispatch the communication to the correct proximity sensor, even if multiple sensors share the same address. Hence, we are able to connect all VCNL4010 proximity sensors to the same I^2C port on the microcontroller. Moreover, each flexible bend sensor requires a voltage divider to condition the signal before being read via the Arduino's ADC port.

Not shown in the diagram is the USB connection between the microcontroller and the robot's central control computer. The latter is responsible, for example, to plan the robot's mission, process vision inputs such as provided by the RGB-D cameras or to control the motion of the mobile base and the manipulator. This USB connection imposes a significant constraint on the system's architecture: the Arduino Nano features only one universal asynchronous receiver-transmitter (UART) that can be used either for the USB connection or the serial communication with the servo motors. The other communication channel must instead rely on a software-based solution to realize the communication protocol, which is colloquially known as "bit banging" and reduces the maximum symbol rate. In the overall, integrated system we deem the link to the control computer as more important, so that we have dedicated the UART to the USB connection.

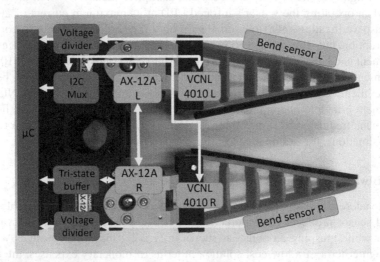

Fig. 3. Data flow between the microcontroller (blue box), the sensors (yellow boxes) and the circuitry conditioners (green boxes). (Color figure online)

3.2 Sensor Analysis and Modeling

The AX-12A servo motors feature a wide range of proprioceptive sensors that provide, among others, measurements of position, velocity, load, voltage or temperature. It should be noted that the motors only offer a position-control interface, i.e. the load measurements are purely available as feedback. Even if the manual [18] remains vague about

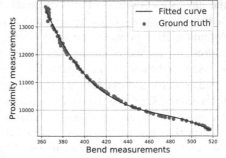

Fig. 4. Flexible finger's minimum and maximum deformation.

Fig. 5. Fitting a 3rd order polynomial to the recorded proximity and bend sensor measurements of the right finger at different deformations.

the concrete computation and representation of the load measurements, they provide valuable information about contact situations that is closely linked to the finger-object interaction. Still, we have observed false positives, for instance, due to contacts with support surfaces or for thin and small objects, in more complex, integrated scenarios such as RoboCup@Work. Additionally, due to the lack of an additional UART – as explained above – our implementation is limited to a symbol rate of 9.6 kBd instead of the theoretically possible 1 MBd.

The proximity sensor and the bend sensor complement each other well. On the one side, the proximity sensor provides a wide measurement range from 0 to 2^{16} and also a high sensitivity. In contrast, the bend sensor is limited by the 10 bit resolution of the microcontroller's ADC. Moreover, the required voltage divider further limits the range to about 200 different measurements from the bend sensor. On the other side, as mentioned above, the proximity sensor provides data at a rate of 250 Hz, whereas the bend sensor can be sampled at around 3.5 kHz.

In our prior work on grasp verification it was possible to calibrate the proximity sensor just before grasping, when it was known that the grippers were not deformed, and then compare the calibration value against the sensor readings considering the (potentially) grasped object, based on a fixed threshold. However, in the current setup we continuously monitor the proximity readings for minor changes. Thus, for the following reasons we have to adapt our previous approach to this new setup. Firstly, the approach we had presented only linearized the proximity sensor measurements, but not the behaviour of the flexible fingers themselves. Secondly, as mentioned above, the proximity sensor is slightly susceptible to the influence of ambient light so that we cannot directly deduce from changes in its signals if they are due to minor deformations of the fingers or just changes in the light conditions.

To tackle those issues, we exploit the linearity of the bend sensors in a simple sensor fusion scheme. This requires a model, to map from the bend sensor measurements to the proximity sensor measurements, which we have experimentally established. To this end, we have manually deformed the finger at its midpoint by exerting a force in the dorsal direction, until maximum bending is achieved as shown in Fig. 4. With the collected data the relation of proximity and bend sensor measurements can be modeled with good accuracy by a 3rd degree polynomial as exemplified in Fig. 5. The concrete parameters depend on the unique characteristics of the involved fingers and sensors. Therefore, they are calibrated offline for each integrated combination of sensor and finger samples.

3.3 Implementation of Manipulation Strategy

Research in human grasping [19], that has also been transferred to robotics [20], suggests that four different types of neurons (so called tactile afferents) provide information about physical interactions between the hand and fingers with the environment. Those afferents are divided into slow-adapting (SA) and fast-adapting (FA), as well as, type I and type II. They are active during different phases of interaction or trigger transitions between those phases. SA-I measures overall force and localizes contacts (0–5 Hz), SA-II reacts to low-frequency tangential forces (0–5 Hz), FA-I is indicative of finger-object contacts or in-hand slippage (5–50 Hz), whereas FA-II detects collisions of the grasped object

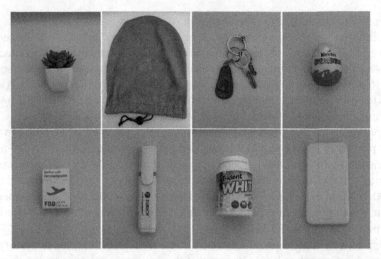

Fig. 6. Test objects with different shape, mass and rigidity.

with other objects (40–400 Hz). Our manipulation strategy concentrates on the initial contact and slippage detection, i.e. the FA-I, during the reach, load, lift and hold phases.

For establishing the initial contact, we focus on the main grasping modes of enveloping and pinch grasps. While the enveloping grasp produces considerable deformation in the fingers this is not the case for the pinch grasp. Thus, the proximity and bend sensor are insufficient to detect the initial contact. Instead, we monitor the measurements of the motor load sensors while closing the gripper stepwise from a pre-defined open configuration until both sensors indicate a contact. This event marks the transition from the reach to the load phase which starts with only very limited force applied to the object.

This transition also engages the slippage detection and reaction for the following lift and hold phases. While slippage in human grasping is associated with rather high frequency vibrations, we have noticed that in our setup it also leads to measurable static deformations as a reaction of the compliant fingers to return to their original shape. Hence, the goal is to monitor the highly sensitive proximity measurements for changes beyond a dynamically-computed threshold. Recalling the linear behaviour of the bend sensor allows us to simply specify a fixed threshold in this domain and then map it to the thresholds in the codomain of the proximity sensor using the 3rd order polynomial that we have established above as the system model. Deviations beyond this threshold are classified as in-hand slippage. Once the robot detects such a situation, it reacts by closing the gripper further so to increase the force exerted on the grasped object and restrict further movement of the object within the hand. By continuously cycling the above steps we are able to close the loop between perception for slippage detection and control. The approach is also tolerant to the grasp position and the object geometry.

4   Evaluation

In the following, we evaluate the integrated hardware and software system that we have described above in a controlled environment. We distinguish between the two phases, i.e. reaching to establish initial contact and lifting with slippage avoidance.

4.1   Initial Contact Detection

For the first scenario, the detection of the initial contact, we consider both grasp modes (enveloping and pinch grasp). Variability in the characteristics of the test objects comprises geometric shape, mass, rigidity, articulation and fragility. The selection of those objects is depicted in Fig. 6. We have performed two attempts of each of the above combinations. The results are reported in Fig. 7.

It can be observed that the load sensors are able to successfully detect when there is an object within the range of the gripper. We can see how even the thinnest object produces the same load measurements in both pinch an enveloping grasping, even when the contact for all objects was made at different joint angles. These results support our hypothesis that the actuator's load measurements are the best candidate to identify the instant of time at which both fingers establish contact with the object.

From the proximity measurements, it can be observed that the output for the pinch grasping hardly deviates from the readings in the flat state (red dashed line). Thus, even if the proximity sensor is very sensitive, it is difficult to derive the moment of initial contact only from the proximity readings. Contrarily, for enveloping grasps those measurements reliably differ from those associated with the empty gripper. A spike can be observed on the proximity value while envelope-grasping the key chain. This result can be attributed to the key chain's articulation, which lets the gripper continue closing until all keys stop moving.

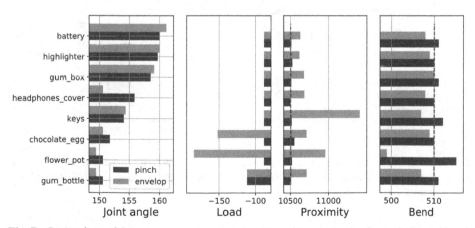

Fig. 7. Comparison of the sensor measurements (motor position, motor load, proximity and bend sensor readings) for the test objects using pinch and enveloping grasps. The dashed red lines indicate the sensor reading for the empty gripper. (Color figure online)

Finally, we can see that the measurements of the bend sensors for most objects are within the sensor's noise threshold. Hence, it is challenging to detect the initial contact based on the curvature values.

4.2 Slippage Detection

To evaluate the integrated system for slippage detection and avoidance we have employed the chocolate egg and the key chain as test objects. The robot closes its gripper from a pre-defined, open configuration while monitoring for the initial contact as described above. Once it has established contact, we manually displace the test objects which in turn triggers the slippage detection.

The chart in Fig. 8 depicts one exemplifying time trace of proximity measurements (red graph) and associated joint angles (blue graph) for the left finger while the robot handles the chocolate egg. Higher proximity measurements indicate increased finger deformation, whereas greater joint angles represent a more closed gripper (this is due to the motor's mounting and its internal position representation). It can be observed that the gripper establishes contact with the object approximately at step 140. After that, the slippage detection algorithm is engaged. Around step 390 the proximity measurements drop below the threshold which indicates that the object is slipping from the fingers. As a reaction the robot continues closing its gripper to increase the force exerted on the grasped object, as can be seen by the increase in the blue graph. Continuing, the robot reacts to two more slippage events at around steps 400 and 500.

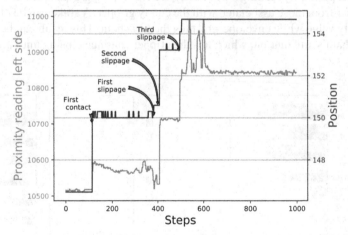

Fig. 8. Time trace of proximity and joint position measurements associated with the left finger while grasping the chocolate egg. The robot's reactions to in-hand slippage are indicated. (Color figure online)

Just like before, the time trace in Fig. 9 shows the measurements of the sensors associated with the left finger, but now while grasping the key chain. Again, the time steps of initial contact and slippage are indicated. It is visible that the general shape of the joint position graph aligns with that of the previous figure (i.e. the gripper is closing

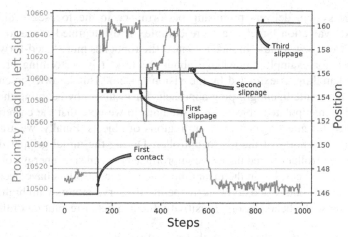

Fig. 9. Time trace of proximity and joint position measurements associated with the left finger while grasping the key chain. The robot's reactions to in-hand slippage are indicated

as a reaction to in-hand slippage). However, in this case the shape of the proximity measurements deviate. Instead of a general increase in the readings there is a trough at around step 375 and a more or less steady decrease from step 500 and onward. Both behaviours are caused by the reconfiguration of the individual keys attached to the key chain as a response to the force that the fingers exert on them. Nevertheless, the key chain remains in the robot's grasp.

5 Discussion and Conclusions

The recent trend in rapid manufacturing has contributed to the progress of robotic grasping using passively compliant materials. Those approaches have not yet converged to preferred gripper designs and even less so to best practices in equipping those grippers with sensors. Additionally, a great amount of research still focuses on planning grasps, instead of controlled grasp execution that exploits continuous sensory feedback.

To tackle those problems, we have proposed an extension of our prior work to now also detect in-hand slippage in such grippers. To this end, we have attached a new bend sensor to the finger. By employing its measurements in conjunction with the motor load and proximity measurements, we are able to reduce the amount of force that the gripper exerts on the grasped objects. Then, by closing the loop between slippage detection and grasp control, the robot can gradually increase the grasp force so as to prevent further slippage. Our approach builds upon commercially available, low-cost flexible fingers and sensors that facilitate cost-efficient and easy integration without relying on advanced manufacturing techniques such as molding the sensors into the fingers. We have successfully evaluated this solution for (*i*) detecting the initial contact between fingers and objects; as well as (*ii*) detecting and reacting to in-hand slippage. The evaluation relies on different objects with distinguished characteristics in terms of geometry, mass and rigidity.

Since the system delivers promising performance in the focused evaluation, an obvious next evaluation target is a more complex and integrated scenario such as a RoboCup@Work benchmark. In such a context the robot has more "feed-forward" context available, for example, knowledge about the task it is performing or about the objects it is handling as extracted by the vision system. This knowledge can help in designing a more intelligent grasping approach, for instance, by adapting the slippage reaction to the manipulated objects. In particular, do we note that the current strategy is better suited for grasping concave (sub)regions of objects. Finally, we are planning to investigate the choice of the microcontroller. During the initial gripper design the current microcontroller offered the best compromise between size, energy consumption and available interfaces, but in the meantime new microcontrollers have become commercially available that would allow us to operate the servo motors with higher symbol rates and increase the bend sensors' sensitivity due to a better resolution of the ADC.

Acknowledgements. The authors gratefully acknowledge the on-going support of the Bonn-Aachen International Center for Information Technology. Sven Schneider received a PhD scholarship from the Graduate Institute of the Bonn-Rhein-Sieg University which is gratefully acknowledged.

References

1. Festo: Adaptive gripper fingers DHAS. [Online]. Available: https://www.festo.com/cat/en-gb_gb/data/doc_ENGB/PDF/EN/DHAS_EN.PDF. Last accessed 18 April 2020
2. Hogan, N.: Impedance control: an approach to manipulation: part I – theory. J. Dyn. Syst. Meas. Control **107**(1), 1–7 (1985)
3. Drake, S.: Using compliance in lieu of sensory feedback for automatic assembly. Ph.D. Dissertation, Massachusetts Institute of Technology (1978)
4. Whitney, D.E.: Mechanical Assemblies: Their Design, Manufacture, and Role in Product Development. Oxford University Press (2004)
5. Bohg, J., Morales, M., Asfour, T., Kragic, D.: Data-driven grasp synthesis – a survey. IEEE Trans. Robot. **30**(2), 289–309 (2014)
6. Sahbani, A., El-Khoury, S., Bidaud, P.: An overview of 3D object grasp synthesis algorithms. Robot. Auton. Syst. **60**(3), 326–336 (2012)
7. Kulkarni, P., Schneider, S., Ploeger, P.G.: Low-Cost Sensor Integration for Robust Grasping with Flexible Robotic Fingers. In: Wotawa, F., Friedrich, G., Pill, I., Koitz-Hristov, R., Ali, M. (eds.) IEA/AIE 2019. LNCS (LNAI), vol. 11606, pp. 666–673. Springer, Cham (2019). https://doi.org/10.1007/978-3-030-22999-3_57
8. Vishay Semiconductors: VCNL4010: Fully Integrated Proximity and Ambient Light Sensor with Infrared Emitter, I2C Interface, and Interrupt Function (2014)
9. Spectrasymbol: Flex Sensor v.2014 Rev A. [Online]. Available: https://www.spectrasymbol.com/wp-content/uploads/2019/07/flexsensordatasheetv2019revA.pdf. Last accessed 18 April 2020
10. Brown, E., et al.: Universal robotic gripper based on the jamming of granular material. Proc. Natl. Acad. Sci. **107**(44), 18809–18814 (2010)
11. Ozel, S., et al.: A composite soft bending actuation module with integrated curvature sensing. In: IEEE International Conference on Robotics and Automation (ICRA), pp. 4963–4968, IEEE, Stockholm, Sweden (2016)

12. Dollar, A.M., Jentoft, L.P., Gao, J.H., Howe, R.D.: Contact sensing and grasping performance of compliant hands. Auton. Robots **28**(1), 65–75 (2010)
13. Homberg, B.S., Katzschmann, R.K., Dogar, M.R., Rus, D.: Haptic identification of objects using a modular soft robotic gripper. In: IEEE/RSJ International Conference on Intelligent Robots and Systems (IROS) (2015)
14. Ho, V., Hirai, S.: Design and analysis of a soft-fingered hand with contact feedback. IEEE Robot. Autom. Lett. **2**(2), 491–498 (2017)
15. Tenzer, Y., Jentoft, L.P., Howe, R.D.: The feel of MEMS barometers: inexpensive and easily customized tactile array sensors. IEEE Robot. Autom. Mag. **21**(3), 89–95 (2014)
16. Zhao, H., O'Brien, K., Li, S., Shepherd, R.: Optoelectronically innervated soft prosthetic hand via stretchable optical waveguides. Sci. Robot. **1**(1), eaai7529 (2016). https://doi.org/10.1126/scirobotics.aai7529
17. Jentoft, L.P., Howe, R.D.: Compliant fingers make simple sensors smart. In: Proceedings of the ASME 2010 Underactuated Grasping Workshop (2010)
18. Dynamixel AX-12A manual: https://emanual.robotis.com/docs/en/dxl/ax/ax-12a/. Last accessed 18 April 2020
19. Johansson, R.S., Flanagan, J.R.: Coding and use of tactile signals from the fingertips in object manipulation tasks. Nat. Rev. Neurosci. **10**(5), 345–359 (2009)
20. Romano, J.M., Hsiao, K., Niemeyer, G., Chitta, S., Kuchenbecker, K.J.: Human-inspired robotic grasp control with tactile sensing. IEEE Trans. Robot. **27**(6), 1067–1079 (2011)

A Method for Realizing the Connection Between the Movements of the Operator's Fingers and the Model of an Anthropomorphic Gripping Device

V. V. Ivanenkov$^{(\boxtimes)}$, G. K. Tevyashov, Y. L. Smirnova, and M. A. Pavlov

BMSTU "Bauman Moscow State Technical University", Moscow, Russian Federation
ivanenkov@bmstu.ru

Abstract. The article poses the problem of managing a virtual model of anthropomorphic capture using a sensor system. The sensors determine the movements of the fingers of the operator's hands in order to formulate the laws of control of the gripper in the copy mode. The analysis of the most famous existing anthropomorphic grips (Robonaut Hand, Shadow Dexterous Hand, EH1 Milano Hand, SVH Hand) is carried out. The obvious advantages of the SVH Hand manipulator from SCHUNK are revealed. The connection of the model in the framework for programming robots – Robot Operating System (ROS) and working out the values of the positions specified using the test file is shown. An experimental system has been developed – a control glove, consisting of rotation sensors to determine the movement of the index finger (by analogy, a model will be developed for four other fingers). The experimental system is connected with the virtual model by connecting the glove to the Arduino Uno board, which in turn is connected to a personal computer to transmit the values of the sensor position changes. In conclusion, the direction of future research is determined, such as developing a design for all fingers and adding feedback to transmit tactile information to the operator from touch sensors.

Keywords: Anthropomorphic capture · Operator movements · Tong · Copying mode · Motion reading methods · ROS

1 Introduction

Currently, in many areas of life there is a steady tendency to transition to robotic technologies. The main advantage of robotic systems is the ability to perform manipulation operations, such as, for example, moving various objects, assembling or disassembling them, with a sufficient distance of a person from the operating area. Particularly relevant are the issues of robotization of operations when working in extreme conditions – in underwater and space space, as well as when working with objects dangerous to humans containing explosive or toxic substances.

At the moment, such robotic operations are implemented mainly through the use of a copy control mode with the operator constantly in the robot control loop. The main

© Springer Nature Switzerland AG 2021
A. Yuschenko (Ed.): MPoR 2020, CCIS 1426, pp. 110–120, 2021.
https://doi.org/10.1007/978-3-030-88458-1_9

problem of the copy mode is the significant complexity of controlling the executive mechanism using the buttons and joysticks located on the control panel. This leads to an increase in the psychological burden on the operator, which increases the risk of erroneous decision-making – the human factor, which in turn can lead to the destruction of the captured object or its loss from the gripper of the manipulator [1]. The force control in the dexterous grippers of robots using an electric drive is provided by current control [2]. Force control is an important technique in programming and safety for collaborative robots [3].

Thus, the task of developing a method for controlling a multi-fingered gripping device, especially in terms of the control interface available for operators with various biometric data, for performing tasks of clever manipulation of objects, is undoubtedly relevant [1].

The main objective of the graduation project is to connect with feedback the controlled model and the operator's hand to ensure the movement of the model in copy mode. Such a connection solves the problem of sensing the capture, for example, during remote clearance, when the operator must be outside the working area.

2 Statement of the Problem

This article presents a way to implement the relationship between the anthropomorphic capture model and the operator's finger motion sensors.

The tasks in the current work are:

1. The choice of a prototype anthropomorphic gripper;
2. Simulate the selected anthropomorphic capture in Robot Operating System (ROS);
3. Link the movement of the operator's hand with the anthropomorphic gripper via ROS.

3 Select a Control Object

Over the past two decades, many anthropomorphic robotic grips have been developed. These devices allow you to capture and manipulate objects [4].

To work, you must choose what to control using a device designed to relieve the movement of the phalanges of the fingers of the operator. Therefore, we consider some of the most famous existing five-fingered anthropomorphic devices.

3.1 Robonaut Hand

Several grippers were developed for use in the cosmos, and some were even tested in space, but not a single robotic arm was used in extra-ship conditions. In Fig. 1 shows Robonaut Hand, one of the first to be developed for use in outer space and closest in size and capabilities to the hand of an astronaut.

Fig. 1. Robonaut hand

Robonaut Hand can reach all parts of the work area and control tools such as a cable hook. Parts of the hands and wrists have dimensions and durability, satisfying the maximum requirements for the crew in outer space. The ability to work in outer space distinguishes Robonaut from all existing robotic arms.

All parts are made of materials that have characteristics that satisfy extreme temperature fluctuations. Brushless motors are used to ensure continuous operation in a vacuum.

Each Robonaut hand has a total of fourteen degrees of freedom. It consists of a forearm, which houses engines, electronics and a drive, a wrist with two degrees of freedom and five fingers of twelve degrees of freedom. The forearm, which is four inches in diameter at its base, is approximately eight inches in length, with fourteen motors, 12 separate circuit boards, and all of the wiring for the hand.

The hand itself is divided into two parts: the part used for manipulation, and the gripping part, which allows the hand to maintain a stable grip during manipulation. The manipulating part consists of two 3 degrees of freedom of the fingers (pointer and index) and 3 degrees of freedom of the opposed thumb. The gripping part consists of two, 1 degrees of freedom of the fingers (ring and little finger) and palms of the degree of freedom [5].

Unfortunately, NASA developments are secret and it is not possible to find Robonaut Hand models in the public domain.

3.2 Shadow Dexterous Hand

Shadow Dexterous Hand is a breakthrough in miniaturization, the appearance of which is shown in Fig. 2. In commensurate with the dimensions of the human hand, the developers packed highly sensitive fingertips, absolute position sensors for each joint and a control panel in the palm of your hand, which allows expanding the system with the help of add-ons. This greatly enhances operational capabilities.

The hand has 20 degrees of freedom and in general 24 connections. Each joint moves the same or very similar to the movements of the human hand, including the thumb and even the fold of the palm for the little finger.

Fig. 2. Shadow dexterous hand

With 129 sensors in total, the hand provides detailed telemetry that can be used to create innovative control systems, manipulations, or to provide a detailed sense of the external environment. In addition to determining the absolute position of each connection, Shadow Dexterous can perceive tactile sensing at your fingertips, temperature and perceive the current and voltage of the motor. All this data is available to the user in the range from 100 Hz to 1 kHz via EtherCAT. Thanks to the high frequency of data transmission, reading the position from the bent to the extended finger is only 0.5 s.

The hand is fully integrated with ROS, and models and code are also available. Development engineers provided the opportunity to work with the Shadow Dexterous model in ROS [6]. Hand control, including position control algorithms, can be changed by the user in ROS. Firmware inside the hand itself is also available for modification [7].

3.3 EH1 Milano Hand

The EH1 Milano Hand series is a programmable anthropomorphic hand similar in size to a human one, able to grab a lot of objects and feel the grip through several force and position sensors (Fig. 3). Modular actuators are located in the flanges, transmission via cable allows for remote control.

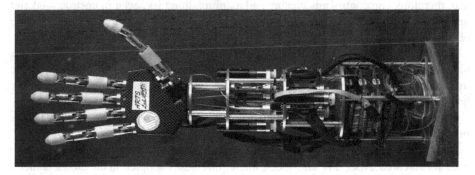

Fig. 3. EH1 Milano Hand

A distinctive feature of this development is weight, one hand weighs only 250 g! Each drive contains a processor, firmware, sensor, electronics, communications electronics, servo controllers and one brush DC motor.

The hand "communicates" through RS232 or USB and can be easily integrated into many research projects, ranging from prosthetics, neurology, human-robot interactions, rehabilitation, etc. EH1 Milano series firmware programs allow you to capture automatically, simply sending one byte from your application. Alternatively, users can implement fully individual control circuits, taking advantage of the integrated 1 kHz servo control circuits [8].

3.4 SVH Hand

The SVH Hand in serial production captures objects almost as well as a human hand. A nine-drive mobile system enables a wide range of delicate gripping operations. Elastic gripping surfaces guarantee reliable retention of items. Electronics are fully integrated in the wrist (Fig. 4).

In addition to new dimensions in the field of capture and manipulation, the SCHUNK manipulator-hand with five fingers provides the ability to communicate with a robot using gestures.

3.4.1 Advantages

- Suitable for mobile use due to low power consumption at 24 V.
- Very compact design thanks to the integration of all control electronics, regulation and power electronics in the wrist
- Standard interfaces for easy connection to industry-standard light industrial robots.

Nine drives allow the 5-finger hand to perform various grip operations. It has been found that many human gestures can be reproduced, so that the visual connection between a person and a service robot is simplified, which increases the acceptability of their use at home.

Using tactile sensors in the fingers, the capture arm has the necessary sensitivity and, therefore, can control any capture and manipulation task, even in unstructured and unforeseen situations. Elastic gripping surfaces provide a secure hold of the gripping objects.

The anthropomorphic handle is fully integrated in the wrist and, therefore, makes particularly compact solutions possible. The grip handle can be connected via specific interfaces to any easy lever available on the market. For mobile applications, a 5-finger hand is designed to be powered by a 24 V DC battery [9].

SVH has 9 degrees of freedom, which are considered as separate channels. Themes that accept the channels will use the following mapping in Fig. 4.

We will use SVH Hand for simulation, because the developers provide open source code for research. Also, this hand meets the requirements adopted in the thesis, namely, each joint of this model is movable, with the ability to control this joint.

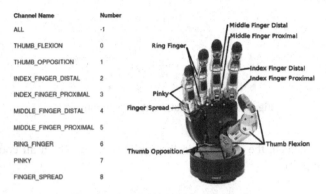

Channel Name	Number
ALL	-1
THUMB_FLEXION	0
THUMB_OPPOSITION	1
INDEX_FINGER_DISTAL	2
INDEX_FINGER_PROXIMAL	3
MIDDLE_FINGER_DISTAL	4
MIDDLE_FINGER_PROXIMAL	5
RING_FINGER	6
PINKY	7
FINGER_SPREAD	8

Fig. 4. SVH hand and her ROS topics

4 Connecting the SVH Hand Model

Robot Operating System (ROS) was chosen as the medium for information processing [5]. ROS provides developers with libraries and tools for building robotic applications, provides hardware abstraction, offers device drivers, libraries, visualizers, messaging, package managers, and much more. ROS is released under the terms of the BSD license and is open source. In ROS, you can create a virtual work environment that fully corresponds to the current work stage in which the manipulator works (for example, a virtual scene model for the manipulator that performs the operation of opening the bag valve) [10].

The schunk_svh_driver package was used for SVH Hand modeling, this package provides a way to control the Schunk Five finger hand (Fig. 5). A driver is used for the low-level interface and makes it easy to control the hand through ROS messages [11].

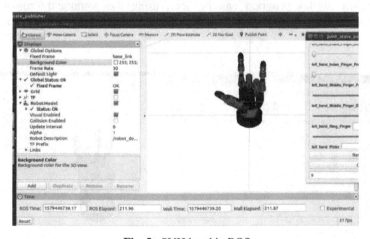

Fig. 5. SVH hand in ROS

To control the model, you need to use the topic "output_joint_state_publisher", which receives the input data for the movement of the SCHUNK model. As an example, let's write a node that will send data to the topic. The basis of this program is the data structure, which consists of the name of the pairing and the meaning of this pairing (Fig. 6).

hello_str.name = ['left_hand_Thumb_Flexion', 'left_hand_Thumb_Opposition', 'left_hand_j5', 'left_hand_j3',
  'left_hand_j4', 'left_hand_Index_Finger_Distal', 'left_hand_Index_Finger_Proximal', 'left_hand_j14',
  'left_hand_Middle_Finger_Proximal', 'left_hand_Middle_Finger_Distal', 'left_hand_j15',
 'left_hand_Ring_Finger', 'left_hand_j12', 'left_hand_j16', 'left_hand_Pinky', 'left_hand_j13',
  'left_hand_j17', 'left_hand_index_spread', 'left_hand_ring_spread', 'left_hand_Finger_Spread']
  hello_str.position = [0.7412885600000001, 0.00187701, 0.00187701, 0.7524894301416001, 1.0740455816984003, 0.1264632, 0.362833856,
0.132154044, 0.14197152200000002, 0.6091044, 0.63675773976, 0.623509425, 0.84722460669, 0.88596324726525, 0.17730405000000002,
0.24092074314000003, 0.2523160744335, 0.04660285499999999, 0.04660285499999999, 0.09320570999999998]

Fig. 6. Topic "output_joint_state_publisher"

Upon initial launch, the model is in the initial state, in which all coordinates are equal to zero (Fig. 7).

Fig. 7. The initial position of the model

The result of this program can be seen using the command "rostopic echo joint_states". The hand itself assumed a position corresponding to the sent coordinates (Fig. 8).

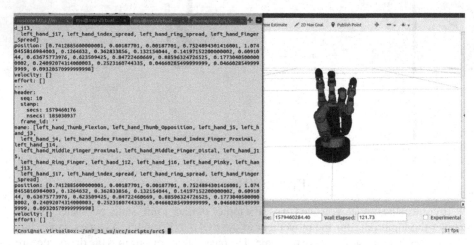

Fig. 8. Model position corresponding to the sent coordinates

5 Development of an Experimental Model

To control the model in ROS, it is necessary to develop an experimental model that will contain sensors for the operator's fingers. In the simplest case, to verify the correctness of the assumption (in this case, to determine the movement of each phalanx of the finger, a rotation sensor is used) it is enough to develop a model for one (index) finger.

We will use a potentiometer as rotation sensors. Potentiometers are adjustable voltage dividers that are designed to regulate the voltage at a constant current, and are made as a variable resistor.

Voltage is applied to the terminals of the resistive element, which is supposed to be regulated. A movable contact is a control element that is actuated by turning the handle (Fig. 9). A voltage is removed from the movable contact, which can range from zero

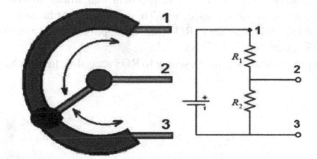

Fig. 9. How the potentiometer works

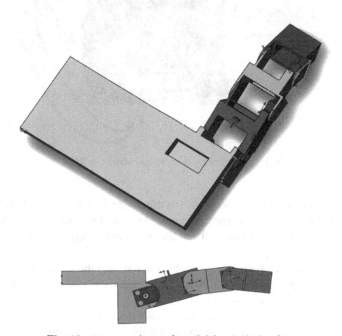

Fig. 10. The experimental model for the index finger

to the largest value equal to the input voltage to the potentiometer, and depends on the current position of the movable contact [12].

The model developed in the SolidWorks CAD software package [13] is presented in Fig. 10.

6 Connecting Sensors with the SVH Hand Model

We will use Arduino UNO as the control board. Arduino is a popular prototyping board, widely used in connection with the notion "smart home" that arose not so long ago and which is an ideal starting point for beginners in the field of microelectronics and robotics [14].

Using the rosserial_arduino package allows you to use ROS in conjunction with the Arduino IDE, rosserial uses a data transfer protocol that works through the Arduino UART (universal asynchronous transceiver). This allows the Arduino to be a full ROS node that can publish and subscribe to ROS messages, publish TF (spatial) conversions, and receive ROS system time.

First, let's try to connect the rotation sensor to ROS according to the scheme presented in Fig. 11.

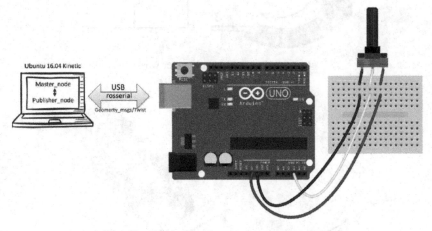

Fig. 11. Connecting the rotation sensor to ROS

To do this, connect the sensor as shown in the diagram above and start the program. The results of the movement of the potentiometer knob and the execution of the program are as follows: the minimum value of 0 and the maximum value when turning the knob 180° is 1023 (Fig. 12).

Now we will connect the anthropomorphic capture and the sensor, that is, the information received from the sensors will be processed on a computer and transmitted directly to a controlled model (Fig. 13).

By analogy with one sensor for one finger phalanx, it will be possible to determine the movements of each phalanx of the operator's fingers. In the future, you need to add

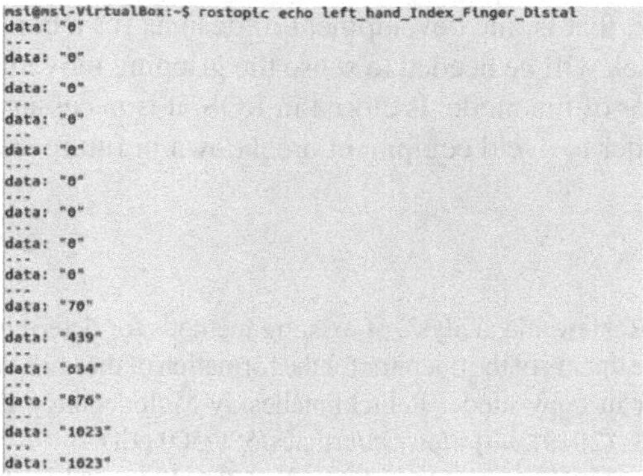

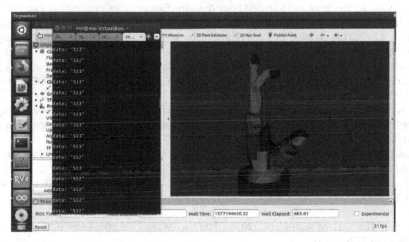

Fig. 12. The result of connecting the sensor to ROS

Fig. 13. The result of receiving information from the sensor and transmitting the model

a capture sensor. It will also be necessary to study the deformation of the object during the capture process [15].

7 Conclusion

As a result of this work, prototypes of an anthropomorphic gripping device were considered and a specific model SVH Hand (from SCHUNK) was selected for further modeling. The operating principle of the Robot Operating System was reviewed, and an anthropomorphic arm was simulated in ROS.

A connection was made between ROS, Arduino and rotation sensors for sensing the movement of the operator's hand and transmitting the movement of the controlled model.

The direction of future research is determined, namely the connection of all fingers of the operators and sensors for each phalanx of the operator. The search for a solution to a constructive task, that is, the development of designs for a control "glove". Search for feedback. Feedback will be needed to sense the gripping movement. In other words, when the touch sensor of the model is closed in ROS, it is necessary to send a signal to the control part in order to avoid equipment breakdown in future studies.

References

1. Tevyashov, G.K.: Review and analysis of existing methods for determining the movement of the phalanges of the fingers of the operator for the formation of the laws of control of the anthropomorphic gripper in copy mode. Politekhnicheskiy Molodezhnyy Zhurnal [Politechnical Student Journal] (8) (2019). http://ptsj.ru/articles/509/509.pdf
2. Serebrennyj, V., Boshlyakov, A., Ogorodnik, A.: Current control in the drives of dexterous robot grippers. In: Ronzhin, A., Rigoll, G., Meshcheryakov, R. (eds.) Interactive Collaborative Robotics. ICR 2018. Lecture Notes in Computer Science, Vol 11097. Springer, Cham (2018)
3. Zabihifar, S., Yuschenko, A.: Hybrid Force/Position Control of a Collaborative Parallel Robot Using Adaptive Neural Network. In: Ronzhin, A., Rigoll, G., Meshcheryakov, R. (eds.) ICR 2018. LNCS (LNAI), vol. 11097, pp. 280–290. Springer, Cham (2018). https://doi.org/10.1007/978-3-319-99582-3_29
4. Bazhinova, K.V., Leskov, A.G., Seliverstova, E.V.: Automatic grasping of objects by a manipulator equipped with a multifinger hand. J. Comput. Syst. Sci. Int. **58**(2), 317–327 (2019)
5. Lovchik, C.S., Diftler, M.A.: The Robonaut hand: a dexterous robot hand for space. In: Proceedings 1999 IEEE International Conference on Robotics and Automation (Cat. No.99CH36288C), vol. 2, Detroit, MI, USA, pp. 907–912 (1999)
6. Joseph, L.: Robot Operating System (ROS) for Absolute Beginners: Robotics Programming Made Easy. Apress (2018)
7. Shadow Robot Company: Design of a Dextrous Hand for Advanced CLAWAR applications. In: CLAWAR Conference 2003, Catania, Italy. http://www.shadow.org.uk/. Accessed 15 Nov 2019
8. P. Srl.: The EH1 Milano Hand (2010). http://www.prensilia.com/index.php?q=en/node/4. Accessed 27 Nov 2019
9. Ruehl, S., Parlitz, C., Heppner, G., Hermann, A., Roennau, A., Dillmann, R.: Experimental evaluation of the schunk 5-finger gripping hand for grasping tasks. In: 2014 IEEE International Conference on Robotics and Biomimetics
10. Leskov, A.G., Illarionov, V.V., Kalevatykh, I.A., Moroshkin, S.D., Bazhinova, K.V., Seliverstova, E.V.: Planning, simulation and experimental research into typical robotic manipulator operation. Vestn. Mosk. Gos. Tekh. Univ. im. N.E. Baumana, Mashinostr. [Herald of the Bauman Moscow State Tech. Univ., Mech. Eng.] (4), 57–70 (2016)
11. SVH Hand: www.roscomponents.com. Accessed 5 Dec 2019
12. Handbook of electrical measuring instruments. In: Ilyunina, K.K. (ed.) L.: Energoatomizdat (1983)
13. Hanafiah, N.M., Sam, R, Buniyamin, N.: Design of an anthropomorphic robotic hand for power grip posture using SolidWorks. In: 2014 IEEE 5th Control and System Graduate Research Colloquium, Shah Alam, pp. 31–36 (2014)
14. Exploring Arduino: Tools and Techniques for Engineering Wizardry; 2nd edn. Jeremy Blum; Wiley, 512 p. (2019)
15. Leskov, A.G., Bazhinova, K.V., Seliverstova, E.V.: Methods of grasp quality evaluation. Vestn. Mosk. Gos. Tekh. Univ. im. N.E. Baumana, Mashinostr. [Herald of the Bauman Moscow State Tech. Univ., Mech. Eng.] (3), 122–139 (2017)

Structure and Control Algorithms of Manipulation Robots Operating Autonomously

A. G. Leskov[1]([⊠]) and V. V. Illarionov[2]

[1] Bauman Moscow State Technical University, Moscow 105005, Russia
leskov@bmstu.ru
[2] Moscow (Dmitrov Branch), Bauman State Technical University,
Moscow Region, Dmitrov 141801, Russia

Abstract. Considerable attention has been paid recently by researchers and developers to manipulator robots (MR) which operate autonomously. Increasing MR autonomy degree allows to significantly reduce, and in some cases, to exclude humans participation in MR management. This issue is especially important if there are restrictions on the communication channels when performing operations in conditions of incomplete information (un-oriented objects, etc.) Tasks of autonomous working are considered related to MR for a wide variety of purposes. One of the most striking manifestations of MR autonomy is space manipulation robots (SMR) which perform assembly operations. Currently, it is planned to perform assembly operations using SMR in autonomous systems when solving problems of constructing and repairing orbital stations, space telescopes and other spacecraft, moreover; in space satellites refueling, etc.

This research discusses some issues of assembling objects using MR in an autonomous system. The main idea of this research is based on the general principles of objects automatic grasping theory using multi-finger gripper (MFG) MR. In this work, an approach for solving the problem of objects automatic grasping as one of the assembly operation phases has been proposed. This research describes an experimental hardware and software system. This system has been created at Bauman Moscow state technical University for solving problems of objects automatic grasping and performing assembly operations in an autonomous system. In this work the simplest examples, that clearly illustrate the proposed approach for solving the problem of automatic grasping in one of the assembly operation phases, have been given.

Keywords: Autonomous manipulator robot · Grasping · Assembly · Space

1 Introduction

Considerable attention has been paid recently by researchers and developers in order to increase the operation autonomy degree of manipulator robots (MR). MR autonomation can drastically reduce, and in some cases, exclude humans from MR control. This

© Springer Nature Switzerland AG 2021
A. Yuschenko (Ed.): MPoR 2020, CCIS 1426, pp. 121–136, 2021.
https://doi.org/10.1007/978-3-030-88458-1_10

is especially important if there are restrictions on the communication channels when working in poorly structured environments, etc.

In this work, issues of MR autonomy in the plane of assembly operation have been discussed. This approach is adopted based on the following considerations.

Relevance of Assembly Operations. Assembly is widely used in the production of automobiles [1, 2] and others. The importance of assembly operations is clear in the space field [3, 4]. Relevance of assembly operations in space and the need for their autonomy have been studied by many authors, such as [5–9]. Following is a list of some well-known space robot assembly projects which are currently under development by both the auspices of NASA (The National Aeronautics and Space Administration) and DARPA (United States Defense Advanced Research Projects Agency) in the major integrated space technology firms:

- Methods of creating satellites directly in space. These satellites do not fit in a standard launch vehicle fairing.
- On-orbit assembly of space telescopes with an aperture in the range of 10–50 m and radio antennas with an aperture of more than 100 m.
- Creating robotic platform that designs, builds, and integrates large spatially optimized systems in space.
- Integrating additive manufacturing technologies with robotic assembly technology in orbit. Where the possibility of additive production and assembly in space is a huge expansion of the modern space technology.
- New key paradigm for efficient and versatile assembly in space.

Prevalence of Assembly Operations and Their Variety. Currently, assembly is one of the most common operations. It has been noticed by researchers in [5] and [5, 6] that significant spread of assembly operations and their diversity with the "generalized" nature of the actions performed during execution allow researchers to consider assembly operations themselves. Moreover; it is possible to consider assembly operations as a basis for design and an incentive for creating fundamentally new designs of MR in space field, and MR of various types and purposes improving their design parameters and technical characteristics.

Presence of a Reserve. Actions performed by MR during assembly operation in an autonomous system include solution of several additional tasks, in addition to the assembly itself. These tasks include automatic location of a manipulated object (MO) in the working area using computer vision systems (CVS), identification of MO, method planning and grasping using MFG when moving MO to a specified area of space. Many studies have been dedicated to solving these problems [10, 11]. Some of these studies have been put into practice, for example the ROS (The Robot Operating System) framework [12]. In particular, the GraspIt! and MoveIt! package systems is widely known [13]. GraspIt! allows (due to the relevant quality criteria) to automatically solve the problem of planning of MO grasping using MFG. MoveIt! in turn allows to plan movement of the grasped objects [14].

One feature of the above developments is the ability to automatically plan individual actions performed during assembly process. It is done separately and without taking into account features of the upcoming task of connecting individual MOs. This approach has a disadvantage. For example, a grasped object, without taking into account the parameters of the subsequent operation of connecting the grasped MO to another MO, can be oriented in space in such a way that before connecting, the grasped MO will have to be «re-grasped». This will require additional time. In this case, it may be necessary to perform additional measures in order to arrange the place of the MO temporary location.

In case of assembling a complex multilink construction, operations of grasp planning, transfer and attachment are repeated many times for each detail of the design [15, 16]. For this case, a set of special planners is used. Grippers are generated and tested for the feasibility in each and every operation. In this case, final selection of the grasp is made based on the possibility of moving OM along any suitable path to the working area.

Thus, usually grasp, movement, and in fact, assembly (MO connection) are planned as separate operations. The approach proposed in this work differs from the traditional one. The difference is clear in assembly operation which is considered as a single process. Parameters of the assembly operation are taken into account at the very beginning i.e. when grasping an MO by a manipulator. This issue speeds up the planning process and makes it more controllable.

In [17], provisions of grasping theory [18, 19] were developed in the direction in which grasp planning is considered by MR as a system that includes not only MFG, but also a multilink executive mechanism MR – the "arm" of the robot (the AHO system – «arm + hand + object»). Using this approach, range of the possible solutions expands both in terms of determining grasping parameters and in terms of subsequent movement of the grasped OM in space.

In the following sections, this approach is developed in a direction in which grasping, movement, and, in the first place, assembly (MO connection) are considered as a single operation.

2 Main Provisions of MO Grasp Planning Theory as Element of Assembly Operation

MR seems to consist of two subsystems—a multilink executive mechanism (MEM— "hands" MR) and a gripper. MEM can have any number of joints. MFG is seen as a multi-finger device. Taking into account [19], vectors that link each other are as follows:

a) The vector ψ of the external forces applied to object mass center, moments relative to mass center and block vector λ formed of λ_i vectors (i = 1,2,..., m). λ_i includes, in the general case, the force vector applied after grasping the object from MFG side at the contact point of the i-th finger of the hand, the object (i-th grasp point), and the moment vector relative to this point. The moment vector is also considered to be applied to the object from the side of the i-th finger MFG. m is the number of grasping points. m is equal to the number of MFG fingers (here, for definiteness, it is assumed that mechanical contact with MO during grasp is carried out only by means of MFG. Manipulator arm is not involved in the grasp). As a result of grasp synthesis, it should be possible to direct the ψ vector *according to assembly technology.*

b) The block vector v which contains the following components: Vectors of the mass center linear velocity, rotation angular velocity of the object relative to the mass center, and the block vector v_c formed of m vectors v_{ci}. v_{ci} contains components-vectors of linear velocity of the i-th grasp point of the object, and rotation angular velocity of the object relative to the mass center. In the case of an assembly operation, it should be possible to direct the vector v *according to the assembly operation technology.*

c) The vector μ of forces and/or moments developed by MFG finger joint actuators, MR, and the vector λ.

d) The vector $\dot{q}$ of time derivatives of the MFG fingers joints coordinates (as well as MEM MR) and the block vector v_c. v_c is formed of the contact points linear velocities and the rotation angular velocities of the object relative to the mass center.

The dimension of each of the vectors ψ and v equals n_v. Value of n_v depends on the space dimension in which the operation is performed. Incidentally, object movement in the plane is considered $n_v \leq 3$, if $3 < n_v \leq 6$ in space. The dimension of each of the vectors μ and $\dot{q}$ is equal to the total number of MFG fingers joints and MEM MR.

These relations have the following forms:

$$G\lambda = -\psi, \tag{1}$$

$$G^T v = v_c, \tag{2}$$

$$J^T \lambda = \mu, \tag{3}$$

$$J\dot{q} = v_c. \tag{4}$$

In expressions (1)–(4), matrix G is called the Grasp Matrix. J is MFG Jacobian matrix or the MEM + MFG system. Components of vectors ψ, v are assumed to be given in the inertial coordinate system (CS) associated with the manipulator base. Components of the vectors λ, v_c are in the coordinate systems CS_i. Beginnings of these systems are located at the grasping points. $x_i CS_i$ axis is directed normally to the tangent plane at the grasping point towards the object. The other two axes are located in a tangent plane and form the right coordinate system. Due to small displacements made by MFG fingers and MEM, when moving the grasping MO at the time of assembly, the relations for velocity vectors v, v_c, $\dot{q}$ remain valid also for motion vectors. In formulas (2), (3) and downwards, the superscript T in matrices notation and vectors means transposition.

In General, the *Grasp Matrix* G has the form:

$$G = \begin{bmatrix} G_{11} & G_{12} & \dots & G_{1m} \\ G_{21} & G_{22} & \dots & G_{2m} \\ \dots & \dots & \dots & \dots \\ G_{nv1} & G_{nv2} & \dots & G_{nvm} \end{bmatrix}. \tag{5}$$

Number of rows in G matrix is equal to n_v which is the number of freedom degrees of the grasping object. Number of columns depends on the number of contact points (m) and the type of contact at each point. Relations (1)–(4) are considered for different types of contacts between hand fingers and the object (point with/without friction, and grasp with "soft fingers" [20]). Matrix G_{ij} dimension depends on the type of contacts.

The *Jacobian matrix* of the MEM + MFG system has the form:

$$J = \begin{bmatrix} J_{h1} & J_1 & ... & 0 \\ J_{h2} & 0 & ... & 0 \\ ... & ... & ... & ... \\ J_{hm} & 0 & ... & J_m \end{bmatrix}. \tag{6}$$

where J_{hi} are elements of the Jacobian matrix, MEM MR for a point is the base of the i-th MFG finger, J_i is Jacobian matrix of the i-th MFG finger (at the grasping point MO). J_{hi} is link to $\dot{q}_{hi}$ which is the time derivative of the i-th MEM coordinate with the velocity vector of the i-th MFG finger base. J_i is link to $\dot{q}_i$ which is derivatives vector of the i-th finger joints coordinates with the angular and linear velocity vector of the i-th finger at the i-th point. v_{ci} is the linear velocity of the i-th grasping point of object and the rotation angular velocity of the object relative to the i-th point. i represents rows numbers of the matrix J. Number of columns is equal to the total number of joints of all MFG fingers and MEM.

3   Grasp Properties as Phases of an Assembly Operation

Grasp properties depend on the properties of the matrices G and J in Eqs. (1)–(4). Theses equations in turn, depend on the choice of points on the MO surface. Briefly, these properties are formulated as follows:

1) A grasp is **sufficient** (in order to hold the object) if N(G) is nontrivial. In this case, λ_i contains "internal" forces and moments that only affect the object intensity compression with fingers.
2) A grasp is termed **uncertain** if $N(G^T)$ is nontrivial. In this case, there are movements of the object. These movements are not associated with fingers movements at the contact points (there is a sliding motion of the object). This refers to lack of control in object movement due to hand's fingers and it is unacceptable.
3) A grasp is termed **defective** if $N(J^T)$ is nontrivial. In this case, $N(J^T)$ contains vectors λ that do not depend on the forces (or moments) of the joints actuators μ.
4) A grasp is termed **redundant** if $N(J)$ is nontrivial. In this case, there are components in the vector $\dot{q}$ that are not associated with the object's movement.

In order to perform assembly operation, grasping must be carried out in the following method. In addition to holding the object (by compressing with MFG fingers, without slipping), it is possible to carry out the necessary movements and force actions on the object according to the assembly operation plan, as well as control these movements and actions.

These conditions can be provided if:

1) $N(G^T)$ is trivial; then, by manipulating the hand's fingers, the object can be moved (velocity vector v), excluding the spontaneous movements (*slipping of the object*).

The formulated conditions are equivalent to the requirement rank (G) = n_v. If the condition rank (G) = n is met, it provides an opportunity for force actions by the hand's fingers on the object to compensate for the action of all vector ψ components.

2) Controlling all movements of object (vector v), using MFG fingers movement of the hand, can be performed under the conditions $dim\ N(G^T) = 0$ and rank $(GJ) = n_v$. These conditions are equivalent to the condition $rank\ (GJ) = rank\ (G) = n_v$. These conditions are also necessary to ensure control of all force acting (components of the vector ψ) on the object.

3) If $N(G)$ is nontrivial; then there exist internal forces that "compress" the object. In this case, not all internal forces in $N(G)$ can be controlled. It was shown in [18] and in [19] that $N(G)$ contains controlled forces if and only if there is no intersection of the null-spaces $N(G)$ and $N(J^T)$ for these forces, i.e., $N(G) \cap N(J^T) = 0$.

4) The grasp object must be oriented relative to the second object accordingly. One of the possible solutions to this problem is considering a certain vector S tied to the structure of the grasped MO, which at the time of assembly, should coincide in direction with the vector v. Orientation of the vector S depends on choosing the contact points on the MO surface and the orientation of the axes of the coordinate systems at the contact points in space. Specific form of this dependence is the shape function of the object which can be very diverse. Finding this dependence in each case is a geometrical problem. An example on solving this problem is presented below.

Formally, the ability to perform an assembly operation is to form MO grasp matrix in such a way that conditions (1)–(4) are satisfied. Moreover; there are values of the vectors $\dot{q}$ and μ for which v and ψ correspond to a given assembly operation. MO in this case is oriented properly in space. This is physically ensured by the actuators operation of joints MEM and MFG MR. The relationship between values of v and ψ, considered as given, and the values of $\dot{q}$ and μ, as the desired variables, is established by Eqs. (1)–(4). In this case, the system of Eqs. (1)–(4) can have a set of solutions.

Generally, different methods can be used to choose a solution from a variety of possible solutions for a particular problem. Computing procedures based on optimization according to certain criteria have become widespread (GraspIt! software package is an example). GraspIt! system allows planning for grasping options but only without considering parameters of the assembly operation. The choice of many suitable options is done by modeling using MoveIt! transfer and assembly operations for each of the grasps. However; both the procedures GraspIt! and MoveIt! have a «discreetness». As a result, the existing solution may be skipped and the task of planning the assembly will not be solved.

The second method is synthesizing (also using GraspIt!, or using another way) of a variety of grasping options. Moreover; grasping options are verified for fulfilling the conditions formulated in this section including the requirement to ensure proper orientation of the grasped MO. This method has less "discreteness", the thing which allows avoiding modeling in some cases and thereby saving time.

In practice, it may turn out that with a given arrangement of MO and given technical means (MEM, MFG), the assembly problem can't be solved. In this case, it will be necessary to somehow change position and orientation of the MO to be assembled, as well as to change hardware structure. The proposed approach allows to identify such a situation.

The formulated conditions are general in nature and can be applied to various MR and MO.

To illustrate the proposed approach, the following is an example of solving grasp planning problem with and without taking into account parameters of the assembly operation. For greater clarity, the simplest objects are considered i.e. MR with one translational pair and two-link MFG.

Example. In Fig. 1, there is a manipulator with one translational sliding pair (q_1 coordinate) using a two-link centering MFG (yellow square, and MFG position of the jaws is indicated by q_2). It should grasp MO (a blue rectangle with two semicircular cutouts) so that it moves along the X axis (vector $v^T = [v_x 0]$) and attach (insert) the "blue" MO to another MO (green). At the time of assembly, the "blue" MO should be oriented in such a way that its longitudinal axis (orientation vector S, indicated by the yellow dotted line) should be parallel to the X axis (vector $v^T = [v_x 0]$). Distance between the centers of the two semicircles is d, while width of the MO is s. MFG contacts with MO is assumed to be pointed: solid fingers with friction.

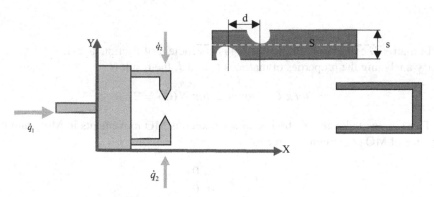

Fig. 1. Manipulator, MFG and objects to be assembled. (Color figure online)

Figure 2 shows the previous manipulator and MO after grasping the "blue" MO using one of the possible methods. Points of contact between MFG and MO are marked with red arrows for clarity.

Analysis shows that matrices G and J have the form.

$$J = \begin{vmatrix} 0 & 1 \\ 1 & 0 \\ 0 & 1 \\ -1 & 0 \end{vmatrix}$$

$$G = \begin{vmatrix} 0 & \Phi & 0 & -\phi \\ -1 & 0 & 1 & 0 \end{vmatrix}$$

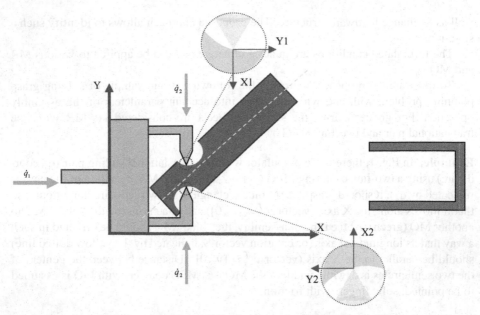

Fig. 2. Change in location of MFG and MO after capturing MO using the first method. (Color figure online)

In matrix G expression, the denoted ϕ is coefficient of friction $\phi < 1$.
By analyzing the properties of matrices G and J, the result is:

$$Rank\ G = nv = 2\ dim\ N(G) = 2.$$

These ratios indicate the absence of spontaneous MO movements in MFG and the presence of MO compression forces.

$$GJ = \begin{vmatrix} 2\phi & 0 \\ 0 & 0 \end{vmatrix}$$

It is easy to see that
$N_1(G) = (0\ z\ 0\ z)^T.$
$N_2(G) = (z\ 0\ z\ 0)^T;$ here z represents arbitrary numbers.
$Rank\ J^T = 2.$
$Rank\ (GJ) = 1.$
$dim\ N(J^T) = 2.$
$N_1(J^T) = (0\ z\ 0\ z)^T.$
$N_2(J^T) = (-z\ 0\ z\ 0)^T.$
$N_2(G) \cap N_2(J^T) = 0.$

Last relations indicate controllability by compression forces of the object.
In this case $Rank(GJ) = 1$. This indicates the possibility of controlling the MO movement in one direction. In this case, it is v_x. There is also the possibility of force

actions along the X axis. The possible direction of movement is determined by the vector $v = [v_x \ 0]^T$. These actions are manageable.

Analysis shows that this grasp satisfies the requirements for the grasp such as: there are controllable compressive forces, there is no slippage of MO.

However; the orientation vector S is not parallel to the X axis. In fact, for the selected grasping points, the inclination angle (denoted by φ) of the axial line MO (vector S) is relative to the horizontal position.

$$\varphi = 90° - \arcsin c/\sqrt{(s^2 + d^2)} \neq 0,$$

and does not match with the direction of the vector v. Therefore; this grasp cannot be used to complete the task.

Figure 3 shows the manipulator and the MO after grasping the "blue" MO in another way. As in the previous case, MFG contact points with MO are marked with red arrows for clarity. It is easy to verify that, in this case, all the grasp properties of the previous case were preserved. However; in this case, orientation requirement is satisfied (the vector S is parallel to the vector $v^T = [v_x \ 0]$. For selected grasping points, the inclination angle is $\varphi = 0$. It coincides with the direction of the vector v. Thus, requirements for grasp as an element of the assembly operation are fully implemented. Assembly operation is complete.

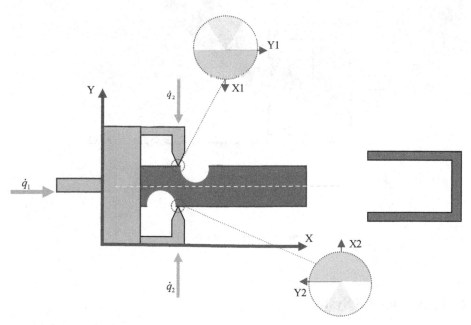

Fig. 3. The object is grasped taking into account the assembly parameters. Assembly operation is complete. (Color figure online)

In practice and as noted earlier, it may turn out that with the existing position of the MO in space and the available technical facility (MEM, MFG), the assembly problem cannot be solved even if all the conditions for the grasp, as such, are met. This case is shown in Fig. 4. In this example, the MOs are oriented one relative to the other in the required way. However; grasp properties correspond to the second case which shows the absence of MEM + MFG system ability to move along the Y axis (since *Rank (GJ) = 1* is not equal to *nv = 2*). This is due to the limitations on the MEM MR kinematics. Using the above formulas, it is easy to show that assembly could be performed while grasping the selected MO. However; for that, it will be necessary to replace this MR with another MR which has a greater degree of freedom (in order to be able to change the orientation of the velocity vector of the grasped MO). In fact, this is due to changes in the composition of technical facilities.

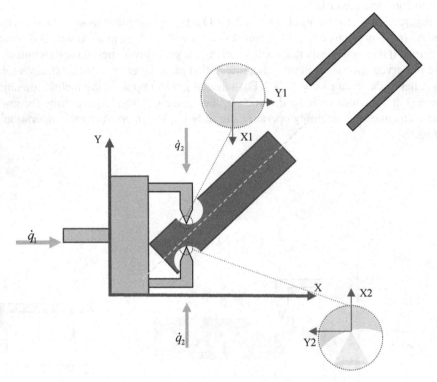

Fig. 4. Assembly is not possible.

4   Experimental System

To test the proposed method of assembly, an experimental stand has been created. General view of this stand is shown in Fig. 5. It includes the following:

- Manipulation robot Kawasaki FS003.
- Gripper Schunk SDH2 equipped with fingers sensed by tactile sensors.

- Computer vision system sensor based on camera with structured light of the PrimeSense family.
- Schunk FTS-Delta wrist force-torque sensor.
- A personal computer (PC), or several computers connected via a network with the software components of a control system (CS) and human-machine interface tools installed on them.

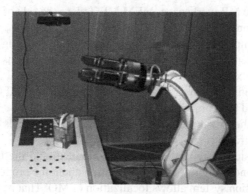

Fig. 5. Appearance of the experimental system.

CS complex includes:

- «arm + hand + object» motion planning system.
- Grasp planning system.
- Vision system.
- Force and tactile sensation system.
- «arm + hand + object» motion control system.

The structure and interaction scheme of the subsystems of the proposed control system are presented in Fig. 6.

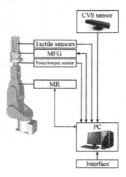

Fig. 6. General structure and interaction scheme of CS subsystems.

Presented CS allows solving tasks of manipulating objects to perform assembly operations in autonomous system.

CS of the AHO manipulation system interacts with various sensors and actuators. Human operator interacts with CS through user interface designed to control the manipulation system when performing assembly tasks in autonomous system.

Components of the executive system in the considered AHO manipulator system for assembly operations are presented in the form of the actuator (MEM) MR and MEM MFG. MEM manipulation robots play the role of "arm" that perform the movement of the end effector in the MR workspace. MEM MFG plays the role of "hand" that ensures the grasp and retention of MO.

The motion planning system of AHO system performs planning of the motion paths of the executive system components with checking the conditions of reachability, the absence of self-intersections of links, and contacts with obstacles.

The grasp planning system is designed to determine the MFG joint coordinates needed to capture and hold objects during assembly operations.

Components of the executive system work out the commands generated by AHO system's motion control system.

The technical vision system, the system of moment, and the tactile sensation are designed to receive and further process information about the properties of the external environment. The vision system allows localization of MO. That is, position determination of the coordinate system of a known MO geometric model in the base coordinate system. In addition, the vision system allows to get a map of the obstacles in the working area of the manipulation system. The obstacle map obtained as a result of processing information from the CVS sensor is a set of points located on the objects surface of the (manipulation system) working area.

The force and tactile sensation system is designed to determine the forces and moments acting on the wrists and fingers of the hands of the AHO manipulation system. Force/torque sensors are designed to measure the main vector components of forces and torques acting on the end effector of the manipulator, in projection on the coordinate system associated with the sensor. Tactile sensors form matrix of strain gauges located on the surface of MFG fingers. They allow determining position and magnitude of the force acting on them.

CS software components in any PC include software modules for sensory and vision systems. They process signals received from the respective sensors, software modules for the trajectory planning system, motion control systems providing control signals for the movement of MEM and MFG links, grasp planning software module, drivers for sensors and other devices. Graphical user interface of this software is designed to visualize the system state and display a three-dimensional virtual scene allowing the operator to set the CS parameters of assembly operation. Moreover; it is designed to control the process of its implementation by interacting with interactive elements of the virtual scene.

CS software structure of the AHO manipulation system for performing assembly operations in autonomous system is depicted in Fig. 7.

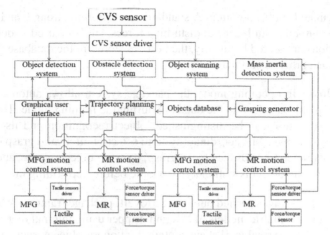

Fig. 7. CS software structure for AHO control system.

The software of this system is built on the basis of ROS meta-operating system. It provides interaction and coordination of all program modules of the system and provides a number of ready-made modules for performing standard tasks.

The system operates in two modes: training mode and manipulation mode (operating mode).

Training Mode. In training mode, all information about a new object is generated and stored in a database which is necessary for further work. It is enough to complete system training for each type of objects only once. Briefly, the system algorithm in the training mode consists of several processes: formation of object geometric model in the form of a set of vertices, edges and faces of its surface; learning CVS object recognition; and planning options for grasping an object by manipulator grasps.

Grasp Planning. Planning is carried out in parallel for all models of gripper devices available in the database and their configurations or for a specific pair of object-MFG at the operator's choice.

Planning is based on the gripper model and the model of the object stored in the database. The gripper model in the database includes: a kinematic scheme; geometric models of links; joint coordinates in the open state; direction of movement of the joints when closing; and the coordinates of the approach vector towards the object in the coordinate system associated with the gripper base. The object model, in addition to the geometry obtained in the previous step, also includes weight and size parameters and orientation parameters at the time of assembly. It is assumed that they are set by the user or measured by an external equipment.

In the planning process, a set of acceptable options for grasping an object is selected. For each of these options, the followings are calculated: coordinates of the gripper joints during grasping; position of the base coordinate system in the object coordinate system at the time of grasping (grasp point); direction of the approach towards the object in the object coordinate system of (vector S) - in case of an assembly operation. Grasp quality is calculated for each option. A standard estimation of strength and stability of the gripper closure under influence of disturbing forces, has been used as defined in [5]. All found options are sorted by quality, the best are stored in the database. The system operator has the ability to sort manually.

Operating Mode. In operating mode, the package system allows automatic grasping and transferring objects added to the database during the training mode. The following phases of the operation can be distinguished: object recognition and its coordinates determination in the base MR coordinate system; selection of a valid grasp option from the database; approach towards the object; grasp; transfer; object release; and departure. It is assumed that the object is stationary on a table before performing the operation.

Trajectories planning is carried out by the MoveIt! package framework based on the kinematic and the geometric models of MR and gripper using internal representation of the working scene. A virtual workstage contains stationary objects, such as equipment table. The geometric model of the object in its current position is also placed on the scene.

If planning is completed successfully (all positions are achievable, there are no self-intersections of MR links and contact with objects in the working area during movement, and OM orientation corresponds to the specified one), then the planned trajectory is transmitted to the input of MR control system. The operator has the ability to confirm or reject the grasp option which is automatically selected.

In the planning phase, the basis for control is modeling operations using computer graphics (Fig. 8).

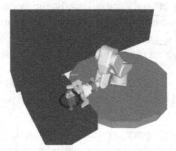

Fig. 8. Virtual scene created by the stand software.

The operation (Fig. 9) is controlled by the operator. At the same time, both the execution phases and the planning phases of operations are monitored. During execution, control is carried out using CVS and directly visualized.

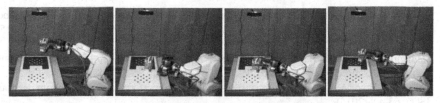

Fig. 9. Phases of the operation.

5 Conclusion

Considerable attention has been recently paid by researchers and developers to increasing autonomy degree of the manipulator robots (MR) that operate autonomously. Autonomous MR systems that perform assembly operations in space are particularly relevant. Autonomy of MR can dramatically reduce, and in some cases, exclude humans from MR control, which is especially important if there are restrictions on communication channels, when working in poorly structured environments, etc.

This work proposes an approach to plan an assembly operation as a whole operation. This operation includes, in addition to grasping, the ability to move MO in a direction specified by the assembly operation technology taking into account orientation of the MO in space corresponding to the assembly technology. This approach simplifies the planning process, which is especially important when assembling complex objects which include a large number of elements. Confirming the validity of the proposed analytical expressions has been achieved using the given examples.

In this work, an experimental stand has been created. On the basis of this stand, the assembly operation was modeled using the proposed technique. The conducted experiments prove validity of the proposed method.

References

1. Hägele, M., Nilsson, K., Pires, J.: Industrial Robotics. In: Springer Handbook of Robotics. Springer, Berlin, pp. 963–986 (2014)
2. Haidegger, T., et al.: Applied ontologies and standards for service robots. Robot. Autonom. Syst. **61**(11), 1215–1223 (2013)
3. Roa, M., Nottensteiner, K., Wedler, A., Grunwald, G.: Robotic Technologies for In-Space Assembly Operations. German Aerospace Center (DLR), 82234 Wessling, Germany (2017)
4. Oegerle, W.R., et al.: Concept for a large scalable space telescope: In-space assembly. In: Proceedings SPIE, 6265, 62652C (2006)
5. Akin, D., Minsky, M., Thiel, E., Kurtzman, C.: Space applications of automation, robotics and machine intelligence systems (ARAMIS) – phase II. NASA Contractor Report 3734 (1983)
6. Barnhart, D., Will, P., Sullivan, B., Hunter, R., Hill, L.: Creating a sustainable assembly architecture for next-gen space: the Phoenix effect. In: National Space Symposium (2014)
7. Artigas, J., et al.: The OOS-SIM: An on-ground simulation facility for on orbit servicing operations. In: Proc. IEEE Int. Conf. on Robotics and Automation (ICRA), pp. 2854–2860 (2015)
8. Hoyt, R., Cushing, J., Slostad, J.: SpiderFab(TM): process for on orbit construction of kilometer-scale apertures. In: NASA Innovative Advanced Concepts (NIAC), Report No. NNX12AR13G (2013)

9. Birkenkampf, P., Leidner, D., Borst, C.: A knowledge-driven shared autonomy human-robot interface for tablet computers. In: IEEE-RAS Int. Conf. Humanoid Robots, pp. 152–159 (2014)
10. Sahbani, A., El-Khoury, S., Bidaud, P.: An overview of 3D object grasp synthesis algorithms. Robot. Autonom. Syst., 326–336 (2011)
11. Suárez, R., Roa, M.: Grasp quality measures: review and performance. J. Autonom. Robots. **38**(1), 65–88 (2015)
12. The Robot Operating System. http://www.ros.org
13. Miller, A.T., Allen, P.K.: GraspIt!: A versatile simulator for robotic grasping. IEEE Robot. Autom. Mag. **11**(4) 110–122 (2005). https://doi.org/10.1109/MRA.2004.1371616
14. Cardon, T.A.: An Introduction. In: Cardon, T.A. (ed.) Technology and the Treatment of Children with Autism Spectrum Disorder. ACPS, pp. 1–2. Springer, Cham (2016). https://doi.org/10.1007/978-3-319-20872-5_1
15. Nottensteiner, K., et al.: A complete automated chain for flexible assembly using recognition, planning and sensorbased execution. In: 47st Int. Symp. on Robotics (ISR), pp. 1–8 (2016)
16. Thomas, U., Stouraitis, T., Roa, M.: Flexible assembly through integrated assembly sequence planning and grasp planning. In: Proc. IEEE Int. Conf. Autom. Science and Engineering, pp. 586–592 (2015)
17. Bazhinova, K.V., Leskov, A.G., Seliverstova, E.V.: Automatic grasping of objects by a manipulator equipped with a multifinger hand. J. Comput. Syst. Sci. Int. **58**, 317–327 (2019). https://doi.org/10.1134/S1064230719020035
18. Bicchi, A., Kumar, V.: Robotic grasping and contact: a review. In: Proceedings of ICRA '00. IEEE Int. Conf. on Robotics and Automation. San Francisco, USA, pp. 348–353 (2000)
19. Prattichizzo, D., Trinkle, J.: Grasping. In: Siciliano, B., Kathib, O. (eds.) Handbook on Robotics. Springer, Berlin, pp. 671–700 (2008)
20. Saxena, A., Driemeyer, J.: Robotic grasping of novel objects using vision. Int. J. Robot. Res. **27**(2), 157–173 (2008)

Inspection of Pipelines of Complex Topology Using an Adaptive, Scalable Multi-segment Mobile Robot

Oleg V. Darintsev[✉], Ildar Sh. Nasibullayev, and Dinar R. Bogdanovv

Mavlyutov Institute of Mechanics UFRC RAS, prosp. Oktyabrya 71, 450054 Ufa, Russia
ovd@uimech.org

Abstract. Existing robotic systems for inspection of pipelines have a strict specialization and are designed to work in areas with a fixed value of the inner diameter. If technical endoscopes are used for pipes of small diameter and small length, then mobile robots are used to control trunk pipelines of large diameters and lengths. City and industrial pipelines are characterized by a complex topology, a variety of sizes, the presence of a large number of transitions, branches, etc., which is a problem for the use of "classical solutions" of inspection robotics. Modular reconfigurable robots are able to successfully move inside randomly oriented tube spaces with variable internal dimensions. Analysis of publications describing technical solutions showed that well-known modular robots do not have the necessary parameters for the effective implementation of monitoring the internal state of pipes. The movement of such robots takes place slowly (the movement is most often realized as a transition from one stable position to another), the outriggers used to adapt to the pipe diameter are limited, and they prevent passage to branches, etc. The proposed technical solution in the form of a mobile multi-link autonomous robot capable of adapting to changing the parameters of the inspected section (diameter, the presence of transitions, slopes, branches, etc.) through a dynamic correction of the relative position of the links and parameters of the movers. Technical and operational characteristics of the robot are determined both by design parameters and the capabilities of the control system. The solution to such a multifactorial problem requires careful mathematical modeling. At this stage, dynamic and kinematic models of the motion of two connected robot elements are constructed and investigated, an algorithmized numerical scheme for an n-link robot is proposed. The results of the experimental testing of the prototype design, ways of adapting the shape of the robot to the pipeline topology are shown. The tasks for the correct synthesis of the control system and information modules are formulated.

Keywords: Inspection robot · Pipeline condition · Rolling and sliding friction · Mechanic · Numerical simulations

1 Introduction

Pipeline systems are the basis for the smooth functioning of various support systems from production to urban (housing) infrastructure. Most of the vital products (clean air,

© Springer Nature Switzerland AG 2021
A. Yuschenko (Ed.): MPoR 2020, CCIS 1426, pp. 137–150, 2021.
https://doi.org/10.1007/978-3-030-88458-1_11

drinking and process water, coolants, gas, oil products) are delivered to consumers using pipes. Piping systems are also used for waste disposal (domestic and industrial effluents, polluted air, garbage, etc.). At present, the Russian Federation is in second place in the world (after the United States) by the length of pipelines, which is more than 233 thousand km, including only gas pipelines – 172.6 thousand km [1]. Only underground pipelines in the Russian Federation have laid more than 2 million km, and the length of internal communal systems is from 3 to 5 million km, half of which falls on the housing and utilities sector (see Table 1). According to statistics, pipeline transport moves more than 100 times more cargo than other transport sectors, so the urgency of the problem of maintaining pipelines in working condition is beyond doubt.

Table 1. The length of the piping of the housing system [2]

Pipelines	Pipelines length, thous. km			
	Sum total	Conduits, sewers, heat distribution networks Ø > 400 mm	Street networks, heat distribution networks, Ø = 200–400 mm	Yard water distribution networks, heat distribution networks Ø up to 200 mm
Water pipes	523	139	320	64
Sewers	163	43	72	48
Heat distribution networks	183	12	29	142
TOTAL	869÷1052	194	421	254

The reliability of the functioning of pipeline systems can be ensured only by comprehensive measures, including the use of modern automated diagnostic methods, carrying out scheduled preventive work and reducing the time for major repairs. These tasks have been successfully solved for main pipelines: for example, since the 80s of the last century, large operators have actively used robotic systems. If at first robots solved only the tasks of cleaning and diagnosing the inner surface of the pipe, now various types of repairs are being successfully performed.

A more difficult task is the inspection of pipelines for production networks and utilities. The main problems in the development and operation of robots in this area are the high size variability and variety of materials used pipes, complex topology, the presence of many branches, various valves, and fittings, etc. The need for the development of diagnostic robotic systems is extremely high, since even official statistics on the degree of deterioration are alarming (see Table 2).

This article analyzes the existing solutions, and also shows one of the options for implementing an alternative method of moving the carrier inside the pipe.

Table 2. The state of the pipelines for water supply and sanitation of the housing and communal services of Russia [2, 3]

Networks	Length, thous. km	Networks ripe for replacement	
		thous. km	%
Water supply			
Conduits	139	20	14
Street networks	320	100	38
Yard water distribution networks	64	38	59
Total	523	158	30
Wastewater disposal			
Sewers	43	6	15
Street networks	73	19	26
Yard water distribution networks	48	33	68
Total	164	58	36
Heating services (in double-pipe dimension)			
Main pipes	12	1	8
Street networks	29	7	25
Yard water distribution networks	142	18	65
Total	183	26	14

2 Robotics in Pipeline Networks

The variety of robotic systems used to diagnose and maintain the operability or repair of pipelines can be reduced to separate classes according to various classification criteria. The difficulty in the classification is that various specific terms are used to describe the same type of in-tube robots – in-tube inspection projectile, crawler, PIG system, etc. The classification below (see Table 3) allows us to separate the systems designed for operation on trunk pipelines with large flow cross-sections over long distances, and the specifics of in-pipe systems for pipe diameters less than 400 mm, most often stand-alone and operating at a much smaller distance from the entry point.

For trunk pipelines, all types of pipe robotic systems can be used and used [4–6], for urban pipelines – only active or pushed systems. Moreover, in recent years there has been a significant increase in the proportion of polymer pipes in the housing and utilities sector, which completely excludes the use of magnetic moving and diagnostic systems in inspection robots. The high plasticity of the material of polymer pipes reduces the likelihood of rupture of systems during soil movement, freezing, etc., but increases the likelihood of geometric deformations: corrugation of the inner surface, ovality of the bore, local slopes and pipe shifts.

Table 3. Classification of pipe robotic systems

Displacement mechanism	Displacement method	Maximum distance from entry point	Equipment
Passive	Product flow	200÷400 km	**Cleaning devices (scrapers):** Brush discs Magnetic disks With drive **Flow detectors:** Magnetic Ultrasonic Combined **Section gauges:** Lever-type Elastic transducer Ultrasonic Devices for determining the position of the pipeline Camcorders Means of communication Telemetry drives Odometers
	Pushed through	up to 300–400 m	Cleaning devices (scraper gauges) Flaw detectors: Magnetic Ultrasonic Section gauges Devices for determining the position of the pipeline Camcorders Active tool
Active	Wheeled, benthonic	up to 10–15 km, depends on energy consumption and capacity of onboard power supplies	Compact cleaning devices Flaw detectors Odometers Active tool Lasers Camcorders&Lighting Memory device
	Wheeled, spacing		
	Tracklaying		
	Wind-driven		
	Creeping		
	Magnetic		
	Original		

Therefore, specific requirements are made for modern pipe robotic systems of small diameters:

1 Ability to work in a wide range of pipe diameters.
2 The ability to fix anywhere in the pipe and deliver the sensor/tool to a given point.
3 Adaptation to changes in the shape, diameter and spatial position of the studied pipe.
4 Ability to transition to arbitrarily oriented branches.
5 The ability to pass through the valves installed in the system.

The passive gimbal system used in trunk multisection systems for connecting indi-vidual modules of a "train" compensates for changes in pipe direction at turning radii of at least 2–3 diameters. A typical topology for the most common pipe systems is shown in Fig. 1, which shows that the transitions between the pipe segments are carried out almost at an angle of 900, therefore, in pipeline systems of small diameter, structures similar to trunk inspection robotic systems are not used.

The absence of inspection systems leads to significant material losses due to the emergency condition of underground utilities: according to official data, "leaks and unaccounted water consumption in water supply systems average 15% (or 3,339.2 mil-lion m^3) of the total water supply per year". The total damage from water leaks in the housing system is estimated at $ 6.5 billion per year.

Currently, existing inspection robots for pipes of small (less than 400 mm) diameter can be divided into 2 classes – self-propelled and pushed. In self-propelled vehicles, a significant proportion of structures is represented by wheeled, tracked bottom-mounted and persistent-spacer robots [7–9]. It is necessary to distinguish snake-like inspection RTS, which, thanks to the active (power) articulation of the links, are able to go into some types of branches.

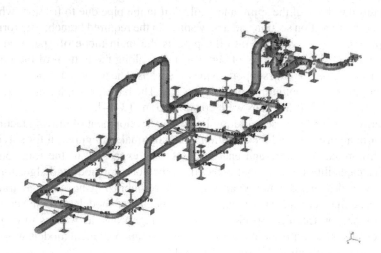

Fig. 1. Topology of a small section of a pipeline with a diameter of 200 mm.

An example of such a design is a robot designed for use in complex pipe systems, including during accidents, natural disasters, in the control systems of technological lines of an enterprise, for rescue operations [10]. The movement of the wheelless snake robot is implemented by programmatically changing the relative position of the robot links based on the pipe walls. In [11], the locomotion capabilities of a wheeled serpentine and ways to control its movement inside the pipes and the bending of the hinges according to the shape of the inner space are considered taking into account the change in the direction of movement, as well as the need for transition to branches.

3   Adaptive Scalable Multi-segment Mobile Robot

Based on the analysis, the authors propose to use new ways to use serpentine multi-segment robots, obtained through the refinement of the movement mechanism and the wider use of static/dynamic stability methods. The proposed design of the robot combines the features, structural elements of wheeled platforms and active hinge elements characteristic of serpentine-like robotic systems.

A robot can consist of a different number of active and passive modules interconnected by controlled hinges, which allow changing the position of the modules relative to each other and providing the necessary force to press the modules to the inner surface of the pipe. Active modules contain a motor-wheel(s), a hinge drive(s), a battery element and a control system, set in motion the entire multi-segment structure, and change the relative position of the modules. The "passive" module does not include motor wheels, but contains the necessary inspection or active tool. To move inside the pipe, the robot, using the hinge drives, forms a spiral from its modules with a predetermined pitch, the diameter of which (or its individual sections) is adapted to the size of the pipe cross-section and provides the wheel pressing force required for reliable adhesion.

In the process of moving inside the pipe when reaching the branch points, part of the robot retains the shape of the spiral and "holds" it in the pipe due to friction, while the other forms the transition section and a new spiral in the required branch. The formation of the spiral and its "screwing" into the pipe is the main mode of operation of the proposed robot design, but the robot can also move along the bottom of the pipe as a typical wheel platform or with support on the pipe walls. The proposed approach is based on the concept of self-configuring modular robots. The basic principles of constructing modules, joints and their fixations were considered in [12–14].

The novelty of the proposed solution lies in the development of moving techniques, robot control algorithms, and the selection of the optimal configuration for solving the tasks with minimal hardware and energy costs. The expansion of the functional and operational capabilities of the robot is based on methods, methods and algorithms that use the specific design and static-dynamic methods of stabilizing the robot on a trajectory or in space. At the moment, experiments with mathematical models are being conducted in order to develop technical specifications and suggestions, as well as to concretize design methods. The verification of the parameters of mathematical models was carried out during field tests with separate robot modules.

4   Models, Computer Modeling and Verification

The design development of a multi-segment robot is a difficult task, since it contains a large number of degrees of freedom and relations, which are affected by many external factors, and, primarily, friction forces. The first stage was the study (numerical computer simulation) of the effect of friction (rolling and sliding) on the parameters of the movement of the robot. Verification of the model, determination of friction coefficients, moment of inertia of the module, etc. conducted on expert evaluations and tests.

4.1 Problem Formulation and Mathematical Model

Suppose that in a pipe of radius R_1 there are N connected robot segments with masses m_i. The mobility of each segment is provided by a pair of coaxial wheels of radius R_2. A polar coordinate system is considered with a reference point O in the geometric center of the pipe, a radial coordinate r and an angular coordinate φ counted counterclockwise from the vertical axis OC. The relative position of the segments is determined by the angle β formed by the radius vectors of the centers of mass of the adjacent segments (Fig. 2).

The forces and moments acting on the i-th module are denoted as follows: gravity force $\mathbf{F}_{gi}$, reaction force $\mathbf{F}_{ri}$, friction force $\mathbf{F}_{fi}$, the engine torque M_i applied to the axis of the i-th module.

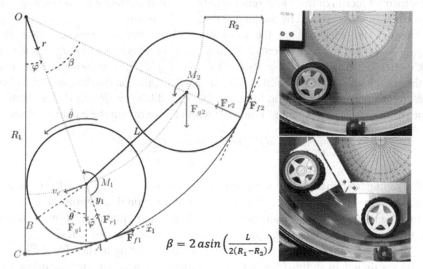

$$\beta = 2\,asin\left(\frac{L}{2(R_1 - R_2)}\right)$$

Fig. 2. The geometric model of the robot (left) and experimental stand with one (top-right) and two modules (bottom-right). (Color figure online)

To determine the rolling condition without slipping (no-slip condition) we consider the arc AB (see Fig. 2, green arc) on the wheel from the point of contact with the pipe A to a certain point B. When rolling at an angular speed O non-slip condition is defined by the equality $\overbrace{AB} = \overbrace{AC}$, i.e. the trajectories of an arbitrary point B and the wheel itself should be equal (see Fig. 2, red arc):

$$R_2(\varphi - \theta) = R_1\varphi \Rightarrow \theta = -(R_1 - R_2)\varphi/R_2 \Rightarrow \dot{\theta} = -(R_1 - R_2)\dot{\varphi}. \qquad (1)$$

Since the location of all robot modules is uniquely determined by the angle φ, this coordinate is hereinafter used as a generalized coordinate.

4.2 The Equation of Motion for One Module

We obtain the equations of motion from Euler-Lagrange equation [15], considering the generalized friction force as external:

$$\mathcal{L} = K - P, \frac{d}{dt}\left(\frac{\partial \mathcal{L}}{\partial \dot{\varphi}}\right) - \frac{\partial \mathcal{L}}{\partial \varphi} = Q, \tag{2}$$

where $\mathcal{L}$ is Lagrangian; $v_c = (R_1 - R_2)\dot{\varphi}$ is the instantaneous linear velocity of the center of mass; Q is the generalized friction force. Kinetic energy is K:

$$K = \frac{1}{2}J_0\dot{\theta}^2 + \frac{1}{2}mv_c^2 - \dot{\theta} \cdot M \cdot t = \frac{1}{2}(J_0 + J_1)\frac{(R_1 - R_2)^2}{R_2^2}\dot{\varphi}^2 + \frac{R_1 - R_2}{R_2}\dot{\varphi} \cdot M \cdot t,$$

where J_0 is the moment of inertia of the wheel relative to the center of mass, $J_1 = mR_2^2$ is the moment of inertia of the wheel relative to the point of contact with the pipe, $\dot{\varphi} \cdot M \cdot t$ is the kinetic energy created by the engine torque M, t is time.

Potential only depends on the position of the center of mass in space $P = -mg(R_1 - R_2)\cos\varphi$. The moment of friction in the wheel is equal to $R_2 F_f$. Elementary work of the friction force is $\delta A = R_2|F_f\ \theta| = (R_1 - R_2)\ |F_f\ \varphi|$ (the modulus sign means that the energy loss due to the friction force does not depend on the direction of motion), therefore, the generalized friction force has the form $\partial A/\partial \varphi = (R_1 - R_2)F_f$. Substituting kinematic energy K and potential P into (2) with (1), we obtain the equation of motion

$$\ddot{\varphi} = -\frac{R_2}{R_1 - R_2}\frac{mgR_2 \sin\varphi - R_2 F_f + M}{J_0 + J_1}. \tag{3}$$

The rolling friction force is determined by the expression [16] $F_f = (f_r/R_2)F_r\ \text{sign}(\dot{\varphi})$, where f_f is the rolling friction coefficient; $sign$ is a function that returns the sign of the argument, and reaction force F_r is determined from the normal projection of forces at the contact point of the wheel and pipe (Oy axis): $F_r = mg\cos\varphi + mR_2\dot{\varphi}^2$.

Note that the rolling friction force cannot exceed the sliding friction force $F_S = f_s mg$ (f_s is the coefficient of sliding friction). When sliding, it is necessary to take into account the effect of velocity on the friction force by introducing a component proportional to the velocity value (with a drag coefficient f_v). Thus, the friction force is selected in the form: $F_f = (f_s sign(\dot{\varphi}) + f_v\dot{\varphi})F_r$.

4.3 The Equation of Motion for a System of Coupled Modules

We obtain the equation of motion for a system of N modules with rigid coupling. In the polar coordinate system, the position of the center of mass depends on the number of modules. The angular coordinate of any module is uniquely determined by the coordinate of the first module φ_1. The center of mass of the ith module is determined by the coordinates $\varphi_i = \varphi_1 + (i - 1)\beta$ and $R_i = R_1-R_2$. We calculate the coordinates of the center of mass of the entire system:

$$R_c = \frac{R_1 - R_2}{M} \sqrt{\left(\sum_{i=1}^{N} m_i \sin \varphi_i\right)^2 + \left(\sum_{i=1}^{N} m_i \cos \varphi_i\right)^2},$$

$$\varphi_c = \frac{1}{N} \sum_{i=1}^{N} m_i\varphi_i, \quad M = \sum_{i=1}^{N} m_i.$$

Note that R_c is independent of the angle φ and is determined only by R_1, R_2 and the design angle β. For example, after transformations with $m_i = m$ one can get: $R_c(N = 1) = R_1 - R_2, R_c(N = 2) = (R_1 - R_2) \cos(\beta/2)$.

The equation of dynamics (3) will change as follows:

$$\ddot{\varphi} = -R_2(R_1 - R_2) \frac{F_g(\varphi)R_2 - F_f(\varphi)R_2 + M}{N\left[(R_1 - R_2)^2 J_0 + R_c^2 J_1\right]}, \tag{4}$$

where $F_g(\varphi) = g \sum_{i=1}^{N} m_i \sin \varphi_i$, $F_f(\varphi) = \sum_{i=1}^{N} C(F_r(\varphi_i)) \frac{f_r}{R_2} F_r(\varphi_i) \text{sign}(\dot{\varphi}_i)$.

The function $C(F_r) = 1$ for $F_r > 0$ and $C(F_r) = 0$ for $F_r < 0$. Using this function, friction force is excluded for modules that lose adhesion to the pipe surface.

For pure sliding $F_f(\varphi, \dot{\varphi}) = \sum_{i=1}^{N} C(F_r(\varphi_i))(f_s \text{sign}(\dot{\varphi}) + f_v\dot{\varphi})F_r$.

4.4 Rolling Movement

The physical and geometric parameters of the system are as follows: module mass $m = 100$ g, pipe radius $R_1 = 18$ cm, wheel radius $R_2 = 3.25$ cm, initial module deviation $\varphi_0 = 31.06°$. To determine the model parameters (the oscillation period T, the moment of inertia of the module J_0, and the rolling friction coefficient f_r), we compared the dependences of the deviation angles of the numerical calculation (φ^n) and the analytical model (φ^a) with the experimental data (φ^e) for rolling of one segment.

In a numerical calculation, Eq. (3) was solved with the initial conditions $\varphi_0^n = \varphi_0^e$, $\dot{\varphi}_0^n = 0$ by the Euler method. To obtain an analytical solution of the dynamics of the module, it is necessary to neglect the centrifugal force $mR_2\dot{\varphi}^2$ and consider the deviation angles from the equilibrium state to be small (then $\sin \varphi \approx \varphi$ and $\cos \varphi \approx 1$). The equation of motion will take the form:

$$\dot{\varphi}^a = -\omega_0^2\left[\varphi^a - f \text{ sign}(\dot{\varphi}^a)\right], \quad \omega_0^2 = \frac{R_2^2}{R_1 - R_2} \frac{mg}{J_0 + J_1}, \tag{5}$$

where ω_0 is the circular oscillation frequency of the module relative to the equilibrium point; $f = f_r/R_2$ is the dimensionless coefficient of rolling friction. We denote the initial conditions by the index "0": $\varphi_0^a = \varphi_0^e$, $\dot{\varphi}_0^a = 0$, $f_0 = f_r/R_2$. Equation (5) includes the sign of the angular velocity $\text{sign}(\dot{\varphi}^a)$ and every half period, at the time of the maximum deviation, when the velocity passes the zero value, the term with the rolling friction force changes stepwise. Equation (5) is solved by the stage-by-stage integration [17] with solution

$$\varphi^a(t) = \left(\varphi_i^a + f_i\right)\cos(\omega_0 t) - f_i \tag{6}$$

with adaptation of parameters every half-cycle $T_0/2 = \pi/\omega_0$ when the direction of movement changes $\varphi_i^a = -\varphi_{i-1}^a + 2f_i$, $\dot{\varphi}_i^a = 0$, $f_i = (-1)^i \cdot f_r \cdot R_2$.

Note that $f_0 > 0$, since the initial deviation in the experiment is negative $\varphi_0^e < 0$. For $\varphi_0^e > 0$, it is assumed that $f_0 = -f_r/R_2$ and $f_i = (-1)^{i+1} f_r/R_2$.

To process the experimental data, the rolling process was recorded on a video camera (time step $\tau = 1/30$ s, see Fig. 2 (right)), followed by processing frames to determine the angle φ.

The oscillation period was determined at the moment the angular velocity changes with the maximum module deviation. At these moments, the time $t_T = t-j\cdot T$, where j is the period number) is small and the expansion in the Taylor series gives: $\cos(2\pi t/T) = \cos(2\pi t_T/T) \approx 2\pi \left(1 - 0.5t_T^2/T^2\right)$, which allows us to use the approximation using the second-order polynomial $\varphi(t) = a\,t^2 + b\,t + c$ with determination of the coefficients a, b and c by three experimental points φ_i (i = 1,2,3 correspond to the previous, current, and next time moment) at times t_i. The extreme value of the function $\varphi(t_T)$ is achieved at times $t = j\cdot T$ and is determined by solving the equation $d\varphi(t)/dt = 0 \Rightarrow j\cdot T = -b/(2a)$, where the coefficients are equal to:

$$a = \frac{(\varphi_1 - \varphi_2)(t_2 - t_3) - (\varphi_2 - \varphi_3)(t_1 - t_2)}{\left(t_1^2 - t_2^2\right)(t_2 - t_3) - \left(t_2^2 - t_3^2\right)(t_1 - t_2)}, \quad b = -\frac{(\varphi_1 - \varphi_2)\left(t_2^2 - t_3^2\right) - (\varphi_2 - \varphi_3)\left(t_1^2 - t_2^2\right)}{\left(t_1^2 - t_2^2\right)(t_2 - t_3) - \left(t_2^2 - t_3^2\right)(t_1 - t_2)}.$$

The average value over five periods of oscillation was $T = 1.017$ s.

To determine the model parameters, the standard deviation between the numerical calculation and experimental data was minimized by the following formula: $\sigma_{ne} = \sqrt{\frac{1}{N}\sum_{i=1}^{N}\left(\varphi_i^n - \varphi_i^e\right)^2}$. The minimum value $\sigma_{ne} = 1.09°$ was obtained for the following parameters: oscillation period $T = 1.017$ s, moment of inertia of the module $J_0 = 0.635$ mg, rolling friction coefficient $f_r = 0.651$ mm. The standard deviations for these parameters are between the analytical calculation and the experiment $\sigma_{ae} = 1.80°$, and between the numerical and analytical calculation of $\sigma_{na} = 1.45°$. The error of the oscillation period in the analytical calculation $T_0 = 0.985$ s was $|1 - T_0/T|\cdot100\% \approx 3.1\%$. Thus, both the numerical calculation and the analytical model are in good agreement with the experimental data. The simulation results are presented in Fig. 3 (left).

In Fig. 3 (right) shows a comparison of numerical and analytical calculations for rolling two modules with a rigid connection and $\beta = 60°$. The initial deviation angle of the left module is $\varphi_0 = 64.2°$. Numerical modeling was carried out using Eq. (7). An analytical solution was found from equation (8) for the motion of the center of mass $\varphi_c = \varphi_1 + \beta/2$ around a circle of radius $R_c = (R_1 - R_2)\cos(\beta/2)$. The rolling friction coefficient $f_r = 2.24$ mm is obtained, which is 3.5 times greater than the similar coefficient for one module, since the rigging introduces additional resistance. An increase in the coefficient of friction leads to the fact that the system comes into equilibrium much faster (2 periods instead of 8). Note that stable equilibrium corresponds to the stagnation interval $[-f_r, f_r]$ determined by the value of the coefficient of friction. Numerical modeling is in qualitative agreement with the experiment. The geometry for the system of two modules is shown in Fig. 2, right.

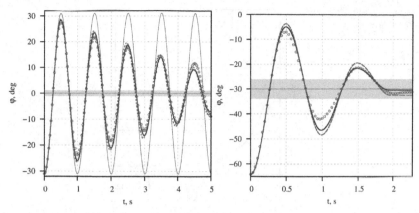

Fig. 3. The dependence of the position of the first module on time when rolling one (left) or two (right) modules. Grey line is numerical results, no friction; blue line is numerical, $f_r = 0.651$ mm; red line is analytical solution (6); green symbols are experimental date; filled area is stagnation interval. (Color figure online)

4.5 Sliding Movement

Consider a system of two modules with a rigid connection with installed engines. The engine increases rolling resistance, which results in the movement of the system with a clean slip. For analytical analysis, we write the equation of motion in the approximation of small angles of deviation of the center of mass from the equilibrium state: $\ddot{\varphi}^a = -\omega_0^2[\varphi^a - f \operatorname{sign}(\dot{\varphi}^a) - f_v\dot{\varphi}^a]$, $\omega_0^2 = g/R_c$. The solutions of the equation are:

$$\varphi^a = C_1 \exp(\lambda_1 t) + C_2 \exp(\lambda_2 t) - f, \lambda_{1,2} = -\beta \pm \sqrt{\beta^2 - \omega_0^2}, \beta = \frac{gf_v}{R_c}. \quad (7)$$

The coefficients C_1 and C_2 are determined from the initial conditions:

$$\varphi_0^a = \varphi_0, \ \dot{\varphi}_0^a = 0 \Rightarrow C_1 = \lambda_2(\varphi_0 + f)/\lambda_2 - \lambda_1, \ C_2 = -\lambda_1(\varphi_0 + f)/(\lambda_2 - \lambda_1).$$

In the numerical calculation was solved (4) with friction force consists of the sliding friction and the drag forces. In Fig. 4 shows the analytical solution (7), the numerical results and experimental data. From a comparison of the numerical results with experimental data were determined: sliding friction coefficient $f_s = 0.4$ and drag coefficient $f_v = 2$ s/m.

The design of the robot involves the use of two types of modules: active, using the engine to move the robot, and passive, on which diagnostic equipment will be installed. Consider a combination of two modules with zero engine torque, one of which is active and the other passive. In the simulation, the sliding friction coefficient and the drag coefficient obtained for pure sliding were used for the active module, and the rolling friction coefficient obtained from pure rolling for the passive module.

In Fig. 5 shows the simulation results and experimental data in the case when the first module is passive (see Fig. 5, left) and when the first module is active (see Fig. 5 right). It can be seen that the current model conveys the nature of the movement.

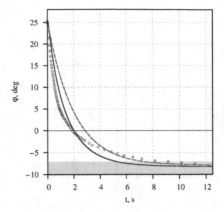

Fig. 4. The dependence of the position of the first module on time when sliding two modules. blue line is numerical results, $f_s = 0.4, f_v = 2$ s/m; red line is analytical solution (7); green symbols are experimental date; filled area is stagnation interval (Color figure online)

Figure 6 shows the results of motion simulation of two connected modules in various combinations of active (with nonzero engine torque M) and passive (engine torque is zero) ones. It can be seen that with the engines turned off, the system rolls down to the border of the stagnation zone. If the master module is active, then the movement stops inside the stagnation zone.

With an active slave module, the system can overcome the stagnation zone. This is because the active module pushes the passive one through the stagnation zone, being outside the zone, and after that enters the zone and stops.

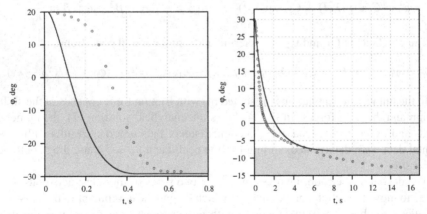

Fig. 5. The dependence of the position on time when moving coupled passive-active (left) and active-passive (right) modules. Blue line is numerical results, $f_s = 0.4, f_v = 2$ s/m; green symbols are experimental date; filled area is stagnation interval; $M = 0$ N·m. (Color figure online)

Two active modules allow you to overcome the stagnation zone twice as fast, but stop in the same position as when the slave active module moves. This is explained by

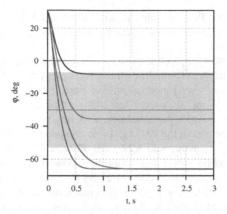

Fig. 6. The dependence of the position on time when moving coupled passive-passive (blue line), active-active (green line), active-passive (purple line) and passive-active modules. Filled area is stagnation interval. Active module has $M = 0.08$ N·m. (Color figure online)

the small reaction force to the leading module and the small tangential component of gravity on the driven module.

5   Conclusion

In the future, it is planned to refine the computer model to increase its accuracy and expand functionality, as well as adding new degrees of freedom.

The experiments carried out with models and their verification made it possible to obtain analytical expressions for choosing the parameters of engines and wheel materials (friction coefficient with the surface) and to prepare the necessary basis for the development of a prototype design. The study of the kinematic model will determine the optimal number of links when performing various types of operations:

- scanning (inspection) of the inner surface of the pipeline with a variable pitch of a spiral path;
- fixing the mobile platform in a given place;
- transitions and movements in arbitrarily oriented branches;
- passage through technological openings of pipeline fittings;
- and so on.

Acknowledgements. This work was supported by the Program of the Presidium of the Russian Academy of Sciences and within the framework of state assignment No. 0246-2018-007.

References

1. Public Joint Stock Company Gazprom, About Gazprom, Operations, Transmission. https://www.gazprom.com/about/production/transportation/. Accessed 9 Apr 2020 (In Russian)

2. Isaev, V.N., Khurgin, R.: Pipeline utility systems. Plumbing **3**, 52–59 (2016). (In Russian)
3. Pipe polymers in urban housing and utilities. http://www.rupec.ru/analytics/32317/. Accessed 9 Apr 2020 (In Russian)
4. In-line inspection services for pipelines with varying diameter. https://www.rosen-group.com/global/solutions/services/service/multi-diameter-technology.html. Accessed 9 Apr 2020
5. Pipeline pigging. https://www.intron.ru/en/development/vnutritrubnaya-diagnostika-magist ralnyix-truboprovodov.html. Accessed 9 Apr 2020 (In Russian)
6. Voronchikhin, S., Samokrutov, A.A., Sedelev, Y.: Using robotized scanners for health estimation of process pipelines at the PAO Gazprom compressor stations. Scientific-Technical Collection book. Vesti gazovoy nauki **3**(27), 120–130 (2016). (In Russian)
7. Schroder wheeled mobile robots pipe inspection crawler for pipeline detection. https://szans.en.alibaba.com/product/60640548594-218977695/Schroder_wheeled_mobile_rob ots_pipe_inspection_crawler_for_pipeline_detection.html. Accessed 9 Apr 2020
8. Dertien, E., Foumashi, M., Pulles, K., Stramigioli, S.: Design of a robot for in-pipe inspection using omnidirectional wheels and active stabilization. In: 2014 IEEE International Conference on Robotics and Automation (ICRA), pp. 5121–5126. Hong Kong (2014). https://doi.org/10.1109/ICRA.2014.6907610
9. OnSpec Custom Solutions. https://eddyfi.com/en/product/onspec-custom-solutions/. Accessed 9 Apr 2020
10. Matsuno, F., et al.: Development of Tough Snake Robot Systems. In: Tadokoro, S. (ed.) Disaster Robotics. STAR, vol. 128, pp. 267–326. Springer, Cham (2019). https://doi.org/10.1007/978-3-030-05321-5_6
11. Sawabe, H., Nakajima, M., Tanaka, M., Tanaka, K., Matsuno, F.: Control of an articulated wheeled mobile robot in pipes. Adv. Robot. **33**, 1–15 (2019). https://doi.org/10.1080/016 91864.2019.1666737
12. Chennareddy, S.S.R., Agrawal, A., Karuppiah, A.: Modular self-reconfingurable robotic systems: a survery on hardware architectures. Hindawi J. Robot. **2017**, 1–19 (2017). https://doi.org/10.1155/2017/5013532
13. Zhong, M., Wang, P., Li, M., Guo, W.: A Modular mobile self-reconfigurable robot. Advanced in Mobile Robotics. In: Proceeding of the Eleventh International Conference on Climbing and Walking Robots and the Support Technologies for Mobile Machines, pp. 71–78. Portugal (2008). https://doi.org/10.1142/9789812835772_0009
14. Memar, A.H.H.A., Bagher, P.Z.H., Keshmiri, M.: Mechanical design and motion planning of a modular reconfigurable robot. Advanced in Mobile Robotics. In: Proceeding of the Eleventh International Conference on Climbing and Walking Robots and the Support Technologies for Mobile Machines, pp. 1090–1097. Portugal (2008). https://doi.org/10.1142/9789812835772_0130
15. Goldstein, H., Poole, C., Safko, J.: Classical Mechanics, 3rd ed. Am. J. Phys. **70**, 782 (2002). https://doi.org/10.1119/1.1484149
16. Hibbeler, R.: Engineering Mechanics: Statics & Dynamics, 11th edn. Pearson, Prentice Hall (2007)
17. Marchewka, A., Abbott, D., Beichner, R.: Oscillator damped by a constant-magnitude friction force. Am. J. Phys. **72** (2004). https://doi.org/10.1119/1.1624113

Robots Control

Adaptive Control System for Industrial Robotic Manipulator

A. P. Rudomanenko[1], N. A. Chernyadev[2], and S. A. Vorotnikov[1(✉)]

[1] Bauman Moscow State Technical University, Moscow 105007, Russian Federation
[2] Skolkovo Institute of Science and Technology, Moscow 121205, Russian Federation

Abstract. The article describes a method for adaptive control of an industrial robotic manipulator in contour control tasks. Such tasks include a large number of technological operations performed by industrial robotic manipulators. These are arc welding, applying sealant, etc. In the conditions of modern robotic production, this problem is solved with the help of CAD-CAM technologies, which make it possible to draw up a description of the trajectory of the working tool using the CAD model of the work object and implement it with a robotic manipulator. Problems arise when implementing this approach in small industrial enterprises, the product range of which changes often. In this case, you have to manually reset the robotic system (RS). In addition, in small-scale production, it is necessary to take into account and compensate for the actual errors in the manufacture of parts and their positioning by verification of the reference points of the trajectory. To automate the solution of these problems, a method for adaptive control of an industrial robotic manipulator is proposed, based on the use of a CAD model of the work object and an RGB-D sensor installed in the area of the manipulator end link to measure the distance to the object marked with a QR code. Comparing the CAD model with the actual position of the work object relative to the working tool allows to make the necessary correction in the contour control process, i.e. ensure the adaptation of this process to real technological conditions. Calibration of the manipulator and generation of trajectories in real time significantly reduces the time of readjustment of the RS and facilitates its operation in small-scale production. The conducted experimental studies have confirmed the effectiveness of the proposed approach, which can find application in small industrial enterprises, with a frequently changing product range.

Keywords: Industrial robotic manipulator · Adaptive manipulator control · CAD-model · RGB-D sensor · Software · QR-code

1 Introduction

Automation of production processes is one of the main trends in the development of world industry, where robots carry out most of the routine operations. Many of them are operations that require a working tool held by the manipulator of an industrial robot along a given contour. These include, in particular, the operations of arc welding, laser cutting, applying sealant, painting, etc. The positional control mode of the manipulator

© Springer Nature Switzerland AG 2021
A. Yuschenko (Ed.): MPoR 2020, CCIS 1426, pp. 153–164, 2021.
https://doi.org/10.1007/978-3-030-88458-1_12

was the most common application in the production of such operations, which is quite simple in execution, and at the same time, helps to solve most real production tasks. In modern robot programming systems, it is implemented by manually setting a finite set of trajectory points [8]. In this case, it is necessary to manually calibrate the robot itself [18], which often requires the use of complex information-measuring devices, such as 3D lasers, gyroscopic devices, etc. [1, 20, 22]. There is information about the use of augmented reality tools for such tasks [13]. During the setup of the manipulator itself, as a rule, it is necessary to ensure the exact positioning of its links at the starting point and at each subsequent point on the path.

The positional control mode is suitable for robots used in large enterprises, where the product range changes rarely, and where the products themselves have a strictly fixed position in the working area of the manipulator during processing [10]. In small manufacturing enterprises, where products are produced in relatively small batches, these conditions are usually not feasible [11]. This is especially problematic for tasks in which the trajectory of the manipulator depends on the shape of the workpiece (laser cutting, arc welding, applying sealant, etc.) [21]. Frequent change in the type of product necessitates the corresponding reprogramming of the robot, since it is impossible to set one processing path for parts of various shapes. It is also impossible to take into account the technological errors of each workpiece and the inaccuracy of its positioning in the working area of the manipulator.

The solution to this problem is using the principles of *adaptive control* of manipulators, which were rarely used in industrial robotics until now [3]. This article describes a method for constructing the desired trajectory of the end effector of the manipulator based on the CAD model of the object [17], as well as an adaptive control algorithm for this manipulator that performs a given programmed motion along a complex contour under conditions of incomplete certainty of the geometric parameters of the work object and its position in the work area.

2 Structure of Adaptive Control System

Figure 1 shows the schematic diagram of the proposed control system. Trajectory of the end effector is generated based on the CAD-model of the work object. A 3D television camera (RGB-D sensor) mounted on an arm in the area of the end link of the manipulator allows to determine the geometric parameters of the object and its actual position within the boundaries of the working area. The mutual orientation of the manipulator and the work object is determined by the QR code that is drawn (or projected through the screen) onto the work object and read by the camera mounted on the manipulator. This approach allows calibrating the manipulator and modifying the trajectory of its movement when replacing work objects in real time, without the need to stop and manually reprogram the robot.

Figure 2 shows the functional diagram of the control system. Let us consider the sequence of operations of this system. First: the operator loads the CAD model of the part using the CAD model loading interface. The result of the work of the CAD-model processing module is the trajectory in the coordinate system of the CAD-model, which is fed to the input of the trajectory verification module. The interface also signals

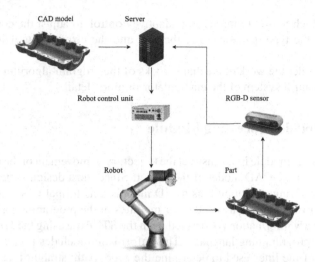

Fig. 1. Schematic diagram of the adaptive control system of an industrial robot

the need for calibration by setting a special calibration flag. After that, the automatic calibration module determines the initial position of the manipulator links using a QR code projected onto the work object. The formation of the trajectory of the end effector of the manipulator (working tool) is carried out by the corresponding module for generating commands associated with both the robot controller and the verification module. The latter, having access to the obtained data of the RGB-D sensor, filters them and corrects the trajectory of the manipulator's end effector depending on the actual position of the work object.

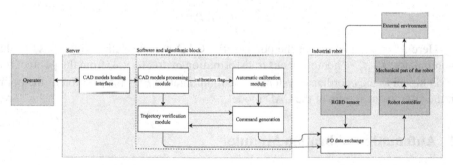

Fig. 2. Functional diagram of an adaptive control system

The proposed system structure allows to automatically calibrate the manipulator and correct its trajectory in real time. The robot controller solves the inverse kinematic problem as in traditional control systems, and the manipulator is controlled by indicating the coordinates of the point at which its end effector should exit.

This approach allows to implement adaptive control, to adjust the control program depending on the type, parameters of the part and the errors of its manufacture and installation.

Let us consider the work of the main blocks of the program-algorithmic complex of the adaptive control system of the manipulator in more detail.

3   CAD Models Processing Module

The purpose of the module is to construct the trajectory of movement of the robot working tool according to the CAD model of the object. Since most design systems use STEP files for data exchange when processing 3D models, this format was used for creating the software environment of this and other modules of the program-algorithm block.

The necessary information is extracted from the STEP file using the *FreeCAD* library of the *Python* programming language. This information includes primitives that characterize each of the lines used to determine the robot path: straight lines, splines, and arcs. All points of these lines are recorded in a specialized array containing trajectory data. In addition, the module receives a transformation matrix T_{Ucad}^{Dcad}, with the help of which each point of the model from the world coordinate system of the CAD system is transferred to the coordinate system of the model. Usually, the main object of *FreeCAD* interaction is the line from which the points that form it are distinguished. Therefore, for example, to describe a straight line, you need only two points - the beginning and the end, while to describe the spline you need many points, determined by its order. When working with the *FreeCAD* library, a spline is defined by a set of points located at an equal distance from each other. The coordinates of the trajectory point in the model coordinate system can be converted into the robot coordinate system using the following expression:

$$P^R = T_{CAD} P^C$$

Here P^R is the position of the point of the CAD model relative to the base of the manipulator; T_{CAD} - a homogeneous transformation matrix (4×4) from the point of the CAD model to the coordinate system of the manipulator; P^C - the position of the point in the coordinate system of the CAD model.

4   Automatic Calibration Module

Manual calibration of the manipulator is usually a difficult task, the complexity of which depends on the shape of the work object [6]. To automate this operation, the object is marked with a unique QR code (Fig. 3a). The module for automatic calibration of the manipulator looks for QR code at the work object using a 3D camera and recalculates the coordinates of the QR code (XYZ in Fig. 3b) into the coordinate system associated with the end effector of the manipulator.

Calibration should be performed only when changing the part, therefore, in order to start this process, it is necessary to project a QR code on the part and set a special

$$a \qquad\qquad\qquad\qquad\qquad б$$

Fig. 3. QR code marker: a - placement on the work object, b - appearance

calibration flag (Fig. 2). After calibration, the flag is removed and the algorithm works as usual.

QR code recognition is carried out using the *zbar* library. The alignment of the end effector of the manipulator occurs along the normal z to the plane of the QR code label, which is restored from the set of points based on the least squares method [2]. The corner points of the QR code can determine the directions of the remaining axes:

$$x_0 = \|(c_{tr} - c_{tl}) + (c_{br} - c_{bl})\|$$

$$y_0 = \|(c_{tr} - c_{br}) + (c_{tl} - c_{bl})\|$$

$$x_{avg} = \|x_0 + y_0 \times z\|$$

$$y = \|z \times x_{avg}\|$$

$$x = \|y \times z\|$$

Here c_{tr}, c_{tl}, c_{br}, c_{bl} are the coordinates of the top right, top left, bottom right and bottom left corner points of the QR code, respectively (Fig. 4b), x_0, y_0 are the directions of the x and y axes of the coordinate system of the QR code label, calculated from RGB-D sensor data, x_{avg} - correction for calculation error of x_0 and y_0.

Knowing the orientation of the plane onto which the QR code is applied, it is possible to transfer its coordinates, and therefore the coordinates of the object itself, into the coordinate system of the manipulator according to the following rule [4, 19]:

$$P^B = T_C^B T_{QR}^C P^{QR}$$

Here P^B is the position of the point on the plane of the QR code, in the coordinate system of the manipulator base; T_C^B - a homogeneous transformation matrix from the coordinate system of the RGB-D sensor to the coordinate system of the manipulator base; T_{QR}^C - matrix of the transition from the coordinate system of the QR code to the coordinate system of the base of the RGB-D sensor; P^{QR} - the position of the center of the QR code label in the coordinate system of the RGB-D sensor.

5 Trajectory Verification Module

The task of the trajectory verification module is to correct the trajectory of the end effector of the manipulator. *Python* and the *openCV* and *pyrealsense2* libraries are used as a development tool for this module. With their help, the RGB-D sensor received and the long-range data are processed.

The coordinates of the next trajectory point obtained by the RGB-D sensor, after filtering the noise [7, 12], are correlated with the calculated ones, taking into account the speed of the manipulator. This is done by extrapolating data from two previously obtained points with coordinates (x_0, y_0) and (x_1, y_1), respectively [9]:

$$(x_{2\,\text{max}}, y_{2\,\text{max}}) = (x_1 + \Delta x_\text{max}, y_1 + \Delta y_\text{max})$$

If $x_2 > x_1 + \Delta x_\text{max}$ or $y_2 > y_1 + \Delta y_\text{max}$, then the position of the measured point is calculated according to the rule, which is illustrated in Fig. 4:

$$y_2 = y_1 + \Delta y_\text{max}$$

$$x_2 = \frac{(x_1 - x_0)(y_2 - y_0)}{y_2 - y_0} + x_0$$

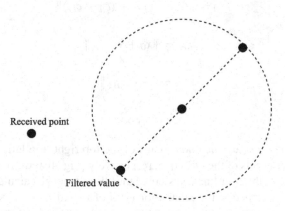

Fig. 4. Illustration of the rule for adjusting the received point coordinates

It is assumed that at each moment of time we know the position and orientation of the manipulator's working tool, as well as the transformation matrix T_S^B between the coordinate system of the manipulator base and the coordinate system associated with the RGB-D sensor [5].

$$T_S^B = T_T^B \, T_S^T$$

Here T_T^B is a homogeneous matrix of transformation of the coordinate system of the end effector of the manipulator into the coordinate system of its base, T_S^T is the matrix of the transformation of the coordinate system of the RGB-D sensor into the coordinate system of the end effector.

Then, the current position of the working tool X_r can be adjusted taking into account the vector X_c calculated from the RGB-D sensor data:

$$X_r - X_c = <x_r - x_c, y_r - y_c, z_r - z_c, \alpha_r - \alpha_c, \beta_r - \beta_c, \gamma_r - \gamma_c>$$

Knowing the difference between the coordinates of the points of the ideal trajectory obtained from the CAD model and the real one determined using the RGB-D sensor, the algorithm corrects the manipulator's movement commands so that they take into account the calculated error. According to indications from the RGB-D sensor, the linear position of the end effector is recalculated using a matrix T_S^T, and its angular orientation using the algorithm described in [16].

The process of automatic calibration, as well as the mechanism for adjusting the trajectory in the *on-line* mode, allow us to consider the proposed method as adaptive with respect to the configuration of the work object, as well as to errors in its manufacture and installation.

6   The Experimental Part

Experimental studies of the adaptive control algorithm of the manipulator were carried out on a hardware-software stand, including the Universal Robotics UR-10 manipulator, Intel's RGB-D sensor D435 RealSense, a sticker with a QR code label and a software package developed by the authors. The purpose of the experiment was to verify the main provisions of the article and to determine positioning errors during calibration of the manipulator using the QR code mark and the errors of working out a given trajectory. The test operation was the application of sealant to the end surface of the door handle. The CAD model of the part is shown in Fig. 5.

Fig. 5. CAD model of the part

The experiment was carried out in two stages. At *the first stage*, the manipulator was calibrated using a label with a QR code and the value of the mean-square value and the maximum positioning error of the manipulator were determined relative to the three linear (x, y, z) and three angular coordinates (θ_x, θ_y, θ_z) of its end effector. The task was to find the position of the object marked with a QR code in the working area of the manipulator using an RGB-D sensor and combine the coordinate system of the end effector with the coordinate system of the QR code mark installed on the work object. During the experiment, the position of the object changed; this allowed us to find and calculate the rms value of the positioning error according to the expression:

$$\sigma = \sqrt{\frac{\sum\limits_{i=1}^{n} (x_i - x_{av})^2}{n}}.$$

Here σ is the rms value of the positioning error, x_i is the measured value of the positioning error, x_{av} is the arithmetic mean value, n is the number of tests.

The results averaged over ten experiments ($n = 10$) are presented in Table 1.

Table 1. Calibration result. Error values

The projection of the positioning error of the end effector of the manipulator in the direction	Rms value	Maximum value
X	0.30 mm	0.57 mm
Y	0.30 mm	0.55 mm
Z	0.31 mm	0.77 mm
θx	0.07°	0.11°
θy	0.07°	0.10°
θz	0.90°	1.60°

As the experiment showed, determining the position and orientation of an object by the label of the QR code provides sufficient accuracy for carrying out this technological process. Thus, the proposed method is a very promising way to calibrate the initial position of the manipulator. This approach significantly reduces the time required to complete this process, and the accuracy of the determination is acceptable for operations such as applying sealant, laser cutting, etc.

At *the second stage*, the accuracy was determined of working out of two test paths by the end effector of the manipulator: ideal and real, where all technological errors must be compensated during operation. The shape of the trajectory was defined by a cubic spline in terms of the Bezier formalism:

$$P(t) = P_0 + 3t(1 - t)^2 P_1 + 3t^2(1 - t) P_2 + t^3 P_3$$

where t is the curve parameter, P_0, P_1, P_2, P_3 are its reference points.

Modification of the curve shape was carried out by changing the parameter t in the above equation.

The main objective of the experiment was to test the algorithm for working out two situations: the real trajectory of the end effector coincides with the ideal trajectory, and the real trajectory does not coincide with ideal one, since there are technological errors that distort it. The trajectory, taking into account the errors in the experiments, was also extrapolated by a cubic spline, the parameters of which were randomly selected from the interval [0–3.0] mm. Trajectory data was determined using an RGB-D sensor (Fig. 6).

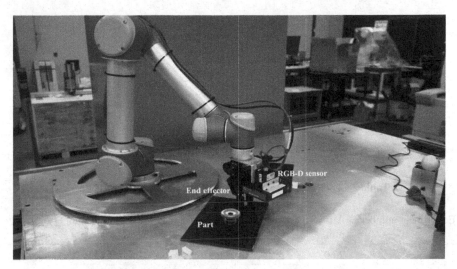

Fig. 6. Laboratory installation

The data preparation consisted of the following stages: translation of a full-color image of the working area in gray gradation, finding contour boundaries using the Canny detector [14], highlighting the specified lines with the Hough transform [15]. The correction of the trajectory itself was carried out according to the method described above. The resulting graph of the trajectory of the end effector reduced to the coordinate system of the plane of the RGB-D sensor (u, v) is shown in Fig. 7. The experiment was carried out 4 times: twice an error was artificially set between the ideal and real trajectories (curves 1 and 2) and twice these trajectories coincided (curves 3 and 4). The task of applying sealant along an arcuate trajectory on a flat horizontal surface was simulated. The solid line indicates the desired trajectory, and the dashed line indicates the actual trajectory. The graph was constructed in the coordinate system of the RGB-D sensor, in which pixels are plotted along the abscissa and ordinate axes. In the experiment, 1 pixel corresponded to 0.264 mm.

Based on the obtained data, the error of the trajectory determination algorithm using the RGB-D sensor for each case was calculated. The results obtained during the second stage of the experiment - the correction of the trajectory, are given in Table 2.

Thus, the obtained values of the maximum error in trajectory refinement in each experiment do not exceed 0.5 mm, which is an acceptable value for many technological operations, such as applying sealant, laser cutting, painting, etc.

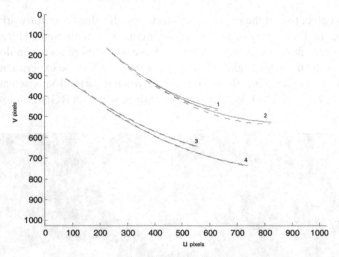

Fig. 7. Plots of the trajectories of the end effector

Table 2. The result of the correction of the trajectory. Error values

Experiment number	Artificial error, max, mm	Real error, max, mm	Algorithm error, max, mm
1	2.60	3.05	0.45
2	2.40	2.90	0.50
3	0	0.50	0.50
4	0	0.40	0.40

7 Conclusion

The proposed method for adaptive control of an industrial robot manipulator in tasks of moving along a trajectory allows reprogramming the robot in *on-line* mode without stopping the process of performing a technological operation. This is achieved by integrating three software modules into the standard robot software that solve the following tasks in real time:

- generation of the trajectory of the end effector;
- calibration of the manipulator;
- verification of the obtained trajectory during the movement of the manipulator.

This approach allows you to get a smoother trajectory of the manipulator than when manually programming it, which is achieved by a large number of points obtained from the CAD model, which is important for tasks where you need to follow along any trajectory.

The proposed method can find application in cases where the company needs to produce products with frequently changing nomenclature. The manual reprogramming of the robot is replaced by simpler operator actions and automatic calibration. Algorithmic correction of the trajectory with small values of technological errors allows us to level the differences between the CAD-model of the object and its real sample, which is processed by an industrial manipulator.

References

1. Zherebyatev, K.V.: Information-Measuring System for Determining the Calibration Parameters of Manipulators of Universal Industrial Robots. Publishing House of SSTU, Samara, p. 180 (2005)
2. Attetkov, A.V., Galkin, S.V., Zarubin, S.V.: Optimization Methods. Publishing House of BMSTU. N.E. Bauman. Moscow, p. 440 (2003)
3. Islam, S., Liu, P.X., Dias, J., Seneviratne, L.D.: Adaptive control for robot manipulators using multiple parameter models. Int. J. Control Autom. Syst. 14(5), 234–241 (2016). https://doi.org/10.1007/s12555-015-0171-3
4. Andersen, R.S., Damgaard, J.S., Madsen, O., Moeslund, T.B.: Fast calibration of industrial mobile robots to workstations using QR codes. In: 44th ISR International Symposium, pp. 123–131 (2013)
5. Bennett, D.J., Geiger, D., Hollerbach, J.M.: Autonomous robot calibration for hand-eye coordination. Int. J. Robot. Res. 10(5), 550–559 (1991)
6. Hvilshøj, M., Bøgh, S., Madsen, O., Kristiansen, M.: Calibration techniques for industrial mobile manipulators: theoretical configurations and best practices. In: Robotics (ISR), 41st International Symposium on and 2010 6th German Conference on Robotics (ROBOTIK), pp. 1–7. VDE (2010)
7. Tellaeche, A., Arana, R., Ángel Pérez, M., Maurtua, I.: Accurate manual guided robot programming and trajectory correction using 3D vision by laser triangulation. J. Adv. Robot. Special Issue Imitative Robot. 81–87 (2008)
8. Frigola, M., Poyatos, J., Casals, A., Amat, J.: Improving robot programming flexibility through physical human - Robot interaction. In: IROS Workshop on Robot Programming by Demonstration, Las Vegas (2003)
9. Picón, M.A., Bereciartua, J.A., Gutiérrez, J.P.: Machine vision in quality control. Dev. 3D Robotized Laser-Scanner Dyna 84(9), 733–742 (2010)
10. Sato, D., Shitashimizu, T., Uchyama, M.: Task teaching to a force controlled high speed parallel robot. In: Proceedings of International Conference on Robotics and Automation, Taipei, Taiwan (2003)
11. Perzylo, A., Rickert, M., Somani, N.: SME robotics. IEEE Robot. Autom. Mag. 26(1), 78–90 (2019)
12. Lin, A.C., Huang, Y.C., Punches, G., Chen, Y.: Effect of a robotic prescription-filling system on pharmacy staff activities and prescription-filling time. Am. J. Health Syst. Pharm. 64(17), 1832–1839 (2007)
13. Schwandt, A., Yuschenko, A.: Robot manipulator programming interface based on augmented reality. Int. J. Recent Technol. Eng. 8(11), 819–823 (2019)
14. Canny, J.: A computational approach to edge detection. IEEE Trans. Pattern Anal. Mach. Intell. 8(6), 679–698 (1986)
15. Hough, P.V.C.: Method and means for recognizing complex patterns. U.S. Patent 3,069,654 D, ec.18 (1962)

16. Noskov, V.P., Kiselev, I.O.: Using the texture of linear objects to build a model of the external environment and navigation. Mech. Autom. Control **20**(8), 490–497 (2019)
17. Neto, P., Norberto, P.J., Moreira, A.: CAD-based off-line robot programming. In: 2010 IEEE Conference on Robotics, Automation and Mechatronics, RAM, pp. 516–521 (2010)
18. Roth, Z.S., Mooring, B.W., Ravani, B.: An overview of robot calibration. Robot. Autom. IEEE J. **3**, 377–385 (2007)
19. Antonov, A.V., Vorotnikov, S.A., Saschenko, D.V., Vukolov, A.V., Shashurin, G.V.: Mathematical model of 3-p wheel-legged mobile robotic platform Int. Rev. Mech. Eng. **11**(5), 311–319 (2017)
20. Marwan, A., Milan, S., Fadi, I.: Calibration method for articulated industrial robots. Procedia Comput. Sci. **112**, 1601–1610 (2017)
21. Korotkov, V.I., Vorotnikov, S.A., Vybornov, N.A.: Management of a mobile manipulation robot in the task of adaptive processing of green spaces. Caspian J. Manage. High Technol. **2**(34), 48–58 (2016)
22. Du, G., Zhang, P., Li, D.: Online robot calibration based on hybrid sensors using Kalman filters. Robot. Comput. Integrated Manuf. **31**, 91–100 (2015)

Logic-Dynamic Control of Assembly Manipulator Under Conditions of High-Energy Impacts

I. N. Egorov[✉] and V. A. Nemontov[✉]

Vladimir State University, Vladimir, Russia

Abstract. Structural and algorithm support of control system of multifunctional installation and assembly robotic complex in conditions of non-stationary arrangement of fuel assemblies and incomplete orientation of their cells is considered. The platform is a portal manipulator with an additional guide cone.

Orientation and movement of platform is provided by logic-dynamic control of nonlinear electric drives of coordinates with position-force control. During process operations it is possible to create exceptions, which are used for switching of manipulator control modes. The orientation and movement of the manipulator with the rod to be installed/removed is realized on the recognition of situations and control of the assembly process.

The results of the simulation and laboratory studies confirmed the operability of the control system under the conditions of uncertainties of the process of contact interaction of the assembly units and the emerging non-stability of the dynamic system.

Efficiency of algorithms of platform orientation and movement during assembly operations is ensured by application of nonlinear control laws during position-force interaction of rod with container.

Keywords: Logic-dynamic control · Position-force control · Adaptive control · Discontinuous control

1 Introduction

Performing assembly operations by automatic manipulators under conditions of uncertainty of coordinate position of mating parts and possible distortion of their shape takes a special place. Automation of such operations is carried out with the help the multipurpose of robotic systems (RTS) similar to reloading manipulators [1–3] and the robotic technological complexes realized on their basis.

The RTS control system shall ensure the following operations: determination of coordinates of mating parts; Transport movements of assembly objects, extraction and installation of parts in appropriate cells under conditions of non-stationary geometry and their possible subtlety; Collecting the debris of the spillways and removing it when the container is destroyed; Drilling and removal of residues when jammed in a container cell; carrying out rescue and recovery operations; Automatic change of gripping, measuring

© Springer Nature Switzerland AG 2021
A. Yuschenko (Ed.): MPoR 2020, CCIS 1426, pp. 165–176, 2021.
https://doi.org/10.1007/978-3-030-88458-1_13

and technological tools. The RTS manipulator shall be controlled in automatic, remote and interactive modes [4–6].

The non-stationary arrangement of assembly units and the incomplete orientation of their cells exclude the use of automatic assembly algorithms when installing and extracting parts and require first solving the problem of determining the coordinates of the container and calculating the centers of the axes of the cells [7]. Shape curves can be of arbitrary form and in setting operations even when the centers of cell axes and grip are aligned, situations of skew and jamming are possible. The appearance of axial and transverse forces can lead to the destruction of mating units. Consequently, the non-stability of the geometry places increased requirements on the accuracy of the trajectory movements and requires the use of force-response sensing of the RTS [8–12]. The subtilarity of the object and its relatively large dimensions impose limits on the speed and acceleration of its movement.

2 Operation to Remove the Rod from the Container Cell

In carrying out transport and control operations, the first is the operation of removing the rod from the container cell and the last is the installation. The inaccuracy of the X and Y positioning of the containers and the ability to rotate them about their axis make it impossible to perform the positioning operations on the pre-stored coordinates of the system, so it is necessary to first solve the problem of accurately finding the coordinates of the cells.

The search task is as follows: In the XYZ container coordinate system, there is a family of design holes in the horizontal plane $\overset{n}{\underset{i=1}{M}} \{X_{i0}, Y_{i0}\}$. Due to container installation errors, the actual coordinates of the container cell centers $\overset{n}{\underset{i=1}{M}} \{X_{i\phi}, Y_{i\phi}\}$ do not coincide with the structural coordinates, i.e. there is inequality

$$\overset{n}{\underset{i=1}{M}} \{X_{i0}, Y_{i0}\} \neq \overset{n}{\underset{i=1}{M}} \{X_{i\phi}, Y_{i\phi}\} \tag{1}$$

Note that the geometry and mutual position of the centers of the cells in the container are strictly defined and it is sufficient to determine the coordinates of only two adjacent cells from which all others can be calculated. In automatic mode, the installation actuator can only be brought to the point where the centre of the container cell is believed to be located. The limited accuracy of the movement drives and the location of the position sensors on the drive mechanisms rather than in the fight of the robot complicates the task. Generation of coordinate data and correction of control program can be performed using algorithms of automatic assembly or adaptive control and measurement.

The enlarged structure of the communication control system in this mode is shown in Fig. 1.

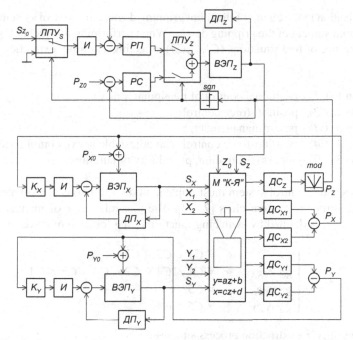

Fig. 1. Structure of the communication system in determining coordinates

Two-channel drive of communication *SRV* [5, 9, 12–16] along *Z* axis contains non-linear functional position regulator (*PLSP* and integrator *I*) with logical control by force, drives *X* and *Y* in tracking mode work out difference signal from corresponding pairs of force sensors. The cone-cell model describes the geometry of the measuring cone contact with the walls of the container cell as it moves.

Operations to remove the rod from the container are only possible after the coordinates of the cell centers have $\overset{n}{\underset{i=1}{M}} \{X_{i0}, Y_{i0}\}$ been determined. The distorted shape of the rod, its fragility and subtilarity significantly complicate the solution of the problem: when vertical movement along the *Z* axis and alignment of vertical axes of the robot grip and the cell due to deviation of the center of mass of the rod from its geometric center, situations of skew and even jamming are possible. Unlike the tasks of automatic assembly of products with deterministic parameters of mating parts, the considered system is uncertain and achievement of the set goal is possible only when using information about the external environment. This requires application along with position control of position-force and even purely force control of robot drives (with tight limitation of developed forces and moments). For change of provision of assembly in a cell at its extraction in a control system movement drives on coordinate axes *X* and *Y* and turn can be used (α) round its pivot-center.

After fixation in the clamp of the robot gripping device, the control system generates a signal for movement of the gripping device. When performing this technological operation emergence of five situations ($C1,...,C5$) reflecting assembly extraction process is possible:

- Situation 1 ($C1$) - positional control of manipulator drives;
- Situation 2 ($C2$) - position-force control;
- Situation 3 ($C3$) - power management;
- Situation 4 ($C4$) - position-force control with adjustable active compliance;
- Situation 5 ($C5$) - abnormal situation, probability of jamming.

Obviously, the control system must implement discontinuous coordinate control in the variable structure system class [7, 12]. The general vector of management $\vec{U} \in \{g_Z, g_X, g_Y, g_\alpha\}$ is defined by switching functions [2] g for each of drives of the robot:

$$
\vec{U} = \begin{cases}
g_Z & \forall\ C1 \vee C2 \vee C3; \\
g_Z \wedge g_X \wedge g_Y & \forall\ C1 \wedge C4 \vee C2 \wedge C4 \vee C3 \wedge C4; \\
g_Z \wedge g_\alpha & \forall\ C5 \\
g_\alpha \wedge g_X \wedge g_Y & \forall\ C5 \wedge C4,
\end{cases}
\tag{2}
$$

Where $C1...C5$ - extraction process situations.

The control $g_Z(z_0, P_Z, P, P_{\max})$ for Z motion is described by the following logic algorithm:

$$
g_Z = \begin{cases}
z_0 \wedge V_z \wedge \Phi_{G_z}(p) & \forall P_Z = G_C; \\
z_0 \cdot k_\pi(P_Z) \wedge V_{Z1}(P_Z) \wedge \Phi_{G_z}(p) & \forall G_C < P_Z \leq P; \\
k_{PC}(P_{\max} - P_Z) \wedge V_{Z2}(P_Z) \wedge \Phi_{V_z}(p) & \forall\ P < P_Z < P_{\max}; \\
-\Delta z \wedge -V_z \wedge \Phi_{G_z}(p) & \forall P = P_{\max},
\end{cases}
\tag{3}
$$

Where $\Phi_{Gz}(p)$, $\Phi_{Vz}(p)$ are the operator equations of the position-closed and velocity-closed drive Z, respectively; V_Z - rod extraction speed; G_C - rod gravity; $k_{P\Pi}$ and k_{PC} are transmission coefficients of Z. drive position and force regulators.

The additional X and Y coordinate components are defined as follows:

$$
x_\partial = \begin{cases}
0 & \forall |P_x| < P_{x0}; \\
+\Delta X & \forall\ \text{sign}(P_x - P_{x0}) = 1; \\
-\Delta X & \forall\ \text{sign}(P_x - P_{x0}) = -1,
\end{cases}
\tag{4}
$$

$$
y_\partial = \begin{cases}
0 & \forall |P_y| < P_{y0}; \\
+\Delta Y & \forall\ \text{sign}(P_y - P_{y0}) = 1; \\
-\Delta Y & \forall\ \text{sign}(P_y - P_{y0}) = -1,
\end{cases}
\tag{5}
$$

where P_{x0}, P_{y0}, P_x, P_y - are threshold and current values of forces on axes X and Y respectively; ΔX and ΔY - the movement diskreta unit fulfilled by coordinate drives.

The X motion control is determined by the view signal $g_X(x_0, x_\partial, P_Z, P_X, S_{max})$:

$$g_X = \begin{cases} x_0 \wedge \Phi_{G_x}(p) & \forall |P_X| < P_{x0}; \\ x_0 + \sum_{i=1}^{n} x_\partial \wedge \Phi_{G_x}(p) & \forall |P_X| > P_{x0} \wedge P_X = 0 \wedge S < S_{max}; \\ k_x(P_Z)\left(x_0 + \sum_{j=1}^{k} x_\partial\right) \wedge \Phi_{G_x}(p) & \forall P_Z > 0 \wedge S < S_{max}; \\ x_0 + x_S \wedge \Phi_{G_x}(p) & \forall P_Z > 0 \wedge S = S_{max}, \end{cases} \tag{6}$$

Where: $\Phi_{Gx}(p)$ is the operator equation of the position-closed drive X; $k_x(P_Z)$ – is a coefficient inversely proportional to the relationship between the Z-axis force and the X-axis displacement; S and S_{max} are, respectively, the current and maximum possible deviations of the robot grip axes and the container cell; x_S - projection of limit deviation S_{max} for the current value of rod lifting on the horizontal axis.

In the same way, a switching function of control of motion provision along Y axis is formed:

$$g_Y = \begin{cases} y_0 \wedge \Phi_{G_y}(p) & \forall |P_Y| < P_{Y0}; \\ y_0 + \sum_{j=1}^{k} y_\partial \wedge \Phi_{G_y}(p) & \forall |P_Y| > P_{y0} \wedge P_Y = 0 \wedge S < S_{max}; \\ k_y(P_Z)\left(y_0 + \sum_{j=1}^{k} y_\partial\right) \wedge \Phi_{G_y}(p) & \forall P_Z > 0 \wedge S < S_{max}; \\ y_0 + y_S \wedge \Phi_{G_y}(p) & \forall P_Z > 0 \wedge S = S_{max}, \end{cases} \tag{7}$$

Where $\Phi_{G_y}(p)$ is the operator equation of the position-closed drive Y; $k_y(P_Z)$ – is the relationship factor; y_S - projection of limit deviation S_{max}.

The control g_X and g_Y occurs only when the total position displacement does not exceed the maximum possible deviation of the cell and rod coordinate axes.

Function of management of turn g_α around an axis of α takes place at impossibility of continuation of operation of extraction and is defined as

$$g_\alpha = \begin{cases} 0 & \forall \quad P_Z \neq G_C; \\ \pm \Delta \alpha \wedge \Phi G_\alpha(p) & \forall P_Z = G_C \wedge z_i = z_{n1}, \end{cases} \tag{8}$$

where $\Phi_{G\alpha}(p)$ - the operator equation of the α drive closed by situation; z_{n1} is the coordinate value.

Functional diagram of the control system along axes Z and X, implementing the proposed operation algorithm, is shown in Fig. 2 (structures of drives along horizontal axes are identical). Here, the nonlinear elements $\Pi\Theta1...\Pi\Theta3$ define the transition thresholds between situations, $\Pi\Theta4$ - the threshold force P_{X0}, $\Pi\Theta5$ - the displacement constraint x_s.

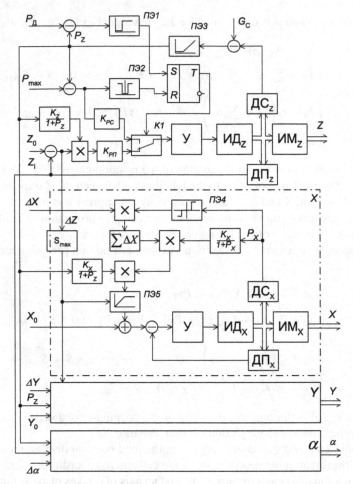

Fig. 2. Structure of the RTC control system when the rod is removed from the container cell

3   To Install a Rod in a Container Cell

Installing a rod in a container cell is the last step of the process. The coordinates of all cells in both containers for their current placement are defined and calculated. The system of rods in the container cells is also not deterministic. This uncertainty is due, on the one hand, to errors in positioning the robot over the container cell, the presence of accumulating kinematic error, plays in mechanical transmissions, etc., and, on the other hand, to distorted shape and changed geometry of the manipulation object. Ideally, the setting operation is a simple task of positioning at a given Z_0 point provided the coordinates x_0 and y_0 are fixed. The transient nature of a dynamic system implies the use of adaptive devices with a variable or parallel structure [7, 18–20]. Information on the progress of the operation are signals from coordinate position sensors, velocity sensors, as well as the magnitude and direction of the force vector arising from contact of the rod with the container cell. The control along the Z axis is carried out by the drive of vertical movement along the Z coordinate, and drives X and Y of horizontal axes are used to form the mode of active compliance (if necessary, the values of speeds V_X and V_Y are specified).

In initial state rod is installed in gripping device and brought out by robot drives to starting point $T_{kH}(x_0, y_0, z_H)$. The installation process is carried out in two steps.

Stage I: "ingress" by the free end of the rod into the opening of the cell; The step is considered complete if the position increment of the cell $\Delta Z \geq l_\phi$ chamfer depth bar.

Stage II: "installation" in the cell; Completion of the process is determined by reaching the specified coordinate along the Z axis.

Define the overall control vector of the system $\vec{U} \in \{g_z, g_x, g_y\}$ through switching functions g_z, g_x, g_y. Let 's make the following assumption: in the analysis we will consider the two-dimensional model of the controlled process $\vec{U} \in \{g_z, g_x\}$, considering the drives X and Y along the horizontal axes identical. The switch function g_Y definitions can be easily derived from g_X substituting the corresponding force and coefficient projection values. Consider the robot control algorithm at the first stage of the interface.

In the absence of contact of mating units, force sensor along Z axis records equality $P_Z = G_C$ of rod gravity force. For the above-mentioned reasons, the end of the rod may not enter the opening of the cell, when contacting the container, the force value $P_Z < G_C$. Then all possible cases can be reduced to three versions of mutual arrangement of rod and cell, represented as A, B and C in Fig. 3, where are indicated: z_{II} - initial position before installation; z_K - position of container surface; $z_{K\phi}$ - cell chamfer depth coordinate; z_0 - final position after installation.

Obviously, although the axes of the grip and the cell are aligned, it is necessary to cause the rod to move along the X axis in the direction towards the center of the cell in the sign and the projection value of the force P_X and moment vector M_T. An analysis of the position of the rod z_i and the magnitude of the force P_Z reveals the contact moment and variant A, B or C of the location of the objects.

Let's determine value of function of traffic control g_z by axis Z and also functions of management $g_{X_A}, g_{X_B}, g_{X_C}$ on axis X for each of the considered options, including their by the equiprobable, but being in the rigid sequence $A \rightarrow B \rightarrow C$.

The control $g_Z(Z_0, P_Z)$ occurring in any variant $A \ldots C$ is determined by a system of equations with logical conditions:

$$
g_Z = \begin{cases} z_0 \wedge \Phi_{G_Z}(p) \quad \forall P_Z = G_C; \\ U_Z k_{PC_k}(G_C - P_Z)\Phi V_Z(p) \quad \forall (G_C - P_Z) < P_{Z0}; \\ k_{PC}P_{Z0} \wedge \Phi P_Z(p) \quad \forall (G_C - P_Z) \geq P_{Z0}, \end{cases} \tag{9}
$$

Where $\Phi_{G_Z}(p)$, $\Phi V_Z(p)$, $\Phi P_Z(p)$, are the operator equations of the position-closed, velocity, and force drive Z, respectively; U_Z - signal of rod installation speed setting; P_{Z0} - P_Z reduction threshold, switching condition; k_{PC_κ} and k_{PC} - coefficients of transfer of regulators of speed and force of drive Z.

Control by Z at setting to initial position is performed in position mode; At contact with container at $(G_C - P_Z) < P_{Z0}$ - in position-force; When $(G_C - P_Z) \geq P_{Z0}$ the developed force is dosed under the action of the rod 's own weight. In the worst case, the system may be in variant A. That in this case it is necessary to arrange movement along the X coordinate depending on the sign of the moment M_T with simultaneous

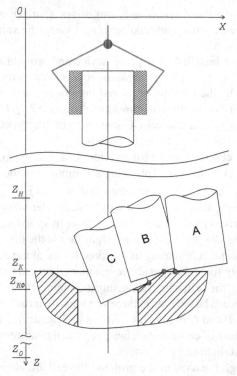

Fig. 3. Mutual position of elements in the first stage of the installation process.

control of the increment along the Z axis or the appearance of the speed of movement V_Z along the same axis under the influence of the weight of the rod, The appearance of which would indicate the transition of the process to option B. The X-axis motion control $g_{X_A}(Z, P_Z, M_T)$ would be:

$$g_{X_A} = \begin{cases} +U_X \wedge \Phi_{V_X}(p) & \forall (G_C - P_Z) \geq P_{Z_0} \wedge M_T > 0; \\ -U_X \wedge \Phi_{V_X}(p) & \forall (G_C - P_Z) \geq P_{Z_0} \wedge M_T < 0; \\ 0 & \forall (G_C - P_Z) < P_{Z0}, \end{cases} \tag{10}$$

Where $\Phi_{V_X}(p)$ - is the operator equation of the velocity-closed drive X; U_X - offset speed setting signal; M_T - calculated moment relative to the center of the robot capture.

In variant B, there is a displacement of the rod along the Z axis due to its weight, so it is advantageous to control the displacement along the X axis as a function of the projection of the force vector $\vec{p}$ on that axis; The condition is $z \geq z_k$ sufficient to determine the transition to option C. Management $g_{X_B}(z, z_k, P_Z, P_X, M_T)$ will take a form:

$$g_{X_B} = \begin{cases} +U_X k_X(P_X) \wedge \Phi_{P_X}(p) & \forall \\ \quad \forall (G_C - P_Z) \geq P_{Z_0} \wedge M_T > 0 \wedge z < z_K; \\ -U_X k_X(P_X) \wedge \Phi_{P_X}(p) & \forall \\ \quad \forall (G_C - P_Z) \geq P_{Z_0} \wedge M_T < 0 \wedge z < z_K; \\ 0 & \forall z = z_K \wedge (G_C - P_Z) < P_{Z0}, \end{cases} \tag{11}$$

Where $\Phi_{P_X}(p)$ - is the operator equation of the force-closed drive X;
$k_X(P_X)$- is the displacement velocity factor.

The cell chamfer motion option C is described by the control $g_{X_C}(z, z_{K\phi}, P_Z, P_X, M_T)$ as

$$
g_{X_C} = \begin{cases}
+U_X k_X(P_X)k_Z(z_{K\phi} - z) \wedge \Phi_{P_X}(p) \quad \forall \\
\qquad \forall (G_C - P_Z) \geq P_{Z_0} \wedge M_T > 0 \wedge z < z_{K\phi}; \\
-U_X k_X(P_X)k_Z(z_{K\phi} - z) \wedge \Phi_{P_X}(p) \quad \forall \\
\qquad \forall (G_C - P_Z) \geq P_{Z_0} \wedge M_T < 0 \wedge z < z_{K\phi}; \\
0 \quad \forall z = z_{K\phi} \wedge (G_C - P_Z) < P_{Z0},
\end{cases} \tag{12}
$$

Where $k_Z(z_{K\phi} - z)$ - is the offset velocity reduction factor when approaching the end of the chamfer, which prevents a jump when leaving the chamfer in the cell hole. The step ends when the rod is shifted along the vertical axis by an amount exceeding the coordinate $z_{K\phi}$. Thus, defining movement control along the horizontal axis as

$$
g_X = g_{X_A} \vee g_{X_B} \vee g_{X_C}, \tag{13}
$$

It is possible to ensure that the first step of the cell installation is carried out at any initial start of the process.

The need to analyze the state of the system when the rod is in contact with the container, to measure the forces that occur during this and the amount of displacement along the Z axis, as well as to organize the displacement along the horizontal axes, leads to the appearance in the system structure (Fig. 4) of the movement control unit (ECU) along the vertical axis and the displacement correction unit (BSC) along the horizontal axes. These units actually combine in their composition the model of the interface process and the logical switching device of coordinate drives control according to the signals of the model.

The use of special orienting and guiding devices makes it possible to significantly simplify the task of the first stage: when extending the rod into a cell, variants A and B of the installation process are excluded; Movement of rod end face along chamfer takes place under action of its own weight; Active compliance along horizontal axes is controlled by sign of corresponding projection of force, not by its value. In this case, the law of traffic control looks like this:

$$
g_Z = \begin{cases}
z_{K\phi} \wedge \Phi_{G_Z}(p) \quad \forall P_Z = G_C; \\
k_{PP}P_{Z0} \wedge \Phi_{P_Z}(p) \, \forall P_Z < G_C.
\end{cases} \tag{14}
$$

$$
g_X = \begin{cases}
+U \wedge \Phi_{V_x}(p) \quad \forall P_Z < G_C \wedge P_X > 0; \\
-U \wedge \Phi_{V_x}(p) \quad \forall P_Z < G_C \wedge P_X < 0; \\
0 \quad \forall \, P_Z = G_C \vee P_X = 0
\end{cases} \tag{15}
$$

$$
g_Y = \begin{cases}
+U \wedge \Phi_{V_Y}(p) \quad \forall P_Z < G_C \wedge P_Y > 0; \\
-U \wedge \Phi_{V_Y}(p) \quad \forall P_Z < G_C \wedge P_Y < 0; \\
0 \quad \forall \, P_Z = G_C \vee P_Y = 0
\end{cases} \tag{16}
$$

Condition of completion of process and transition to the second stage is $PZ = P_Z = G_C$ and $z = z_{K\phi}$.

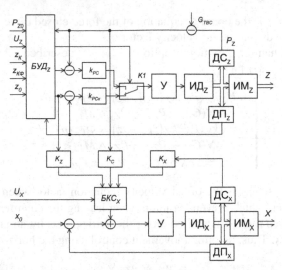

Fig. 4. Functional diagram of the plant control system (Z and X coordinates)

The task of RTK control at the second stage of installation is to organize the grip movement along the vertical axis. When the shape is deviated from the mating axis, it is possible to contact the rod with the cell walls and to generate additional forces of resistance to movement, which leads, as in the first stage, to the need to shift the grip along horizontal axes. If P_{Z1} - restriction on force for drive Z, then a vector of management of $\mathbf{U} \in \{g_Z, g_X\}$ for this mode:

$$g_Z = \begin{cases} z_0 \wedge \Phi_{G_Z}(p) \quad \forall \ P_Z = G_C; \\ U_Z k_{PC}(G_C - P_Z) \wedge \Phi_{V_Z}(p) \quad \forall (G_C - P_Z) \leq P_{Z1}; \\ 0 \quad \forall (G_C - P_Z) > P_{Z1}, \end{cases} \quad (17)$$

$$g_X = \begin{cases} +U_X k_X(P_X) \wedge \Phi_{P_X}(p) \quad \forall \\ \qquad \forall (G_C - P_Z) \geq P_{Z1} \wedge P_X > 0 \wedge V_X \neq 0 \wedge z < z_0; \\ -U_X k_X(P_X) \wedge \Phi_{P_X}(p) \quad \forall \\ \qquad \forall (G_C - P_Z) \geq P_{Z1} \wedge P_X < 0 \wedge V_X \neq 0 \wedge z < z_0; \\ 0 \quad \forall_X = 0 \wedge P_X = 0 \vee z = z_0, \end{cases} \quad (18)$$

Where V_X is the X-speed, a controlled parameter that allows you to determine whether an offset can be performed.

In case of deviations in the form, implementation of the proposed control does not exclude the probability of jamming, and incorrect setting of the P_{Z1} threshold can cause unmanaged oscillations in the system; In addition, the need to accurately determine the projection values of the force vector increases the amount of calculations required.

4   Conclusion

There are control systems that allow you to mate parts without accurately calculating forces and moments. In these systems, periodic movements on all axes except the feeder are deliberately formed, causing the mating objects to be released from the links at some mutual location and, at this point, the installation to continue. Laws of movement of manipulator degrees of mobility are generated by special program.

References

1. Dmitriev, S.M.: Osnovnoe oborudovanie AES//S.M. Dmitriev, D.L.Zverev, O.A. Byh i dr. pod red. S.M.Dmitrieva. -Minsk: Vyshejshaya shkola, 288 s (2015)
2. Budov, V.M., Farafonov, V.A.: Konstruirovanie osnovnogo oborudovaniya AES.-M.:Energoatomizda, p. 264 s (1985)
3. Shiyanov, A.I., Gerasimov, M.I., Murav'ev, I.V.: Sistemy upravleniya peregruzochnyh manipulyatorov atomnyh elektrostancij s VVER. – M.: Energoatomizdat, p. 239 s (1987)
4. Vukobratovic, M., Kircanski, N.: Real-time Dynamics of Manipulation Robots, Springer-Verlag, Berlin (1985). https://doi.org/10.1007/978-3-642-82198-1
5. Kuleshov, V.S., Lakota, N.A., Distancionno, V.A.: upravlyaemye roboty i manipulya-tory/Andryunin i dr.; Pod obshch. red. E.P. Popova. - M.: Mashinostroenie, p.328 s (1986)
6. Zenkevich, S.L., Yushchenko, A.S.: Upravlenie robotami. Osnovy upravleniya manipuly-acionnymi robotami: Ucheb. pos. dlya vuzov – M.: MGTU im. N. E. Baumana, p. 440 s (2000)
7. Veselov, O.V., Kobzev, A.A., Egorov, I.N., Nemontov, V.A.: TVELov Ustrojstvo i algo-ritm opredeleniya centrov otverstij kontejnerov pri razbrakovke Robototekhnika dlya ekstremal'nyh uslovij: VI-ya Mezhdunarod. nauch.-tekhn. konf.: Sb. tr. /S.-PbGTU. S.-Peterburg, pp. 111–114 (1996)
8. Gorinevskij, D.M., Formal'skij, A.M., Shnejder, A.Yu. Upravlenie manipulyacionnymi sis-temami na osnove informacii ob usiliyah/Pod red. V.S. Gurfinkelya i E.A. Devyanina.-M. Fizmatlit, p. 368s (1994)
9. Egorov, I.N.: Sistemy pozicionno-silovogo upravleniya tekhnologicheskimi robo-tami/Mekhatronika, avtomatizaciya i upravlenie, №10 – pp. 15–20 (2003)
10. Brock, O., Kuffner, J., Xiao, J.: Motion for manipulation tasks. In: Siciliano, B., Khatib, Q. (eds.) Springer Handbook of Robotics, pp. 615–645. Springer, Berlin, Heidelberg, (2007)
11. Luigi Villani, Joris De Schutter. Force Control. In: Siciliano, B., Khatib, Q. (eds.) Springer Handbook of Robotics, pp. 161–185. Springer, Berlin, Heidelberg (2007)
12. Egorov, I.N.: Pozicionno-silovoe upravlenie robototekhnicheskimi i mekhatronnymi ustro-jstvami : monografiya/Vladim. gos.un-t. – Vladimir: Izd-vo Vladim. gos. un-ta, p. 192 s (2010)
13. Nevill, H.: Impedance control: an approach to manipulation. Part 2 – implementation. Trans. ASME, **107,** 8–16 (1985)
14. Kazerooni, H.: Automated robotic deburring using impedance control. IEEE Control Syst. Mag. **8**(1). 21—25(1988)
15. Parr a-Vega, V., Arimoto, S.: A passivity-based adaptive sliding mode position-force control for robot manipulators. Int. J. Adapt. Control Sig. Proc. **10,** 365–377 (1996)
16. Kiguchi, K., Fukuda, T.: Position/force control of robot manipulators for geometrically unknown objects using fizzy neural networks. IEEE Trans. Ind. Electr. **47**(3), 641–649 (2000)
17. Zuev, A.V., Filaretov, V.F.: Osobennosti sozdaniya kombinirovannyh pozicionno-silovyh sistem upravleniya manipulyatoram. Izvestiya RAN. Teoriya i sistemy upravleniya № 1, pp. 154–162 (2009)

18. Kravchenko, P.D., Yablonovskij, I.M.: Sravnenie konstruktivnyh skhem mashin peregru-zochnyh s zhestkim i gibkim podvesom ispolnitel'nogo organa//Sbornik trudov mezhdunaro-dnoj XIII NTK «Mashinostroenie i tekhnosfera XXI veka» v g. Sevastopole, 2006g. Doneck: DonNTU, Tom 2, pp. 213–217 (2006)
19. Merlet, J.-P., Gosselin, C.: Parallel mechanisms and robots. In: Siciliano, B., Khatib, Q. (eds.) Springer Handbook of Robotics, pp. 269–285. Springer, Berlin, Heidelberg (2007)
20. Glazunov, V.A., Yesin, M.G., Bykov, R.E.: Control of mechanisms of parallel structure at transition through special positions. Probl. Mech. Eng. Reliab. Cars. № 2, pp. 78–84 (2004)

Algorithms of Self-control of the Underwater Walking Device According to Information on a Collision of Feet with an Unorganized Support Surface

V. V. Chernyshev[1]([envelope]) [iD], V. E. Pryanichnikov[2,3] [iD], and V. V. Arykantsev[1,4] [iD]

[1] Volgograd State Technical University, Lenin Avenue, 28, Volgograd 400005, Russia
[2] Keldysh Institute of Applied Mathematics of RAS, Miusskaya pl., 4, Moscow 125047, Russia
[3] International Laboratory "Sensorika", Miusskaya pl., 4, Moscow 125047, Russia
[4] Innopolis University, Universitetskaya Street, 1, Innopolis 420500, Russia

Abstract. In underwater conditions walking machines have better ground and shape passability. Control of almost all robotic systems moving on a bottom (underwater bulldozers, cable layers, self-moved ground mining units, etc.) is executed from a surface by the operator according to the visual information from onboard video sensors. Such approach to control of the multi-legged walking machines is not appropriate. The operator cannot to control effectively all legs at the same time and does not manage to make good decisions at emergence of any obstacle in the direction of movement, because of poor visibility. Results of investigation of information opportunities of foot of the cyclic walking mover during collision with an unorganized support surface are discussed. Shown that on the type of self-adapting of foot to an unorganized support surface during collision with an obstacle and the relative movement of the mechanism of walking it is possible to obtain some indistinct information about external working space and the current situation. It can be used at adoption of the correct decisions on control in the conditions of absence of external control signal. In particular, on the basis of fuzzy control algorithms, realization of the standard typical movements which are independently executed by the underwater walking robot for an exception of capsizing and other emergencies is possible.

Results of the work can be demanded in developing of the walking robotic systems intended for underwater technical works and for new technologies of mining of seabed resources.

Keywords: Underwater units · Bottom-moved machines · Robotic system · Mobile robot · Sensors · Walking mover · Subsea tests

1 Introduction

When carrying out underwater technical works and when introducing new industrial technologies for the development of seabed resources, robotic systems moving along the bottom are used. There are already various types of robotic underwater bulldozers,

A. Yuschenko (Ed.): MPoR 2020, CCIS 1426, pp. 177–191, 2021.
https://doi.org/10.1007/978-3-030-88458-1_14

excavators, cable layers, as well as self-moved bottom mining units [1–3]. Existing machines moving along the bottom have, as a rule, a tracked or wheeled mover. At the same time, the rough shape of the seabed and the low bearing capacity of underwater soils significantly limit the capabilities of traditional types of movers in underwater conditions. Even tracked vehicles can work under water only on relatively flat and fairly dense soils with small slopes of the bottom [1–5]. Walking machines and robots are more suitable for underwater operations, as they can provide higher traction properties and cross-country ability [6–11]. Almost all robotic systems moving along the bottom (underwater bulldozers, cable layers, self-moved bottom mining units, etc.) are controlled from the surface by the operator using visual information coming from the onboard video sensors [2, 3, 11]. This approach to controlling multi-legged walking machines is not applicable. First, the operator cannot effectively control all legs at the same time. Second, due to poor visibility under water, the operator often does not have time to make adequate decisions when there is any obstacle in the direction of travel. Such a situation, for example, arose during underwater tests of the MAK – 1 walking device [12]. The walking device (modular hardware complex) MAK-1 (Fig. 1) was specially developed at Volgograd State Technical University for developing methods for controlling the movement of underwater walking robotic systems and optimization of the parameters of their walking mechanisms at the design stage.

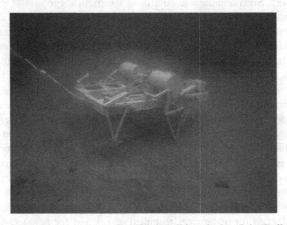

Fig. 1. Underwater tests of MAK-1 walking device (lake Baikal).

Underwater tests of the device confirmed the superiority of walking machines in terms of traction, soil and cross-country ability in comparison with traditional vehicles [7, 8, 13, 14]. However, tests revealed a number of problems associated with the management of the device. In movement control, the following approach was used. The operator was outside the workspace (on the shore or escort ship) and controlled the operation of an autonomously working device according to visual information received via cable from the onboard video sensors. The operator can change the speed and direction of movement, and also has certain opportunities to adjust the length and height of the step. The task of coordinated control of the legs in the straight modes of movement was solved without the participation of the operator. He intervened in controlling the movement of the legs only when necessary, for example, when overcoming local obstacles. However, as tests have shown, due to poor visibility under water, as a rule, no more than 1–3 m, the operator in straight modes of movement (at speeds about 1.5–2 m/s) did not manage to receive adequate decisions in case of any obstacles in the direction of motion (decision time was from 0.5 to 2 s). As a result, when encountering obstacles, there were cases of destruction of the feet and elements of the walking mover. Even with a relatively small mass of the apparatus (about 200 kg), the feet received significant damage (Fig. 2). Loss of stability and tipping of the device is also possible (Fig. 3).

Fig. 2. Damaged feet after encountering of obstacles.

Fig. 3. Tipping of walking device after encountering of unrecognized obstacles.

In such conditions, short-range information-measuring and control systems become extremely important. In walking robots, supporting elements (feet) often serve as contact sensors. In the work, using the example of the MAK-1 robot, the methods of self-control of an underwater walking vehicle using information of feet meeting with an obstacle with previously undefined parameters are studied.

2 Design Features of the Underwater Walking Robot

Underwater walking robot MAK-1 (Fig. 4) includes walking modules of right and left board. They are connected by changeable frame, which can be modified depending on required additional equipment. Walking modules are was equipped with on-board power electrical drive with connected walking mover on a shaft. On-board electrical drives designed as power modules, placed in water resistant cases. Drive power is provided via cable from external stand-alone power supply (for example, gasoline power generator or industrial power line). The total power of on-board drives is about 2 kW. Frequency regulation of smooth velocity changing has been provided. Mass of the whole device is about 200 kg, with the size 1,8 × 1,8 × 0,9 m. Highest speed under water is 3–5 km/h, depends on movement conditions. The device was developed for works at depths up to 300 m, but it has been tested at small depths so far (up to 60 m). The robot can be disassembled for easier transportation. Modular technology, used in MAK-1 device design, allows to easily upgrade it for a special task. For example, it is possible to connect a manipulator or cable reel.

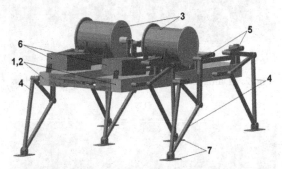

Fig. 4. Underwater walking robot MAK-1 (a) and its design scheme (b): 1—walking modules; 2—bearing beam; 3—on-board electrical drive in water resistant boxes; 4—walking mechanisms; 5, 6—suspension point mover mechanism and its linear electrical drive; 7—changeable feet.

The walking mover of cyclic type was used in the robot. Mover consists of 3 kinematically connected walking mechanisms of cyclic type, arranged along the board. Outer walking mechanisms works in inphase, middle one—in antiphase. As a result, in each moment of time at least one of legs of the mover is in support phase. Movers of each board of the machine have independent electric engines. The robot has just 2 controlled degrees of freedom. Limbs of the robot Crabster CR200 with movers of adaptive type, for comparison, has more than 30 controlled actuators [15]. Usage of cyclic movers allows not to be concerned about safety of the gait and makes stability providing easier. Machine with cyclic movers has a minimal number of controlled actuators and significantly simpler, more reliable and cheaper than analogues with adaptive control.

To adapt to the supporting surface, the legs of the MAK-1 device are equipped with articulated feet. Due to the kinematics of the feet, in each cycle it makes a strictly defined "program" movement. In the phase of transfer, the toe of the foot is lifted [16, 17].

The trajectory of the reference point of the walking mechanism in direct and reverse motion is shown in Fig. 5b and c, respectively.

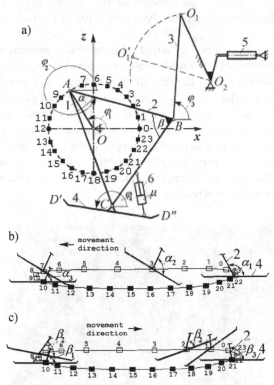

Fig. 5. Walking mechanism scheme (a) and its support point trajectory with featured positions of foot in straight (b) and reverse (c) movement of machine: 1 – winch; 2 – crank rod; 3 – rocking arm; 4 – changeable foot; 5 – linear drive of rocking arm supporting point shifting; 6 – damper.

Points on the trajectory are located through 1/24 of the cycle period, filled points correspond to the reference phase. On the points 10–22 of the trajectory (Fig. 5a), the foot is in the phase of support on the ground. At the end of the support phase, points of the trajectory 22–3, the foot 4 is located at an angle α_1 relatively to the support link 2. In the transfer phase, there are points of the trajectory 3–7, the foot moves together with the support link and the angle α_1 does not change. Damper 6 (Fig. 5a) reduces the influence of random factors on the programmed movement of the articulated foot at this stage. As a result, the toe of the foot will be raised during the transfer. The change in the angle of inclination of the foot φ_4 per cycle depending on the rotation angle of the leading crank φ_1 is shown in Fig. 5a. In the figure, the angle φ_4, for clarity, is counted from the ground (for $\varphi_4 > 0$, the toe of the foot is raised, and for $\varphi_4 < 0$ it is lowered). If the foot is ski-shaped, then at the beginning of the transfer phase - at point C of the trajectory, there will be a contact of the heel of the foot D'' with the ground. In this case, the angle α_1 will decrease to α_2, but even so, the toe of the foot in the phase of transfer will be raised, although to a lesser extent. After the transfer - at the points 7–10 of the trajectory, the foot descends to the ground and takes a horizontal position. The angle α_2 decreases to α_3. In the contact phase, at the trajectory points 7–10, the angle of inclination of the foot does not change, and the angle between the foot and the supporting link gradually increases to α_1. Then the cycle repeats. As a result, toe of the foot D' in transfer phase is always raised (Fig. 6).

Raising the toe of the foot is also carried out with reverse movement (Fig. 5c). In this case, after the completion of the contact phase - at the end of the 10–22 points section of the trajectory, the heel first leave the support on the ground and then the toe of the foot. The angular position of the foot with respect to the support link varies from angle β_1 to angle β_2. As a result, the angle $\varphi_4 < 0$ on the trajectory points 22–2 and then on the 2–8 trajectory points, the angle φ_4 again becomes greater than zero. Points 8–10 of the trajectory in time occupies a small part of the cycle, in the main part of the transfer phase of the toe of the foot is still raised. After the transfer, the foot - in the points 10–22 of the trajectory, falls to the ground. The angle β_2 increases to β_3, and the angle φ_4 becomes equal to zero. Then the cycle repeats.

Fig. 6. The toe of the foot in the phase of transfer is always raised.

Legs are supplied with passive feet control of cyclic mover. This is significantly increase abilities of walking machines with cyclic type of mover to adjust to rough ground and allows to overcome obstacles, which higher than height of the step by more than two times [17]. Passive adaptation of the foot allows to pass obstacles with height more than step length by 2 times (Fig. 7).

For decreasing of impact load in walking mechanism introduced an additional damping unit, which provide dissipative connection of the foot with support link of walking mechanism (Fig. 5a). The damper, in addition to decreasing of impact load influence, also decrease influence of random factors to software movement. Moment of viscous friction foot in hinge determined by viscous friction coefficient in damper and angular speed of foot relatively to support link.

For full realization of abilities of cyclic mover on adaptability and shape passableness in walking mechanisms of the MAK-1 was realized an ability to correct the trajectory of support points [17]. It was achieved by implementation of the additional rotary link in mechanism (Fig. 5a). Changing of its angular position leads to shifting of arm point

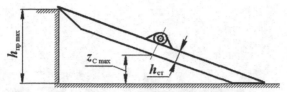

Fig. 7. Scheme for determining the maximum height of a local obstacle: z_{Cmax}—maximum lifting height of the reference point of the walking mechanism in absolute motion; h_{cm}—foot thickness.

of support of the walking mechanism and to transformation of forward movement base trajectory (Fig. 8a), which provides movement with lower energy costs, into obstacles passage mode with increased height and length of step (Fig. 8b, c). Thereby, control of supporting points trajectory of the MAK-1 robot is achieved in quite wide range. Moreover, articulated feet due to the kinematics of the mechanism at each step make a strictly defined "program" movement of the rocker: "small" (a), "medium" (b) and "big" (c) step length.

3   Information Opportunities of Articulated Feet

When developing the control system of the MAK-1 robot, the possibility to use information about the position of the articulated foot when meeting an unknown obstacle to make the right control decisions was also explored. The MAK-1 internal information sensors allow you to unambiguously determine the "program" angular speeds of the feet and links of the walking mechanisms, as well as the position and speeds of the nodal points of the mechanisms in the reference system rigidly connected to the device's body. In determining the angle of inclination of the foot, the differential equations for the angular velocity of the foot were added to the kinematic equations of the kinematics of the links of the walking mechanism. In the contact phase, its angular velocity is zero $\omega_4 = 0$. In the transfer phase, the angular feet velocity is equal to the angular velocity of the reference link $\omega_4 = \omega_2$. At the exit and entry into the contact phase, the angular velocity of the foot is determined by the angular velocity of the support link ω_2 and the vertical component of the absolute velocity v_{Cz} of the foot hinge of point C (Fig. 9).

When the heel of the foot (point D') comes into contact with the supporting surface, the following options are possible.

a) If $v_{Cz} > 0$ (foot is lifting) and $\omega_2 > 0$ (counterclockwise), then

$$\omega_4 = \begin{cases} \dfrac{v_{Cz}}{l_4 \cos \varphi_n} \ where \ v_{Cz} \leq \omega_2 \, l_4 \cos \varphi_4 \\[2mm] \omega_2 \quad where \ v_{Cz} > \omega_2 \, l_4 \cos \varphi_4 \end{cases} \tag{1}$$

where l_4—half foot length, φ_4—foot angle.

b) If $v_{Cz} > 0$ (foot is lifting) and $\omega_2 < 0$ (clockwise), then

$$\omega_4 = \omega_2 \tag{2}$$

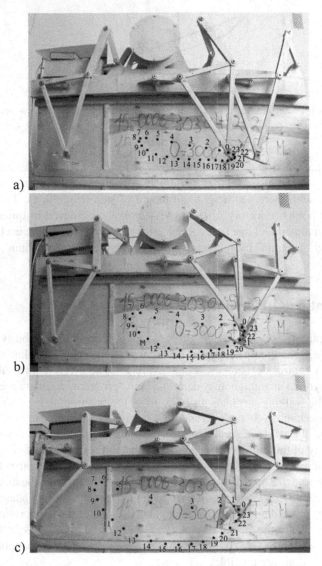

Fig. 8. Transformation of the trajectory of reference point C with a shift of the suspension point

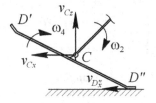

Fig. 9. Speeds of the foot points during the contact of heel with the ground.

c) If $v_{Cz} < 0$ (foot is descending) $\omega_2 > 0$ (counterclockwise), then

$$\omega_4 = \begin{cases} \dfrac{v_{Cz}}{l_4 \cos \varphi_4} & \text{where } v_{Cz} \geq \omega_2 \, l_4 \cos \varphi_4 \\[2ex] \omega_2 & \text{where } v_{Cz} < \omega_2 \, l_4 \cos \varphi_4 \end{cases} \tag{3}$$

d) if $v_{Cz} < 0$ (foot is descending) and $\omega_2 < 0$ (clockwise), then

$$\omega_4 = \frac{v_{Cz}}{l_4 \cos \varphi_4} \tag{4}$$

Thus, articulated foot in this case makes a strictly defined "program" movement in the transfer phase. Any deviation of the foot's behavior from the "program" one when the walking device is moving, for example, when meeting an obstacle, allows you to determine some information about the workspace and the current situation.

Consider, for example, the situations presented in Table 1, where U_k—unit function describing the state of the k-th walking mechanism ($k = 1, 2$), which is equal to 1 in contact phase and 0 in transfer; ω_{4k}^r—relative angular velocity of the k-th foot in relation to the support link; z_{Ck},—vertical coordinates of reference points (hinges of the foot) in the reference system associated with the body; $z_{D'k} = z_{Ck} + l_4 \sin \varphi_{4k}$ and $z_{D''k} = z_{Ck} + l_4 \sin(\varphi_{4k} + \pi)$—coordinates of the toe and heel of the foot in the reference system associated with the body of the device.

By combining the above conditions and introducing a number of linguistic variables (obstacle high, not high, deep, shallow, wide, not wide, etc.), based on information about the movement of the foot, we can form the rules of behavior of the robot in the form of fuzzy conditional propositions like «If A ..., then B...». For example, for the situation of Table 1a, "if the 1st foot in the transfer, the 2nd in the phase of contact and the toe and the heel of the 1st foot are higher than the reference point of the 2nd foot and there is a positive relative angular velocity of the 1st foot, relative to the supporting link of that legs, the obstacle is "high", it cannot be overcome in the marching mode of movement. If, under the same conditions, the relative angular velocity of the 1st foot with respect to the supporting link is negative (Table 1b), then the obstacle is "low" and the movement can be continued in marching mode. For a situation at Table 1c, "if the 1st foot is in the transfer, the 2nd in the phase of contact and the toe of the 1st foot is higher than the reference point of the 2nd foot, the heel of the 1st foot is at the level of the reference point of the 2nd foot and there is a positive relative angular the speed of the 1st foot in relation to the support link, then there is no obstacle", there is a "program" foot movement. For a situation presented at Table 1d, "if the 1st foot is in the transfer, the 2nd in the phase of contact and the toe of the 1st foot is higher than the reference point of the 2nd foot, the heel of the 1st foot is lower than the level of the reference point of the 2nd foot and there is a positive relative angular the speed of the 1st foot, the obstacle is "shallow" and you can continue to move in marching mode. If under the same conditions the first foot does not rotate in relation to the support link (Table 1e), the obstacle is "deep" and an emergency stop of the device and transfer of control to the operator is necessary.

Table 1. Examples of situations when meeting an obstacle.

Possible situations	Characteristic of the situation
a)	obstacle is "high" Characteristic of the situation: $U1 = 0$ и $U2 = 1$; $zD'1 > zC2$, $zD''1 > zC2$; $\omega_{41}^r > 0$
b)	obstacle is "not high" Characteristic of the situation: $U1 = 0$ и $U2 = 1$; $zD'1 > zC2$, $zD''1 > zC2$; $\omega_{41}^r < 0$
c)	there is no obstacle Characteristic of the situation: $U1 = 0$ и $U2 = 1$; $zD'1 > zC2$, $zD''1 = zC2$; $\omega_{41}^r > 0$
d)	obstacle is "not deep" Characteristic of the situation: $U1 = 0$ и $U2 = 1$; $zD'1 > zC2$, $zD''1 < zC2$; $\omega_{41}^r > 0$
e)	obstacle is "deep" Characteristic of the situation: $U1 = 0$ и $U2 = 1$; $zD'1 > zC2$, $zD''1 < zC2$; $\omega_{41}^r = 0$

Thus, by the relative motion of the articulated feet of a walking device with cyclic type of movers, the nature of which is completely determined by the sensors of internal information, some information about the external workspace and the current situation can be obtained.

4 Possible Management and Self-control Solutions

Obviously, the information obtained by the relative movement of the articulated feet of the walking device, as a rule, is incomplete and ambiguous. Despite this, it can be used in making the right management decisions. In particular, based on fuzzy control algorithms, it is possible to implement typical reflex movements autonomously performed by an underwater walking robot to eliminate emergency situations [9, 16, 18–20]. For example, in situation, presented in Table 1a, possible control solutions in this case are an emergency stop, a step backward, switching to a mode with an increased step height, a repeated attempt to overcome an obstacle at a low speed in an autonomous mode, or giving control to an operator. In situations presented at Table 1(b, c, d) it is possible to continue autonomous movement in marching mode. For situation from Table 1e, possible control decisions are a step back, switching to a mode with an increased step length, a second attempt to overcome the obstacles at low speed in stand-alone mode, or transferring control to the operator.

Assessing the profile passability of a walking device, it should be taken under consideration that it depends on the initial position of the reference points on the profile. Therefore, various situations are possible when overcoming one and the same obstacle (Table 2). In case (a), the obstacle was not noticed, but was overcome. In case (b) at the 1st step, the obstacle was not noticed, but was detected only at the 2nd step. In case (c), at the 1st step, the toe of the 1st foot took out the opposite wall of the ditch. In case (d) at the 1st step, the 1st foot did not reach either the opposite wall or the bottom of the obstacle.

Despite the fact that the information received about the external workspace and the current situation is incomplete and unreliable, it can be used in making the right management decisions. Despite the fact that the obstacle is the same, in each case considered, management decisions will be different.

Possible management solutions. In situation from Table 2a: continuation of autonomous movement in straight mode. In situation from Table 2b: locking of the damper of 1-st foot and continuation of autonomous movement in straight mode. In situation from Table 2c: emergency stop, increasing of step length, next attempt to pass the obstacle in autonomous mode. In situation from Table 2d: emergency stop, step behind, increasing of step length, next attempt to pass the obstacle in autonomous mode with low speed or transfer of control to the operator.

Thus, even incomplete and inaccurate information about an obstacle can be used in making the right management decisions. In particular, based on fuzzy control algorithms, it is possible to implement typical reflex movements autonomously performed by an underwater walking robot to eliminate emergency situations.

Table 2. Different situations during passing the same obstacle.

Possible situations	Characteristic of the situation
a)	Characteristic of the situation: There is no obstacle
b)	Characteristic of the situation: Obstacle is "not wide"
c)	Characteristic of the situation: Obstacle is "deep" and "not wide"
d)	Characteristic of the situation: Obstacle is "deep" and "wide"

5 Experimental Verification of the Analysis

An experimental verification of some of the results was carried out on the basis of the MAK-1 underwater walking robot. The experiments were carried out both on land and in real water objects conditions (Fig. 10). During the experiments, various obstacles were overcome in an autonomous mode.

The experiments carried out confirmed the feasibility of the proposed approach to the control of walking robotic systems in underwater conditions. However, it should be noted that the conclusions drawn from the test results are preliminary. For a more complete understanding of the phenomenon under consideration, of course, a more significant amount of experiments is needed.

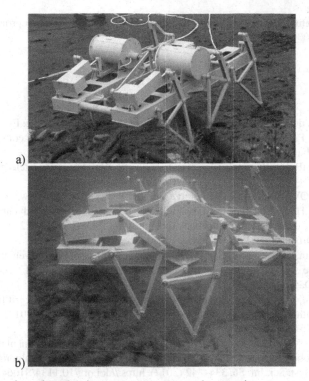

Fig. 10. Overcoming obstacles in an autonomous mode: stepping over an obstacle (a), an emergency stop when meeting a "high" obstacle (b).

6 Conclusion

By the nature of the self-adaptation of the foot to an unorganized supporting surface, for example, when changing the "programmatic" movement of the foot when meeting an obstacle and the relative movement of the walking mechanism, the nature of which is completely determined by the sensors of internal information, you can get some fuzzy information about the external workspace and the current situation. Despite the fact that information, as a rule, is incomplete and ambiguous, it can be used in making the right management decisions in the absence of external control actions. In particular, based on fuzzy control algorithms, it is possible to implement typical reflex movements autonomously performed by an underwater walking robot to prevent rollovers and other emergency situations. The proposed situational approach to the organization of the behavior of underwater walking robots with cyclic type propellers makes it easier to control the movement in conditions of an incomplete and ambiguous idea of the current situation caused by the underwater environment.

The results of the work can be claimed in the development of underwater walking robotic systems for underwater technical work and new industrial technologies for the development of the seabed resources.

Acknowledgements. Research was partially supported by RFBR, research projects No. 19-08-01180, 19-48-340007.

References

1. Verichev, S., de Jonge, L., Boomsma, W., Norman, R.: Deep sea mining: from exploration to exploitation. Presented at the Minerals of the Ocean - 7 & Deep-Sea Minerals And Mining-4, Saint-Petersburg, Russia (2014)
2. Teledyne SeaBotix: Remotely Operated Vehicles (ROVs). http://www.teledynemarine.com/seabotix
3. VideoRay ROVs: Underwater Remotely Operated Vehicles. https://www.videoray.com/
4. Kim, H.-W., Hong, S., Choi, J.: Comparative study on tracked vehicle dynamics on soft soil : single-body dynamics vs. multi -body dynamics. In: ISOPE-M-03-022, p. 7. International Society of Offshore and Polar Engineers, Tsukuba (2003)
5. Hong, S., Kim, H.W., Choi, J.-S.: Transient dynamic analysis of tracked vehicles on extremely soft cohesive soil. In: ISOPE-P-02-016, p. 8. International Society of Offshore and Polar Engineers, Daejeon (2002)
6. Briskin, E.S., Kalinin, Ya.V.: On energetically efficient motion algorithms of walking machines with cyclic drives. J. Comput. Syst. Sci. Int. **50**, 348–354 (2011). https://doi.org/10.1134/S1064230711020043
7. Briskin, E.S., Kalinin, Ya.V., Maloletov, A.V., Shurygin, V.A.: Assessment of the performance of walking robots by multicriteria optimization of their parameters and algorithms of motion. J. Comput. Syst. Sci. Int. **56**, 334–342 (2017). https://doi.org/10.1134/S1064230717020058
8. Briskin, E.S., Kalinin, Ya.V., Maloletov, A.V.: Estimates of efficiency of cycle mechanisms. Mech. Solids **52**, 128–133 (2017). https://doi.org/10.3103/S0025654417020029
9. Briskin, E.S., Kalinin, Ya.V., Maloletov, A.V., Serov, V.A., Ustinov, S.A.: On controlling the adaptation of orthogonal walking movers to the supporting surface. J. Comput. Syst. Sci. Int. **56**, 519–526 (2017). https://doi.org/10.1134/S1064230717030078
10. Comanescu, A., Comanescu, D., Dugaesescu, I., Ungureanu, L.M.: Optimal inverse models for bi-mobile mechanisms of walking robot legs. Presented at the 24th DAAAM International Symposium on Intelligent Manufacturing and Automation (2013)
11. Kubota, T., Katoh, H., Toyokawa, T., Nakatani, I.: Multi-legged robot system for deep space exploration. In: Proceedings World Automation Congress, pp. 203–208 (2004)
12. Chernyshev, V.V., Pryanichnikov, V.E., Arykantsev, V.V., Vershinina, I.P., Kalinin, Y.V.: Research of the walking type of movement in underwater conditions. In: OCEANS 2019, Marseille, pp. 1–6. IEEE, Marseille (2019). https://doi.org/10.1109/OCEANSE.2019.8867233
13. Silva, M.F., Machado, J.T.: A literature review on the optimization of legged robots. J. Vib. Control **18**, 1753–1767 (2012). https://doi.org/10.1177/1077546311403180
14. Smirnaya, L.D., Briskin, E.S.: The interaction of the foot walking propulsion of mobile underwater robot with the bottom soil. In: Proceedings of the 30th International Scientific and Technological Conference «Extreme Robotics – 2019», pp. 213–219. The Russian State Scientific Center for Robotics and Technical Cybernetics, Saint-Petersburg, Russia, 13–15 June 2019 (2019)
15. Yoo, S.Y., Jun, B.H., Shim, H.: Design of static gait algorithm for hexapod subsea walking robot: crabster. Trans. Korean Soc. Mech. Eng. A. **38**, 989–997 (2014). https://doi.org/10.3795/KSME-A.2014.38.9.989

16. Chernyshev, V.V., Arykantsev, V.V., Vershinina, I.P.: Fuzzy control of underwater walking robot during obstacle collision without pre-defined parameters. In: Radionov, A.A., Karandaev, A.S. (eds.) RusAutoCon 2019. LNEE, vol. 641, pp. 347–356. Springer, Cham (2020). https://doi.org/10.1007/978-3-030-39225-3_38

17. Chernyshev, V.V., Arykantsev, V.V., Vershinina, I.P.: Minimization of energy costs for movement resistance of ground for walking device by the control of support points motion. In: Radionov, A.A., Kravchenko, O.A., Guzeev, V.I., Rozhdestvenskiy, Y.V. (eds.) ICIE 2019. LNME, pp. 839–848. Springer, Cham (2020). https://doi.org/10.1007/978-3-030-22063-1_89

18. Briskin, E.S., Vershinina, I.P., Maloletov, A.V., Sharonov, N.G.: On the control of motion of a walking machine with twin orthogonal rotatory movers. J. Comput. Syst. Sci. Int. **53**, 464–471 (2014). https://doi.org/10.1134/S1064230714020038

19. Briskin, E.S., Zhoga, V.V., Maloletov, A.V.: Control of motion of a legged locomotion machine with minimal-power motor. Mech. Solids. **44**, 828–836 (2009). https://doi.org/10.3103/S002565440906003X

20. Volodin, S.Yu., Mikhaylov, B.B., Yuschenko, A.S.: Autonomous robot control in partially undetermined world via fuzzy logic. In: Ceccarelli, M., Glazunov, V.A. (eds.) Advances on Theory and Practice of Robots and Manipulators. MMS, vol. 22, pp. 197–203. Springer, Cham (2014). https://doi.org/10.1007/978-3-319-07058-2_23

Distributed Data-Sensor Systems in Wall Climbing Robotic Complexes

Gradetsky Valery, Knyazkov Maxim, Semenov Eugeny, and Sukhanov Artem[✉]

Laboratory of Robotics and Mechatronics, Ishlinsky Institute for Problems in Mechanics RAS, Prospect Vernadskogo 101-1, 119526 Moscow, Russia

Abstract. The strategy of rational use of distributed information-sensor systems in mobile technological robotic complexes, including complexes based on vertical movement robots designed for operations in extreme environments and situations, is considered. The analysis of the use of information-sensor systems in the following mobile robotic complexes of vertical movement, in which a robot and a technological machine are used:

1. A mobile complex, including a wheeled robot for movement on a horizontal surface and a robot for vertical movement mounted on it. The complex is designed to decontaminate vertically located surfaces.
2. A complex for cutting and welding products, which includes two interacting mobile robots with on-board manipulators.
3. A technological robot of vertical movement, which is part of an automat-ed complex for performing inspection and repair work on surfaces under water.

The control systems of each of the complexes interact with distributed networks of information-sensor systems, which include sensors distributed over nodes and mechanisms, designed to control the movements of the robot and technological equipment. Each of the control networks for various movements includes sensors for position, vacuum, force, pressure, and corresponding drive mechanisms. The technological networks include process sensors. Structures, schemes, and cyclograms of the operation of information-sensor networks of the complexes under consideration are given.

Keywords: Robotic complex · Distributed data and sensor system · Vertical movement robot · Technological equipment · Sensors and converters · Physical quantities · Survey algorithms · Survey cyclograms · Block diagrams

1 Introduction

Modern information-measuring systems can be equipped with both individual mobile robots that are part of the operational groups, and interconnected industrial robots, systems, or complex technological tasks. The main feature of such groups of mobile robots is that the robots themselves and their information-measuring systems are distributed in

© Springer Nature Switzerland AG 2021
A. Yuschenko (Ed.): MPoR 2020, CCIS 1426, pp. 192–206, 2021.
https://doi.org/10.1007/978-3-030-88458-1_15

the space of movement of mobile robots, and the received information about the situation or changes in the environment from the information-measuring systems is transmitted to form the databases of the required data and control individual robots or the entire group.

When performing technological tasks, the sensors and converters of physical quantities of information-measuring systems are distributed in the space of actuators intended for the production of technological operations and their execution at technological processing facilities, as well as the formation of algorithms for the robot control system and technological equipment.

Of particular interest is the use of distributed tactile sensors of force vectors in human-machine interfaces of interaction between an operator and a robot [1]. It is shown how the developed sensors can be used in the recognition technique, using the developed algorithms.

The capabilities of the created architecture of the information system, which operates on the basis of integrated distributed sensors integrated in the network, for use in navigation and control systems of robots, are analyzed in [2], where attention is paid to the need for clear synchronization when reading sensory information when working in difficult underwater conditions the technology offers a distributed 3D-system of technical vision according to the degree of mobility of a seven-degree hydraulic manipulator based on built-in telecoms p for the purpose of object recognition and semiautomatic control [3].

In [4], a hybrid control system architecture is proposed for navigating autonomous mobile robots in the presence of obstacles. The architecture of the information-sensory and control systems is characterized by the properties of hybridity and adaptability, depending on the incoming information about changes in the environment with a distributed sensor system. A large number of works have been devoted to solving similar problems of avoiding obstacles of varying degrees of difficulty using a distributed sensor system in space.

The information-measuring systems under consideration as part of technological complexes and processes are distributed in the space of drives, actuators, objects for performing technological operations and are widely used in industry. Industrial robots with distributed information-measuring systems are characterized by features related to the implementation of specific technological processes and the conditions for their implementation.

This article is devoted to the role and importance of distributed information-sensor systems in a number of developed technological complexes of vertical movement.

2   Method and Statement of the Problem

Among various modern mobile robots and robotic complexes, mobile robots of vertical movement and technological systems built on their basis find a certain rational use, especially in extreme working conditions and environmental environments that are dangerous for humans, such as increased radiation, high temperature, gas contamination, underwater environment [5]. Technological systems developed in Japan, England, China, the USA and other countries are used for non-destructive testing of facilities and decontamination of rooms and equipment of nuclear power plants [5, 6], under water for diagnostics of pipelines [7, 8], for extinguishing fires and fires, to detect cracks in buildings and structures [8], to perform such various technological operations as welding in pools of nuclear power plants and laser cutting [9, 10].

When designing robotic complexes of vertical movement, considerable attention is paid to information-measuring systems, which are necessary to ensure control, stabilization and stability of the movement of robots on vertically located surfaces, as well as to perform technological operations.

The article provides an analysis of the use of information-sensor systems in mobile technological robotic complexes of vertical movement, in which a robot and a technological machine are used. Information-sensor systems are analyzed for each of the following robotic systems:

1. A mobile complex, including a wheeled robot for movement on a horizontal surface and a robot for vertical movement mounted on it. The complex is designed to decontaminate vertically located surfaces.
2. A complex for cutting and welding products, which includes two interacting mobile robots with on-board manipulators.
3. A technological robot of vertical movement, which is part of an automated complex for performing inspection and repair work on surfaces under water.

The control systems of each of the complexes interact with distributed networks of information-sensor systems, which include sensors distributed over nodes and mechanisms, designed to control the movements of the robot and technological equipment. Each of the control networks for various movements includes sensors for position, vacuum, force, pressure, and corresponding drive mechanisms. The technological networks include process sensors.

3 Distributed Information-Sensor System of a Robotic Complex for Decontamination and Cleaning of Vertically Located Surfaces

The robotic complex for decontamination of vertically located surfaces [11] includes: a mobile horizontal movement complex, a vertical movement robot mounted on it, a device for sending a vertical movement robot over the surface to be processed, an information-sensor and control system.

The following designations are introduced on the scheme of the robotic complex for decontamination and cleaning of surfaces (Fig. 1): 1 - horizontal movement robot. 2 - a robot for vertical movement with technological equipment, 3, 4, - an interface unit for interfacing robots of vertical and horizontal movements, 5 - a power supply unit, 6 - a sensor for contact with a vertical surface, 7 - vacuum contact devices with sensors for vacuum and pressure of a robot for vertical movement, 8 - navigation sensors of the information-sensor system, 9 - on-board control system, 10 - remote control panel, 11 - operator, 12 - surface intended for processing, 13 - control channel, 14 - container A cleaning fluid.

The information-sensor system (ISS) of the complex (Fig. 2) is distributed in space by the functions performed in accordance with the design features, and distributed in time

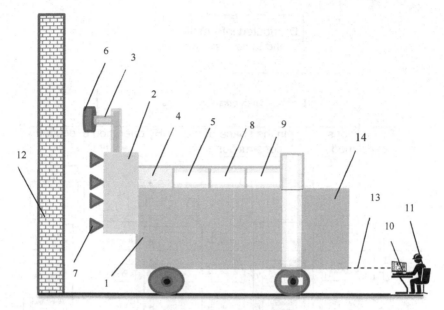

Fig. 1. Robotic complex for decontamination and surface cleaning.

by the sequence of functional movements of the robots and technological equipment. All system transformations are subordinate to one set goal and tasks for its implementation - decontamination and surface cleaning.

The distribution of sensors according to the functions performed depends on the purpose of the robot included in the complex. The movement of the horizontal movement robot (HMR) is determined by the navigation sensors, the sensors of the angle of rotation of the wheels and their angular velocity. Ultrasonic position sensors relative to the approach to a horizontally located wall, a vision system for monitoring the position of a mounted vertical movement robot (VMR). The movement of the RVP is recorded by touch sensors of the vertical surface and vacuum in vacuum contact devices (VCD), angle sensors relative to the center of mass and the end positions of the drive devices, information sensors in the feedback loops of the control system. The functions of technological equipment (TE) are carried out by means of scanning converters of angular movements of the cleaning brushes and indicators of the beginning and end of the supply of the cleaning solution, as well as monitoring the cleaning operation.

The distribution of sensors built into the HMR, VMR and TE structural units is determined by their design features, and the distribution of actions over time is characterized by cyclograms and operation algorithms. The synchronization of the operation of ISS elements is carried out using a polling algorithm that allows for the exchange of information with the control system of the complex.

The cycle of turning on the sensors of the information-sensor system (Fig. 3) determines the beginning, end and control of the movements and the sequence of turning on the drives through the control system and converters of physical quantities of actuators.

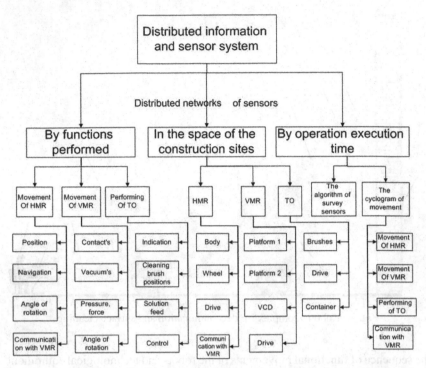

Fig. 2. The structure of a distributed information-sensor system of a mobile complex for decontamination and cleaning of vertically located surfaces.

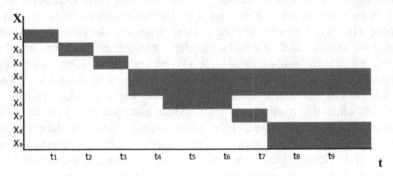

Fig. 3. Cyclogram of the inclusion of sensors of the information-sensor system for the implementation of the movements and actions of HMR, VMR and TE.

On the cyclogram of Fig. 3, the designations $x_1, \ldots, x_9$ are introduced for the following information signals from the sensors of the information-sensor system about the movement of the HMR drives mounted on it by the VMR and the inclusion of TE:

X_1 – movement HMR
X_2 – touching vertical surface while movement HMR
X_3 – VMR extension to vertical surface

X_4 – vertical contact of VMR
X_5 – vacuum activation VCD VMR
X_6 – contact of the lower VMR platform with a horizontal surface
X_7 – angular movement of the upper VMR platform before TE starts
X_8 – TE on indication
X_9 – TE work

In the cyclogram, there are no time delays between the commands from the sensors to the control system of the actuators and signals about the execution of movements by the HMR, VMR and TE drives.

Fig. 4. General view of the cleaning and decontamination complex

In the foreground, photographs of a general view of the cleaning and decontamination complex (Fig. 4) are presented by the HMR with a system of sensors that are mounted on its body. Technological equipment in the form of cleaning brushes with a decontamination solution supply device is shown in Fig. 5.

4 Distributed Information-Sensor System of a Robotic Complex for Cutting and Welding Products

The robotic complex for cutting and welding products includes: two interacting mobile robots with on-board technological manipulators, a distributed information-sensor system and a control system.

Fig. 5. Cleaning brush with decontamination solution feeder

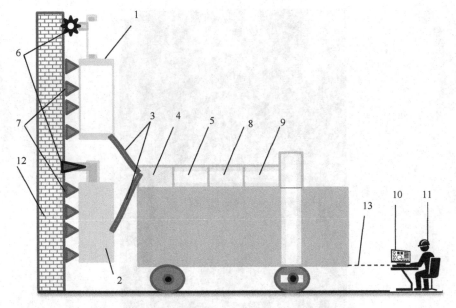

Fig. 6. Robotic complex for cutting and welding products

The following designations are introduced on the scheme of the robotic complex for cutting and welding products (Fig. 6): 1 - vertical movement robot with technological equipment 1, 2 - vertical movement robot with technological equipment 2, 3, 4, - interface unit for interfacing robot of vertical movement 1 and 2, 5 - power supply unit, 6 - contact sensor with a vertical surface, 7 - vacuum contact devices with vacuum and pressure sensors of a vertical movement robot, 8 - navigation sensors of the information-sensor system, 9 - onboard control system, 10 - remote control panel, 11 - operator, 12 - surface intended for processing, 13 - control channel.

The information-sensor system (ISS) of the complex is distributed in space by the functions performed in accordance with the design features, and distributed in time by the sequence of the movements of the functional purpose of the movement of robots and technological equipment. All system transformations are subject to the following goals and objectives - cutting and welding of products (Fig. 7).

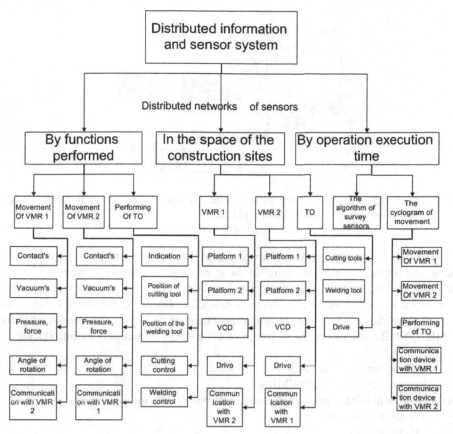

Fig. 7. The structure of a distributed information-sensor system of a robotic complex for cutting and welding products.

The distribution of sensors according to the functions performed depends on the purpose of the robot included in the complex. The movement of the VMR for cutting and welding is determined by contact sensors with the displacement surface, VCD vacuum sensors, force and pressure sensors of the drives, angle sensors of rotation of one axis of one robot platform relative to another. The movement of the VMR is also controlled by sensors of the end positions of the drive devices and information sensors in the feedback loops of the control system, a vision system for monitoring the technological operation of welding or cutting provides quality control of technological operations.

The distribution of VMR designs for cutting (VMR 1), VMR for welding (VMR 2) and TE sensors built into the nodes is determined by their design features, and the distribution of actions over time is characterized by cyclograms and operation algorithms.

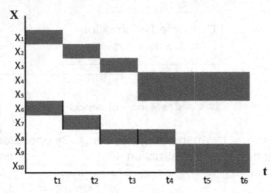

Fig. 8. Cycle diagram for activating sensors of the information-sensor system for performing movements and actions of VMR 1, VMR 2 and TE.

The cycle of turning on the sensors of the information-sensor system (Fig. 8) determines the beginning, end and control of the movements and the sequence of turning on the drives through the control system and converters of physical quantities of actuators. On the cyclogram of Fig. 8, the designations $x_1,...,x_{10}$ of the following information signals from the sensors of the information-sensor system about the movement of the VMR 1, VMR 2 drives and the inclusion of TE cutting and welding are introduced:

X_1 – vertical contact VMR 1
X_2 – vacuum activation VCD VMR 1
X_3 – movement of the upper VMR 1 platform before TE cutting
X_4 – TE cut-in indication
X_5 – TE cutting work
X_6 – vertical contact of VMR 2
X_7 – switching on vacuum VKU VMR 2
X_8 – movement of the upper VMR 2 platform before the start of TE welding
X_9 – TE start indication for welding
X_{10} – TE welding work

The general view of a complex for cutting and welding products (Fig. 9) shows a VMR with a VCD and a sensor system. Technological equipment in the form of a cutting machine and a manipulator for welding equipment is mounted on an external VMR platform.

Fig. 9. General view of the complex for cutting and welding products.

5 Technological Robot of Vertical Movement, Which Is Part of an Automated Complex for the Inspection and Repair of Surfaces Under Water

The technological robot for vertical movement for inspection and repair work on surfaces under water includes: a mobile robot with on-board technological equipment, a distributed information-sensor system and a control system.

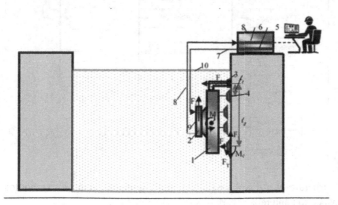

Fig. 10. Scheme of a technological robot for performing inspection and repair work of surfaces under water.

The following designations are introduced on the scheme of the robotic complex for cutting and welding products (Fig. 10): 1 - vertical movement robot, 2 - on-board control system, 3 - technological equipment, 4 - vacuum contact devices with vacuum and pressure sensors of the vertical movement robot, 5, 6 - interface unit for interfacing robots of the vertical and operator control posts, 7, 8 - control and power channels of the robot, 9 - navigation sensors of the information-sensor system, 10 - exposure pool at nuclear power plants.

ISS technological VMR for performing inspection and repair work on surfaces under water, like the other robots described above, is distributed in space by the functions performed in accordance with the design features, and distributed in time by the sequence of functional movements of the robot and technological equipment. All system transformations are necessary for the following purposes and tasks - inspection and repair of surfaces under water (Fig. 11).

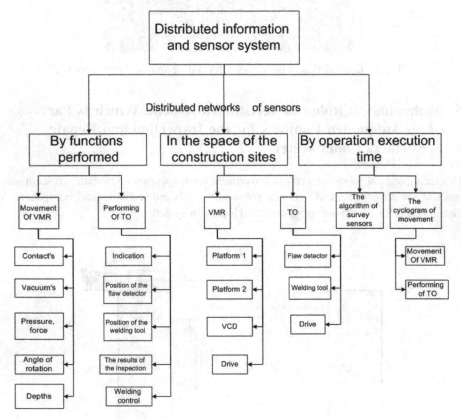

Fig. 11. The structure of a distributed information-sensor system of a technological robot for performing inspection and repair work of surfaces under water.

The distribution of sensors according to their functions depends on the purpose of the VMR included in the complex. VMR movement for inspection and repair work of surfaces under water is determined by contact sensors with the moving surface, VCD vacuum sensors, force and pressure sensors of the drives, sensors of the angle of rotation of the robot and its immersion depth. The immersion depth of the robot must be controlled to adjust the pressure level of the VCD supplying the vacuum generators. VMR movement is also monitored by end position sensors of drive devices and information sensors in the feedback loops of the control system. The vision system is used to control the work performed.

The distribution of the VMR structures built into the assemblies for inspection and repair work of surfaces under the water of sensors is determined by their design, and the sequence of actions in time is characterized by cyclograms and operation algorithms.

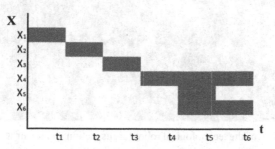

Fig. 12. Cyclogram of the inclusion of sensors ISS technological robot for inspection and repair work on surfaces under water.

The cycle diagram for switching on ISS sensors is presented in Fig. 12. The designations $x_1,...,x_6$ of the following information signals from the sensors of the information-sensor system about the movement of VMR drives are introduced on the cyclogram:

X_1 – VMR immersion depth

X_2 – vertical contact of VMR

X_3 – setting the pressure level of the supplying vacuum generator VCD with adjustment for the depth of immersion VMR

X_4 – inclusion of vacuum VCD VMR

X_5 – indication of the inclusion of inspection and repair TE

X_6 – inspection and repair work TE

The photograph of a general view of a technological robot for performing inspection and repair work on surfaces under water (Fig. 13) shows a VMR with a VCD and a sensor system and technological equipment in the form of a structurescope.

The algorithm for survey sensors of a distributed sensor system looks as follows (Fig. 14):

The algorithm for survey sensors of a distributed sensor system [12–20] provides for sending signals from the sensors shown in Fig. 7 and Fig. 11, to the complex control system. The algorithm provides for receiving feedback signals from the drive system of VMR 1, VMR 2, and TE.

Fig. 13. General view of the technological robot for inspection and repair work of surfaces under water.

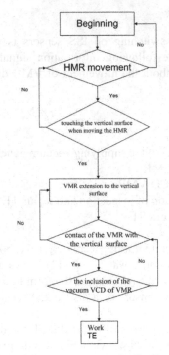

Fig. 14. Algorithm for survey sensors of a distributed sensor system

6   Conclusion

The following systems have been developed:

1. A mobile complex, including a wheeled robot for movement on a horizontal surface and a robot for vertical movement mounted on it. The complex is designed to decontaminate vertically located surfaces.
2. A complex for cutting and welding products, which includes two interacting mobile robots with on-board manipulators.
3. A technological robot of vertical movement, which is part of an automated complex for performing inspection and repair work on surfaces under water.

Acknowledgements. The present work was supported by the Ministry of Science and Higher Education within the framework of the Russian State Assignment under contract No. AAAA-A20-120011690138-6.

Reference

1. Cirillo, A., Cirillo, P., De Marie, G., Natale, C., Pizozzi, C.: A distributed tactile sensor for intuitive human-robot interfacing. J. Sens. **2017**, 14. Article ID: 1357061. https://doi.org/10.1155/2017/1357061
2. Jie, S., Dong, Z., Pand, X.: Distributed intelligent assistance robotic system with sensor networks based on robot technology middleware. Int. J. Distrib. Sens. Netw. 1–11 (2014). https://doi.org/10.1155/2014/908260
3. Hildebrandt, M., Kerdels, J., Albier, J., Kirchner, F.: Robust vision-bared semi-autonomous underwater manipulation. In: Burgard, W., et al. (eds.) Intelligigent Autonomous System 10, pp. 308–315. IOS Press (2008). https://doi.org/10.3233/978-1-58603-887-8-308
4. Adouance, L.: An adaptive multi-controller architecture for mobile robot navigation. In: Intelligent Autonomous System 10. https://doi.org/10.3233/978-1-58603-887-8-342
5. Satan, T.S.: CORDIS, Final report – RIMINI, development of new and novel low cost robot inspiration methods for in-service inspection of nuclear installation (2015)
6. Al Rashed, M., et al.: Climbing robots for NDT applications. In: Proceedings of 20th International Conference of Climbing and Walking Robots and the Support Technologies for Mobile Machines, Human-Centric Robotics, pp. 285–292 (2017)
7. Ribeiro, M.S., et al.: Pipeline inspection robotic solutions. In: Proceedings of 20th International Conference of Climbing and Walking Robots and the Support Technologies for Mobile Machines, Human-Centric Robotics, pp. 293–308 (2017)
8. Euro Garages UK: Eco wrap immediately stops splash zone corrosion. http://www.eccossegl obaluk.com/anti-corrosion.html. Accessed 20 Feb 2017
9. Sattar, T.P., Leon-Rodrigeur, E.H., Shang, J.: Amphibious NDT robots. In: Zhang, H. (ed.) Climbing and Walking Robots: Towards New Application, pp. 128–136 (2013). https://doi.org/10.5772/5078
10. Gradetsky, V.G., Knyazkov, M.M., Semenov, E.A., Sukhanov, A.N.: Adaptive gripping device of mobile robots with miniature ejectors. Mechatron. Autom. Control **17**(1), 172–176 (2016)
11. Gradetsky, V.G., Rachkov, M.Y.: Wall Climbing Robots, p. 223. IPM RAS, Ministry of Education, Moscow (1997)
12. Gradetsky, V.G., Knyazkov, M.M., Semenov, E.A., Sukhanov, A.N.: Control system of wall climbing robots in complex environments. In: Proceedings of Local Conference "Robotics and Mechatronics - 2019", XII Multiconference of Problem in Control, vol. 2, pp. 61–63 (2019)

13. Gradetsky, V.G., Knyazkov, M.M., Semenov, E.A., Sukhanov, A.N.: Development of control algorithms for wall climbing robots. In: Proceedings of Local Conference "Robotics and Mechatronics - 2019", XII Multiconference of Problem in Control, vol. 2, pp. 58–61 (2019)
14. Briskin, E., Charonov, N.: Control motion of mobile robots with step and like step drivers. In: Proceedings of Local Conference "Robotics and Mechatronics - 2019", XII Multiconference of Problem in Control, vol. 2, pp. 119–121 (2019)
15. Kalyaev, I.A., Kaliaev, I., Kapustyan, A.G.: Models and Algorithms of Collective Control in Groups of Robots. Fizmatlit, Moscow (2009)
16. Yuksel, C., Schaefer, S., Keyser, J.: On the parameterization of Catmull-Rom curves. In: 2009 SIAM/ACM Joint Conference on Geometric and Physical Modeling, San Francisco, California (2009). https://doi.org/10.1145/1629255.1629262
17. Yin, S., Yuschenko, A.S.: Collaborative robot - surgeon assistant. Extreme Robot. 1(1), 568–575 (2019)
18. Tachkov, A.A., Kalinichenko, S.V., Malykhin, A.Yu.: Modeling and evaluating the effectiveness of the retention system of a small-sized autonomous robot of vertical movement with vacuum grips. Mechatron. Autom. Control (3), 178–186 (2016)
19. Watanabe, M., Tsukagoshi, H.: Snail inspired climbing robot using fluid adhesion to travel on rough concrete walls and ceilings. In: Proceedings of CLAWAR-2016. Advanced in Cooperative Robotics, London, UK, 12–14 September 2016, pp. 79–87 (2016)
20. Sattar, T.P., Hilton, P., Howlader, M.F.: Deployment of laser cutting head with wall climbing robot for nuclear decomissioning. In: Proceedings of CLAWAR 2016 International Conference. Advance in Cooperative Robotics, London, UK, September 2016, pp. 725–732 (2016)

Adaptive System of Compensation of Motors' Partial Degradations of Multirotor UAVs

Oleg N. Gasparyan$^{(\boxtimes)}$ and Haykanush G. Darbinyan

National Polytechnic University of Armenia, Yerevan, Armenia

Abstract. Multirotor unmanned aerial vehicles (MUAVs) are widely used in military tasks, as well as in various civilian areas such as agriculture, search and rescue operations, detection of fires in forests, traffic monitoring, etc. In real flights of the MUAVs some unexpected situations may occur bringing to failures of various elements or devices of the MUAV's control system. This, in turn, can lead to the crush and complete collapse of the entire vehicle. First of all, it concerns the DC motors and propellers, which, as opposed to electronic devises and sensors, cannot be duplicated. A new method of the design of an adaptive control system which compensates the MUAVs' motors' partial degradations (not complete failures) is developed in the paper. The design procedure is based on the method of direct model reference adaptive control, on the assumption that the angles and angular velocities of the MUAV are so small that the nonlinear terms in the dynamics equations of rotational motions of the vehicle can be neglected. The numerical simulation of the designed adaptive control system in the MATLAB package environment confirms the theoretical results.

Keywords: Multirotor UAV · Motors efficiency degradation · Model reference adaptive control · Lyapunov's second method

1 Introduction

Multicopters, or N-rotor copters, also called multirotor unmanned aerial vehicles (MUAV), are widely used in various military and civilian fields [1–3]. Therefore, the safety and survivability of MUAVs are nowadays of paramount importance. Especially, it concerns the applications carried out in urban areas, since any failure or fault occurred in a MUAV may not only bring to its crash, but also cause damage in its surroundings and even expose human beings to injury risks.

That is why the fault-tolerant control problem has attracted much interest among researchers in recent years [4–7]. Many advanced control methodologies have been proposed to overcome that problem, including optimal LQR control [8, 9], model predictive control [10, 11], model reference and L_1 adaptive control [12–16], sliding mode control and backstepping [17–21], nonlinear dynamic inversion (called also feedback linearization) [22–24], and some others [25–27].

In this paper, some essential design considerations concerning the application of the direct model reference adaptive control (MRAC) to the fault-tolerant control systems of MUAVs are discussed, where a fault implies a partial degradation (or partial loss) of effectiveness of the DC motors or propellers.

© Springer Nature Switzerland AG 2021
A. Yuschenko (Ed.): MPoR 2020, CCIS 1426, pp. 207–219, 2021.
https://doi.org/10.1007/978-3-030-88458-1_16

2   Rigid-Body Dynamics and Conventional Control of MUAVs

Let $\{I\}$ denotes a right-hand inertial frame with axes x_I, y_I, z_I, and $\{B\}$, a body-fixed frame with axes x_B, y_B, z_B aligned along principal axes of inertia (Fig. 1). The position of the center of mass of the MUAV in $\{I\}$ is given by the vector $\xi = (x, y, z)^T$, and the orientation of $\{B\}$ with respect to $\{I\}$ is described by an orthogonal rotation matrix which depends on conventional Euler ψ (yaw), ϕ (roll), and θ (pitch) angles [1, 24, 28].

Let us denote m the mass of the MUAV; g, the gravitational constant; J, the constant inertia tensor of the MUAV expressed in $\{B\}$; $\omega = [\omega_x, \omega_y, \omega_z]^T \in \{B\}$, the angular velocity of $\{B\}$ with respect to $\{I\}$; $\Omega_i (i = 1, 2, ..., N)$, the angular velocities of N rotors.

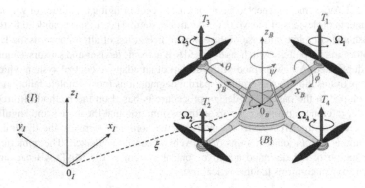

Fig. 1. Schematic representation of the MUAV (for $N = 4$).

Then, assuming for simplicity the MUAV's flight in hover, i.e. assuming that the angles and angular velocities of the MUAV are so small that the nonlinear terms in standard equations of motion can be neglected, the dynamics of the N-rotor MUAV can be written in the form [24, 28]

$$m\frac{d^2\xi}{dt^2} = -mgz_I + F, \tag{1}$$

$$J\frac{d\omega}{dt} = \tau, \tag{2}$$

The vectors $F, \tau = [\tau_x, \tau_y, \tau_z]^T \in \{B\}$ in the Eqs. (1), (2) combine, assuming no external disturbances, the principal non-conservative forces and moments applied to the MUAV's body by the aerodynamics of the N rotors [28]. Each i th rotor generates a thrust T_i which is proportional to the square of Ω_i and acts along the body-fixed axis z_B. Denoting the total thrust at hover by T_Σ ($T_\Sigma = \sum_{i=1}^{N} T_i$), and by $\overline{T}$, the N-dimensional vector of thrusts T_i, the mapping of $\overline{T}$ to the vector $[T_\Sigma, \tau]^T$ can be written in the following matrix form:

$$\begin{bmatrix} T_\Sigma \\ \tau \end{bmatrix} = D_M \Lambda_M \overline{T}, \quad \Lambda_M = diag\left\{\lambda_i^M\right\}, \tag{3}$$

where the $4 \times N$ full-rank numerical matrix D_M depends on the geometry of the MUAV, number of rotors N, etc. [24, 28], and λ_i^M $(0 < \lambda_i^M \le 1)$ are the motors' unknown degradation parameters. For properly functioning motors, the matrix Λ_M is equal to the $N \times N$ identity matrix $I_{N \times N}$. Note that the case $\lambda_i^M = 0$ for any i, which corresponds to the complete failure of the i th motor, is excluded.

Given the needed controls T_Σ and τ, the Eq. (3) allows one to compute the required thrusts T_i of rotors. For $N = 4$, it is done by inverting the matrix B_M, and the Moore-Penrose pseudoinverse must be used for $N = 6$ or $N = 8$ [24, 28].

Irrespective of the number of rotors N, the flight altitude z and the vector of rotations $\eta = [\phi, \theta, \psi]^T$ are usually chosen as four control variables in the underactuated control systems of MUAVs.

Based on the Eqs. (1)–(3) and disregarding, for simplicity, the dynamics of DC motors, the block diagram of the MUAV's linear (linearized) control system can schematically be depicted in the form shown in Fig. 2.

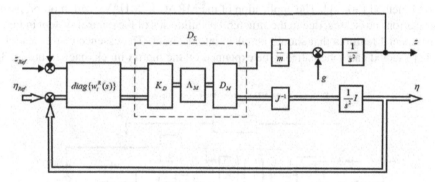

Fig. 2. Matrix block diagram of the linearized control system of the MUAV.

The scalar signals (lines) in the block diagram in Fig. 2 correspond to the vertical motion z of the MUAV along the inertial axis z_I, the double lines designate vectors of appropriate dimensions (3 or N), and s is the Laplace operator.

The control system in Fig. 2 belongs to the class of multi-input multi-output (MIMO) feedback control systems [29]. Structurally, the numerical matrix D_M in (3) describes kinematic cross-connections between separate channels of the MIMO system, or, more correctly (if $N > 4$), the kinematic relations between N thrusts T_i and four control signals T_Σ, τ_x, τ_y, τ_z.

Commonly, the matrix regulator $K_{\mathrm{Reg}}(s)$ in such systems is taken in the form

$$K_{\mathrm{Reg}}(s) = K_D diag\{w_i^R(s)\}. \tag{4}$$

In (4), $K_D = D_M^{-1}$ for $N = 4$, and $K_D = D_M^+$ for $N = 6$ or $N = 8$, where D_M^+ is the Moore-Penrose pseudoinverse of D_M, and $w_i^R(s)$ are the transfer functions of regulators in separate channels. Usually, the conventional PID regulators are used as $w_i^R(s)$ in (4).

Let us denote $D_\Sigma = \{d_{ij}^\Sigma\}$ the following matrix:

$$D_\Sigma = D_M \Lambda_M K_D = D_M \Lambda_M D_M^+. \tag{5}$$

In case of no motors' degradations (i.e. $\Lambda_M = I_{N \times N}$), we have $D_\Sigma = I_{4 \times 4}$ for any N, i.e. the kinematic cross-connections between four separate channels of the linear MIMO system in Fig. 2 are compensated and the system reduces to four independent single-input single-output (SISO) control systems [24], where the dynamics of each channel is described by a double integrator (i.e. by two zero poles at the origin of the complex plane). In case of motors' partial degradations, i.e. for $\Lambda_M \neq I_{N \times N}$ and $D_\Sigma \neq I_{4 \times 4}$, the linear MIMO system in Fig. 2 becomes cross-coupled.

3   Direct Model Reference Adaptive Control of MUAVs with Motors' Partial Degradations

Assume now that the motors' partial degradations occur, i.e. $\Lambda_M \neq I_{N \times N}$. One of the possible approaches to compensating their influence on dynamics of the control system consists in application of the direct MRAC, which, in turn, is based on the Lyapunov's second method [30, 31]. The application of the MRAC to MUAVs with motors' partial degradations possesses, due to the structural peculiarities of the control system in Fig. 2, some special features that should be taken into account. The essence of the described further method can schematically be explained by the matrix block diagram in Fig. 3.

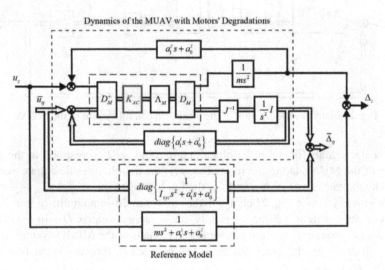

Fig. 3. Schematic block diagram of the MUAV with the adaptive controller K_{AC} and the reference model.

The task is posed to design such an adaptive controller K_{AC} that the differences Δ_z, $\overline{\Delta}_\eta$ between the outputs of the real plant (MUAV's dynamics) and the diagonal reference model, as well as the derivatives of these differences, would tend to zero irrespective of the unknown (but constant) motors' degradations λ_i^M. In other words, the MRAC is used here only for compensating the influence of motors' degradations on the MUAV's dynamics, in which we incorporate, for convenience, the decoupling regulator $K_D = D_M^+$

(see Fig. 3). The required performance of the overall MUAV's feedback control system with the adaptive controller K_{AC} in this case is provided by the choice of the diagonal regulator $diag\{w_i^R(s)\}$ in (4). Another essential point concerns the application of the Lyapunov's second method. As is known [30, 31], the Lyapunov's second method can be applied in MRAC only to the plants with a Hurwitz system matrix, i.e. to plants having no zero poles, whereas the linearized MUAV dynamics in Fig. 2 has eight zero poles. To circumvent this issue, a local matrix feedback loop is introduced into the system, the coefficients $a_1^i, a_0^i, a_1^z, a_0^z$ ($i = \phi, \theta, \psi$) of which are selected from the condition of shifting the mentioned zero poles to any prescribed locations in the left-hand plane. The loss of zero poles (integrators) that predetermine the dynamical properties of the rigid body motion is then recovered by introducing integrators in the regulators $w_i^R(s)$ in (4).

To apply the MRAC to the compensation of motors' degradations within the above-described framework, the dynamics of the MUAV must be presented in the state-space. Define the components of the eight-dimensional state-space vector x as

$$x_1 = z, x_2 = dz/dt, x_3 = \phi, x_4 = d\phi/dt, x_5 = \theta, x_6 = d\theta/dt, x_7 = \psi, x_8 = d\psi/dt \tag{6}$$

Then the dynamics equations of the MUAV with motors' degradations can be written in the form

$$\frac{dx}{dt} = Ax + BD\Lambda_M u_c,$$
$$y = \begin{bmatrix} z \\ \eta \end{bmatrix} = Cx, \tag{7}$$

where u_c is the signal at the output of the adaptive controller, and matrices A, B und C are of the form

$$A - \begin{bmatrix} 0 & 1 & 0 & 0 & 0 & 0 & 0 & 0 \\ 0 & 0 & 0 & 0 & 0 & 0 & 0 & 0 \\ 0 & 0 & 0 & 1 & 0 & 0 & 0 & 0 \\ 0 & 0 & 0 & 0 & 0 & 0 & 0 & 0 \\ 0 & 0 & 0 & 0 & 0 & 1 & 0 & 0 \\ 0 & 0 & 0 & 0 & 0 & 0 & 0 & 0 \\ 0 & 0 & 0 & 0 & 0 & 0 & 0 & 1 \\ 0 & 0 & 0 & 0 & 0 & 0 & 0 & 0 \end{bmatrix}, \quad B = \begin{bmatrix} 0 & 0 & 0 & 0 \\ 1/m & 0 & 0 & 0 \\ 0 & 0 & 0 & 0 \\ 0 & 1/I_x & 0 & 0 \\ 0 & 0 & 0 & 0 \\ 0 & 0 & 1/I_y & 0 \\ 0 & 0 & 0 & 0 \\ 0 & 0 & 0 & 1/I_z \end{bmatrix}, \tag{8}$$

$$C = \begin{bmatrix} 1 & 0 & 0 & 0 & 0 & 0 & 0 & 0 \\ 0 & 0 & 1 & 0 & 0 & 0 & 0 & 0 \\ 0 & 0 & 0 & 0 & 1 & 0 & 0 & 0 \\ 0 & 0 & 0 & 0 & 0 & 0 & 1 & 0 \end{bmatrix}. \tag{9}$$

All eight eigenvalues of the matrix A in (8) are zero, i.e. A is not Hurwitz. In accordance with the above-stated, the plant must be encompassed by a feedback loop with the constant matrix

$$
K_{FL} = \begin{bmatrix}
-a_0^z & -a_1^z & 0 & 0 & 0 & 0 & 0 & 0 \\
0 & 0 & -a_0^\phi & -a_1^\phi & 0 & 0 & 0 & 0 \\
0 & 0 & 0 & 0 & -a_0^\theta & -a_1^\theta & 0 & 0 \\
0 & 0 & 0 & 0 & 0 & 0 & -a_0^\psi & -a_1^\psi
\end{bmatrix}.
\tag{10}
$$

This matrix is equivalent to the dynamical local feedback in Fig. 3, i.e. it provides shifting of all zero eigenvalues of the matrix A to any predetermined positions in the left-hand plane.

In case of no motors' degradations, i.e. if $\Lambda_M = I_{N \times N}$ and $D_\Sigma = I_{4 \times 4}$, the dynamics of the MUAV is described by the following equation:

$$
\frac{dx}{dt} = \overbrace{(A - BK_{FL})}^{A_{\text{Ref}}} x + Bu_{In},
\tag{11}
$$

where $u_{In} = \left[u_z, \bar{u}_\eta\right]^T$ (see Fig. 3), and the matrix A_{Ref} in (11) is equal, accounting for (8) and (10), to

$$
A_{\text{Ref}} = \begin{bmatrix}
0 & 1 & 0 & 0 & 0 & 0 & 0 & 0 \\
-a_0^z & -a_1^z & 0 & 0 & 0 & 0 & 0 & 0 \\
0 & 0 & 0 & 1 & 0 & 0 & 0 & 0 \\
0 & 0 & -a_0^\phi & -a_1^\phi & 0 & 0 & 0 & 0 \\
0 & 0 & 0 & 0 & 0 & 1 & 0 & 0 \\
0 & 0 & 0 & 0 & -a_0^\theta & -a_1^\theta & 0 & 0 \\
0 & 0 & 0 & 0 & 0 & 0 & 0 & 1 \\
0 & 0 & 0 & 0 & 0 & 0 & -a_0^\psi & -a_1^\psi
\end{bmatrix}.
\tag{12}
$$

This matrix is the system matrix of the reference model in Fig. 3, the dynamics equation of which in state-space has the form

$$
\frac{dx_{\text{Ref}}}{dt} = A_{\text{Ref}} x_{\text{Ref}} + B_{\text{Ref}} u_{In},
\tag{13}
$$

where B_{Ref} is equal to the matrix B in (8), i.e. $B_{\text{Ref}} = B$.

In the state-space representation of the MUAV dynamics, the signal u_c at the output of the adaptive controller in Fig. 3 is given by the following expression:

$$
u_c = K_{AC}(t)D^+(u_{In} - K_{FL}x),
\tag{14}
$$

in which we emphasize that the matrix $K_{AC}(t)$ is time-dependent.

Substituting (14) in (7) yields

$$
\frac{dx}{dt} = \left[A - BD\Lambda_M K_{AC}(t)D^+ K_{FL}\right]x + BD\Lambda_M K_{AC}(t)D^+ u_{In}.
\tag{15}
$$

Suppose now that there exists an "ideal" constant matrix K_{AC}^* such that

$$A - BD\Lambda_M K_{AC}^* D^+ K_{FL} = A_{Ref},$$
$$BD\Lambda_M K_{AC}^* D^+ = B_{Ref}. \tag{16}$$

Then, defining the error signal as

$$e = x - x_{Ref}, \tag{17}$$

and following the derivations given in [31], it can be shown that

$$\frac{de}{dt} = \frac{dx}{dt} - \frac{dx_{Ref}}{dt} = A_{ref}e - BD\Lambda_M \tilde{K}_{AC} D^+ (K_{FL}x - u_{In}), \tag{18}$$

where $\tilde{K}_{AC} = K_{AC}(t) - K_{AC}^*$.

To derive the adaptation law, let us introduce the following Lyapunov function candidate:

$$V(e, \tilde{K}_{AC}) = e^T Pe + trace\left(\Lambda_M \tilde{K}_{AC}^T \Gamma^{-1} \tilde{K}_{AC}\right), \tag{19}$$

where Γ ($\Gamma = \Gamma^T > 0$) is a symmetric positive definite matrix often called *adaptation gain* (matrix Γ is chosen by the developer), and the symmetric positive definite matrix $P(P = P^T > 0)$ is the unique solution of the algebraic Lyapunov equation

$$PA_{Ref} + A_{Ref}^T P = -Q \tag{20}$$

for any symmetric positive definite matrix $Q = Q^T > 0$.

It can be shown that the time derivative of the Lyapunov function $V(e, \tilde{K}_{AC})$ (19) is given by the expression:

$$\frac{dV(e, \tilde{K}_{AC})}{dt} = -e^T Qe + 2trace\left\{\Lambda_M \tilde{K}_{AC}\left[D^+(u_{In} - K_{FL}x)e^T PBD + \Gamma^{-1}\frac{d\tilde{K}_{AC}^T}{dt}\right]\right\}. \tag{21}$$

From (21), it follows that if we choose the adaptation low such that

$$D^+(u_{In} - K_{FL}x)e^T PBD + \Gamma^{-1}\frac{d\tilde{K}_{AC}^T}{dt} = 0, \tag{22}$$

or

$$\frac{d\tilde{K}_{AC}^T}{dt} = -\Gamma D^+(u_{In} - K_{FL}x)e^T PBD, \tag{23}$$

then the time derivative (21) of the Lyapunov function $V(e, \tilde{K}_{AC})$ (19) becomes semi-definite negative:

$$\frac{dV(e, \tilde{K}_{AC})}{dt} = -e^T Qe \leq 0. \tag{24}$$

From (21), it can be stated, based on Barbalat's lemma [30, 31], that $\lim \|e(t)\| \to 0$ as $t \to \infty$, and, consequently, $x(t) \to x_{\text{Ref}}(t)$ as $t \to \infty$.

Hence, the adaptation low (23) provides asymptotic convergence of the dynamics of the MUAV with motors' degradations to the dynamics of the reference model. It is essential here to note that the adaptive control law (23) depends explicitly on the matrix K_{FL} of the local feedback. This is due to the structure of the MUAV's control system, in which the output of the local feedback can be applied only to the points preceding the degradation matrix Λ_M (3). Note also that the reference model (13) represents, structurally, a set of four independent SISO systems of the second order.

The state-space representation of the MUAV dynamics with the incorporated adaptive controller is presented in Fig. 4, and the corresponding block diagram of the overall MUAV's control system is given in Fig. 5.

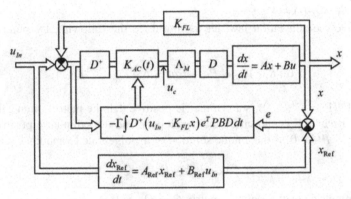

Fig. 4. Block diagram of the MUAV with the adaptive controller (state-space representation).

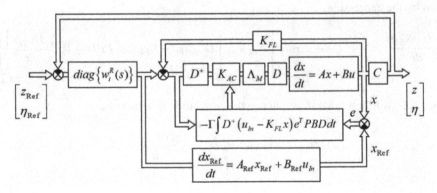

Fig. 5. Block diagram of the control system of the MUAV with the adaptive controller (state-space representation).

In ideal case, if complete compensation of the motors' degradations is achieved, the adaptive control system in Fig. 5 reduces to four independent linear SISO systems. As an illustration, the block diagram of the roll channel of the MUAV's control system with completely compensated motors' degradations is shown in Fig. 6.

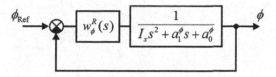

Fig. 6. Block diagram of the ideally compensated control system (the roll channel ϕ).

It should be especially emphasized once more that the local feedback loop by the matrix K_{FL} removes the integrators from the MUAV's dynamics. Therefore, as is pointed above, the scalar transfer functions of the regulators in the separate channels $w_i^R(s)$ $(i = z, \phi, \theta, \psi)$ must contain pure integrators.

Numerical Simulation. Consider the control system of the quadcopter with the following specifications: $m = 2.5$ kg, $I_x = I_y = I_z = 0.005$ kg $\cdot$ m^2, $J_R = 5 \cdot 10^{-6}$ kg $\cdot$ m^2, $\Omega = 10$ s^{-1},

$$D = \begin{bmatrix} 1.5 & 1.5 & 1.5 & 1.5 \\ 0 & 0.1 & 0 & -0.1 \\ -0.1 & 0 & 0.1 & 0 \\ -1.3 & 1.3 & -1.3 & 1.3 \end{bmatrix}. \tag{25}$$

The coefficients of the local feedback loop in (10) and (12) are chosen as $a_0^i = 400$, $a_1^i = 40$, and the transfer functions $w_i^R(s)$ of the PID regulators in separate channels are taken in the form:

$$w_i^R(s) = 10000\left(0.1 + \frac{2.5}{0.005s + 1} + \frac{1}{s}\right), \qquad (i = z, \phi, \theta, \psi). \tag{26}$$

The dynamics of that control system was modelled in the MATLAB package environment, based on the MUAV's matrix block diagram in Fig. 5.

The results of simulation of the control system in the ideal case of no motors' degradations ($\Lambda_M = D_\Sigma = I_{4\times4}$) and step (reference) input signals $z_{Ref} = 0.001$ m, $\phi_{Ref} = \theta_{Ref} = \psi_{Ref} = 5.0°$, where all these signals are applied at $t = 0.5$ s, are shown in Fig. 7. Note that, in this case, the transient responses of all rotational channels in Fig. 7(b) coincide since for $D_\Sigma = I_{4\times4}$ these channels are identical and independent.

Suppose now that there are motors' degradations given be the following diagonal matrix: $\Lambda_M = diag\{0.8, \ 0.7, \ 0.6, \ 0.4\}$. The results of simulation of the same, non-adaptive control system in this case are shown in Fig. 8, where the black dotted lines represent the transient responses of the ideal control system in Fig. 7. As can be seen from Fig. 8, the above-given values of the motors' degradations considerably affect the dynamics of the control system.

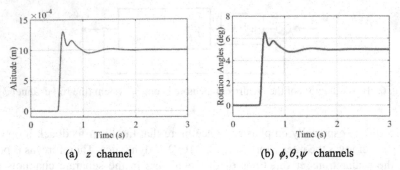

(a) z channel

(b) ϕ, θ, ψ channels

Fig. 7. Transient responses of the quadcopter's control system to step inputs for $\Lambda_M = I_{4\times4}$.

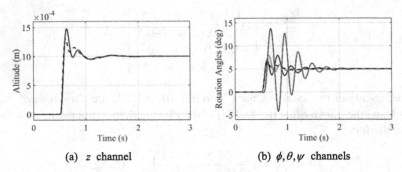

(a) z channel

(b) ϕ, θ, ψ channels

Fig. 8. Transient responses of the non-adaptive system for $\Lambda_M = diag\{0.8, \ 0.7, \ 0.6, \ 0.4\}$.

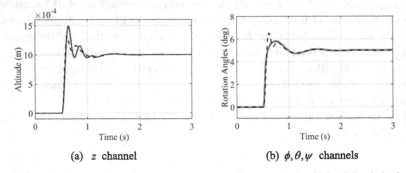

(a) z channel

(b) ϕ, θ, ψ channels

Fig. 9. Transient responses of the adaptive system for $\Lambda_M = diag\{0.8, \ 0.7, \ 0.6, \ 0.4\}$.

Introducing into the MUAV's control system the adaptive controller $K_{AC}(t)$ governed by the Eq. (23) (see also Fig. 4 and Fig. 5) results in the transient responses presented in Fig. 9. The matrix $K_{AC}(t)$ was calculated for the adaptation gain matrix $\Gamma = \gamma I_{4\times4}$, where $\gamma = 0.02$, and for the matrix Q in the Lyapunov Eq. (20) equal to the identity matrix $I_{8\times8}$. The solution P of that equation for $Q = I_{8\times8}$ is given by the following matrix:

$$
P = 10^{-3}
\begin{bmatrix}
62.5 & -500 & 0 & 0 & 0 & 0 & -0.5 & -6.2 \\
-500 & 5\,01\,2 & 0 & 0 & 0 & 0 & 6.2 & 62.7 \\
0 & 0 & 62.5 & -500 & 0 & 0 & 0 & 0 \\
0 & 0 & -500 & 5\,01\,2 & 0 & 0 & 0 & 0 \\
0 & 0 & 0 & 0 & 62.5 & -500 & 0 & 0 \\
0 & 0 & 0 & 0 & -500 & 5\,01\,2 & 0 & 0 \\
-0.5 & 6.2 & 0 & 0 & 0 & 0 & 62.6 & -500 \\
-6.2 & 62.7 & 0 & 0 & 0 & 0 & -500 & 5014
\end{bmatrix}.
\qquad (27)
$$

Comparison of the transient responses in Fig. 8 and Fig. 9 clearly demonstrates the effectiveness of the discussed adaptive controller in compensating the unknown (but constant) motors' partial degradations. In fact, the transient responses of the adaptive control system in Fig. 9 converge quite rapidly to the responses of the ideal control system in Fig. 7, i.e. of the system with no motors' degradations. It should also be noted that the rate of convergence can essentially be regulated by an appropriate selection of the adaptation gain matrix Γ in (23).

4 Conclusions

In this paper, some issues concerning the application of the MRAC to the compensation of the influence of the motors' efficiency partial degradation on the dynamics of the MUAVs are discussed. It is shown that due to the specific structural features of the MUAVs' control systems, the adaptive control low depends explicitly on the constant matrix of the local feedback, which is introduced in the system to shift the zero eigenvalues of the plant (i.e. of the linearized MUAV's dynamics equations in the state-space) to the predefined positions in the left-hand plane. The derived adaptive control low provides convergence of the dynamics of the MUAV with motors' partial degradations to the dynamics of the reference model, which represents a set of four independent linear systems of the second order. The numerical simulations confirm the validity of the theoretical results.

References

1. Hassanalian, M., Abdelkefi, A.: Classifications, applications, and design challenges of drones: a review. Prog. Aerosp. Sci. **91**, 99–131 (2017)
2. Huang, Y., Thomson, S.J., Hoffmann, W.C., Lan, Y., Fritz, B.K.: Development and prospect of unmanned aerial vehicle technologies for agricultural production management. Int. J. Agric. Biol. Eng. **6**(3), 1–10 (2013)
3. Yushu, Y., Yiqun, D.: Global fault-tolerant control of underactuated aerial vehicles with redundant actuators. Int. J. Aerosp. Eng. 1–12 (2019)

4. Schneider, T.: Fault-tolerant multirotor systems. Swiss Federal Institute of Technology, Zurich (2011)
5. Peng, L., Erik-Janvan, K., Bin, Y.: Actuator fault detection and diagnosis for quadrotors. Concordia University, Montreal (2014)
6. Sadeghzadeh, I.: Fault tolerant flight control of unmanned aerial vehicles. Concordia University, Montreal (2015)
7. Lanzon, A., Freddi, A., Longhi, S.: Flight control of a quadrotor vehicle subsequent to a rotor failure. AIAA J. Guidance Control Dyn. 37(2), 580–591 (2014)
8. Adîr, V., Stoica, A.: Integral LQR control of a star-shaped octorotor. INCAS Bull. 4(2), 3–18 (2012)
9. Bouabdallah, A., Roland, S.: PID vs LQ control techniques applied to an indoor micro quadrotor. In: 2004 IEEE/RSJ International Conference on Intelligent Robots and Systems (IROS), Sendai, Japan, vol. 3, pp. 1–6 (2004)
10. Zhang, Y., Minchala, I., Qu, Y.: Fault tolerant control with linear quadratic and model predictive control techniques against actuator faults in a quadrotor UAV. In: 2013 Proceedings of the Conference on Control and Fault Tolerant Systems, Nice, France, pp. 661–666 (2013)
11. Izadi, A., Zhang, Y., Gordon, B.: Fault tolerant model predictive control of quad-rotor helicopters with actuator fault estimation. In: Proceedings of the 18th IFAC World Congress. The International Federation of Automatic Control, Milan, vol. 44, pp. 6343–6348 (2011)
12. Falconi, G., Jorg, A., Florian, H.: Adaptive fault–tolerant position control of a hexacopter subject to an unknown motor failure. Int. J. Appl. Math. Comput. Sci. 28(2), 309–321 (2018)
13. Mühlegg, M., Niermeyer, P., Falconi, G., Holzapfel, F.: fault tolerant adaptive control of a hexacopter with control degradation. In: Proceedings of the IEEE Conference on Control Applications (CCA), Sydney, Australia, pp. 750–755 (2015)
14. Gasparyan, O., Darbinyan, H.: adaptive control of quadcopters. In: CSIT Conference 2019, pp. 137–140. IIAP, Yerevan (2019)
15. Sadeghzadeh, I., Ankit, M., Youmin, Z.: Fault tolerant control of a quadrotor helicopter using model reference adaptive control. In: IDETC/CIE 2011, Washington, vol. 48755, pp. 997–1004. IEEE (2011)
16. Ghaffar, A., Richardson, T.: Model reference adaptive control and LQR control for quadrotor with parametric uncertainties. World Acad. Sci. Eng. Technol. Int. J. Mech. Mechatron. Eng. 9(2), 244–250 (2015)
17. Yang, H., Jiang, B., Zhang, K.: Direct self-repairing control of the quadrotor helicopter based on adaptive sliding mode control technique. In: Proceedings of the 2014 IEEE Chinese Guidance, Navigation and Control Conference, Yantai, China (2014)
18. Kacimi, A., Mokhtari, A., Kouadri, B.: Sliding mode control based on adaptive backstepping approach for quadrotor unmanned aerial vehicle. Przegląd Elektrotechniczny 88, 188–193 (2012)
19. Chen, F., Jiang, R., Zhang, K., Jiang, B., Tao, G.: Robust backstepping sliding-mode control and observer-based fault estimation for a quadrotor UAV. IEEE Trans. Ind. Electron. 63(8), 5044–5056 (2016)
20. Zhang, G., Taha, H.: Adaptive back-stepping control applied on octocopter under recoil disturbance. J. Eng. Sci. Mil. Technol. 1(1), 12–21 (2017)
21. Das, A., Frank, L., Kamesh, S.: Backstepping approach for controlling a quadrotor using lagrange form dynamics. J. Intell. Robot. Syst. 56(1), 127–151 (2009). https://doi.org/10.1007/s10846-009-9331-0
22. Freddi, A., Longhi, S.: A feedback linearization approach to fault tolerance in quadrotor vehicles. In: Proceedings of 18th IFAC World Congress, pp. 5413–5418. Elsevier, Milan (2011)

23. Du, G., Quan, Q., Cai, K.-Y.: Additive state decomposition based dynamic inversion stabilized control of a hexacopter subject to unknown propeller damages. In: Proceedings of the 32nd Chinese Control Conference, Xi'an, China, pp. 6231–6236 (2013)

24. Gasparyan, O.N.: On application of feedback linearization in control systems of multicopters. In: Misyurin, S.Y., Arakelian, V., Avetisyan, A.I. (eds.) Advanced Technologies in Robotics and Intelligent Systems. MMS, vol. 80, pp. 343–351. Springer, Cham (2020). https://doi.org/10.1007/978-3-030-33491-8_41

25. Zhang, Y., Chamseddine, A., Rabbath, C., Apkarian, J., Gosselin, P.: Development of advanced FDD and FTC techniques with application to an unmanned quadrotor helicopter testbed. J. Franklin Inst. 350(9), 2396–2422 (2013)

26. Zeghlache, S., Saigaa, D., Kara, K.: Fault tolerant control based on neural network interval type-2 fuzzy sliding mode controller for octorotor UAV. Front. Comp. Sci. 10(4), 657–672 (2016). https://doi.org/10.1007/s11704-015-4448-8

27. Saied, M., Lussier, B., Fantoni, I., Shraim, H., Francis, C.: Passive fault tolerant control of an octorotor using super-twisting algorithm: theory and experiments. In: 3rd Conference on Control and Fault-Tolerant Systems (SysTol), Barcelona, pp. 361–366 (2016)

28. Mahony, R., Kumar, V., Corke, P.: Multirotor aerial vehicles: modeling, estimation, and control of quadrotor. Robot. Autom. Mag. 19(3), 20–32 (2012)

29. Gasparyan, O.N.: Linear and Nonlinear Multivariable Feedback Control: A Classical Approach. Wiley, Hoboken (2008)

30. Nguyen, N.T.: Model-reference adaptive control. In: Nguyen, N.T. (ed.) Model-Reference Adaptive Control, pp. 83–123. Springer, Cham (2018). https://doi.org/10.1007/978-3-319-56393-0_5

31. Lavretsky, E.: Adaptive control: introduction, overview, and applications, robust and adaptive control workshop (MT-1). In: 2008 American Control Conference, Seattle, Washington, USA, 9–10 June 2008 (2008). http://acc2008.a2c2.org/

Author Index

Printed in the United States
by Baker & Taylor Publisher Services